# 1st Workshop on Ecology, Environment, and Natural Language Processing (NLP4Ecology 2025)



Tallinn, Estonia
2 March 2025

ISBN: 979-8-3313-1888-8

**Printed from e-media with permission by:**

Curran Associates, Inc.
57 Morehouse Lane
Red Hook, NY 12571

**Some format issues inherent in the e-media version may also appear in this print version.**



Printed with permission by Curran Associates, Inc. (2025)

For permission requests, please contact the Association for Computational Linguistics at the address below.

Association for Computational Linguistics
209 N. Eighth Street
Stroudsburg, Pennsylvania 18360

Phone: 1-570-476-8006
Fax: 1-570-476-0860

acl@aclweb.org

**Additional copies of this publication are available from:**

Curran Associates, Inc.
57 Morehouse Lane
Red Hook, NY 12571 USA
Phone: 845-758-0400
Fax: 845-758-2633
Email: curran@proceedings.com
Web: www.proceedings.com

NLP4Ecology 2025

# 1st Workshop on Ecology, Environment, and Natural Language Processing

## Proceedings of NLP4Ecology2025

March 2, 2025

# Introduction

We are pleased to welcome you to NLP4Ecology 2025, the 1st International Workshop on Ecology, Environment, and Natural Language Processing. This first edition debuts in a hybrid format on March 2nd, 2025, co-located with the Joint 25th Nordic Conference on Computational Linguistics and the 11th Baltic Conference on Human Language Technologies (NoDaLiDa/Baltic-HLT 2025) in Tallinn, Estonia.

The NLP4Ecology workshop provides a venue for publication and exchange between the Natural Language Processing (NLP) community and stakeholders from different disciplines. It aims to explore how computational linguistics and NLP tools, methods, and applications can contribute to addressing urgent environmental challenges—not only climate change, which has received the most research attention so far due to its visibility and quantifiability, but also broader ecological crises affecting humans, non-human animals, and ecosystems worldwide. Tackling these issues requires interdisciplinary action, and the NLP community has a crucial role to play. The responsibility to address these challenges extends beyond scientists directly involved in climate and environmental studies—it is a shared duty.

NLP4Ecology aims to attract a highly interdisciplinary audience, welcoming contributions at the intersection of linguistics, ecology, and computer science, especially from fields such as AI, computational linguistics, digital humanities, ecolinguistics, ethics, philosophy, and environmental humanities. Our goal is to expand research and collaboration and to empower the NLP community to take an active role in addressing the ecological crisis through innovative and collective action.

This year's program includes a keynote lecture and three presentation sessions. We received 21 submissions, including 10 long papers, 7 short papers, and 4 research communications. Our Program Committee (PC) consisted of 11 early-career and 5 senior researchers, each responsible for reviewing two to three papers. Every submission was double-blind reviewed by two PC members, and we carefully considered their assessments in making our final selection. The PC members did an outstanding job, and we sincerely thank them for their invaluable contributions to maintaining a high-quality program. In the end, we accepted 15 papers: 7 long papers, 6 short papers, and 2 research communications (the latter not included in the proceedings). These numbers yield an overall acceptance rate of 71.4

In organizing this hybrid workshop, we sought to preserve as much as possible the engagement and interaction of a fully in-person event. The program includes 7 oral presentations in the opening and closing sessions, while the poster session in between features 9 poster presentations.

Topic-wise, the workshop includes contributions on the development and evaluation of NLP models for ecological and environmental applications, including Green NLP efforts and mitigating anthropocentric biases in large language models. Several papers focus on corpus creation, entity recognition for environmental concepts, and information extraction in the contexts of biodiversity, climate change, and sustainability. Other studies investigate topic modeling and discourse analysis of environmental narratives, covering online discussions, policy documents, and scientific texts. We also feature work on sentiment and emotion analysis in ecological discourse, multilingual approaches to environmental communication, recommender systems for renewable energy communities, and NLP methods for environmental monitoring and advocacy.

Regarding language diversity, the accepted papers explore datasets and experiments involving 6 languages, including English, Finnish, Portuguese (Brazilian), Russian, Spanish, and Italian. By discussing environmental issues from a multilingual perspective, the workshop provides a valuable opportunity to highlight cultural differences in how ecological challenges are framed and addressed across languages.

A workshop of this scale requires the advice, support, and enthusiastic participation of many individuals, to whom we express our deepest gratitude. We especially thank our keynote speaker, Tommaso Caselli (University of Groningen), for his inspiring talk on "Climate Crises, Vegan Meat, and Sustainable Fuels:

How Words Shape Reality". We also extend our appreciation to the Program Committee members for their time and dedication in shaping an excellent technical program. Finally, we thank all the authors and participants for making the first edition of NLP4Ecology a success and contributing to the growth of research at the intersection of NLP, ecology, and environmental discourse.

**The NLP4Ecology Program Chairs** (in Alphabetical Order)

Valerio Basile, University of Turin, Italy

Cristina Bosco, University of Turin, Italy

Francesca Grasso, University of Turin, Italy

Muhammad Okky Ibrohim, University of Turin, Italy

Maria Skeppstedt, Uppsala University, Sweden

Manfred Stede, Potsdam University, Germany

# Organizing Committee

**Chair**

Valerio Basile, University of Turin, Italy
Cristina Bosco, University of Turin, Italy
Francesca Grasso, University of Turin, Italy
Muhammad Okky Ibrohim, University of Turin, Italy
Maria Skeppstedt, Uppsala University, Sweden
Manfred Stede, Potsdam University, Germany

# Program Committee

## Program Committee

Davide Audrito, University of Turin, Italy
Luca Brigada Villa, University of Pavia, Italy
Tyler A. Chang, University of California San Diego, USA
Luigi Di Caro, University of Turin, Italy
Steffen Frenzel, University of Potsdam, Germany
Sara Gemelli, University of Bergamo, Italy
Frederikus Hudi, Nara Institute of Science and Technology, Japan
Stefano Locci, University of Turin, Italy
Stella Markantonatou, Athena Research Center, Greece
Lucia Passaro, University of Pisa, Italy
Maximos Skandalis, University of Montpellier, France
Ivan Spada, University of Turin, Italy
Amanda Starling Gould, Duke University, USA
Masashi Takeshita, Hokkaido University, Japan
Karolina Zaczynska, University of Potsdam, Germany
Fabio Massimo Zanzotto, University of Rome "Tor Vergata", Italy

## Invited Speaker

Tommaso Caselli, University of Groningen, Netherlands

## Keynote Talk

# Climate Crises, Vegan Meat, and Sustainable Fuels: How Words Shape Reality

**Tommaso Caselli**
University of Groningen

**Abstract:** The words we choose, the contexts in which they are uttered, and the actors conveying these utterances all have a critical role in the way we create narratives that influence our perception of reality. In some cases these narratives can be so strong that they defy the appearance: referring to the increase of the earth's temperature as "global warming" hinders the destructive effects that higher temperatures have on the climate and the livability of the planet. "Vegan meat" is an oxymoron but the anchoring between the established concept (animal-based food) and the new one (plant-based alternative) can favor the acceptance of the latter in the protein transition debate. When presenting "sustainable fuels" as green solutions for mobility, companies fail to specifiy that sustaianbility is just a reduction of CO2 production when compared to fossil fuels. This talk is focused on the linguistic devices and their use to convey narratives where NLP is a methodology to uncover how the use of words affect the perceptions of different issues related to the ecological transition.

**Bio:** Dr. Tommaso Caselli is Assistant Professor in Computational Semantics at the Center for Language and Cognition (CLCG) of the Faculty of Arts of the University of Groningen. His main research interests are in event extraction and framing, hate speech and misinformation detection and countering. He is one of the founders of the "Event and Stories in the News" workshop series and the co-editor of the volume "Computational Analysis of Storylines" (CUP, 2021). He has been involved in the organization of several semantic evaluation campaigns for NLP for English and Italian. He has covered (senior) area chair positions (COLING, ACL, EMNLP, EACL) and his work is featured in major *CL conferences and journals. He has been awarded two "Outstanding Paper Award" (COLING 2022; ACL 2023) and one "Best Paper Award" (AACL 2022). Since November 2024, he is the coordinator of the theme "AI and Language" of the Jantina Tammes School of Digital Society, Technology, and AI of the University of Groningen.

# Table of Contents

# From Data to Grassroots Initiatives: Leveraging Transformer-Based Models for Detecting Green Practices in Social Media

**Anna Glazkova**
Carbon Measurement Test Area in Tyumen' Region (FEWZ-2024-0016),
University of Tyumen
Tyumen, Russia
a.v.glazkova@utmn.ru

**Olga Zakharova**
Carbon Measurement Test Area in Tyumen' Region (FEWZ-2024-0016),
University of Tyumen
Tyumen, Russia
o.v.zakharova@utmn.ru

## Abstract

Green practices are everyday activities that support a sustainable relationship between people and the environment. Detecting these practices in social media helps track their prevalence and develop recommendations to promote eco-friendly actions. This study compares machine learning methods for identifying mentions of green waste practices as a multi-label text classification task. We focus on transformer-based models, which currently achieve state-of-the-art performance across various text classification tasks. Along with encoder-only models, we evaluate encoder-decoder and decoder-only architectures, including instruction-based large language models. Experiments on the GreenRu dataset, which consists of Russian social media texts, show the prevalence of the mBART encoder-decoder model. The findings of this study contribute to the advancement of natural language processing tools for ecological and environmental research, as well as the broader development of multi-label text classification methods in other domains.

## 1 Introduction

Growing environmental challenges and climate change have led governments to develop adaptation and mitigation policies. These policies are expected to influence people's behavior, shaping what are known as social practices (Giddens, 1984). However, it is unclear whether these practices are becoming more eco-friendly or how they can be improved to better address the environmental crisis.

Green practices are social actions aimed at harmonizing the relationship between people and the environment by reducing resource consumption, waste, pollution, and emissions (Zakharova et al., 2021). Studying the prevalence of green waste practices is crucial to give people new ideas for promoting and expanding these actions (Lamphere and Shefner, 2018; van Lunenburg et al., 2020). Despite this, awareness of these practices in society remains limited.

To fill this gap, researchers need to collect and analyze large amounts of data on green waste practices. Social media provides a rich repository of environmental information, but manually reviewing posts is time-consuming and inefficient. Automated approaches, such as deep learning and content analysis, can contribute to solving this problem. However, to date, only a limited number of studies have used big data tools to investigate green waste practices (Haines et al., 2023; Zakharova et al., 2023; Sivarajah et al., 2020).

In this work, we explore the possibilities of natural language processing (NLP) tools for detecting mentions of green waste practices in social media. This task is framed as a multi-label text classification problem. Since large language models (LLMs) demonstrate superior performance across various NLP tasks, the focus of our research is on applying pre-trained language models (PLMs) to detect mentions of green waste practices. We seek to answer the following research questions (RQs):

- How effective can PLMs be in detecting mentions of green waste practices in social media?
- Which transformer-based model architectures are the most effective for this task?

The contributions of this paper can be summarized as follows. To address RQs, we present the first large-scale comparison of encoder-only, encoder-decoder, and decoder-only transformer-based models for the task of detecting mentions



*Proceedings of the 1st Workshop on Ecology, Environment, and Natural Language Processing (NLP4Ecology2025)*, pages 1–9
March 2, 2025 ©2025 University of Tartu Library

of green waste practices in social media. Several label descriptors to represent data for generative models were evaluated. The presented evaluation has revealed that encoder-decoder models, namely mBART, can outperform both encoder-only and decoder-only models for detecting mentions of green waste practices. The obtained results provide insights into the potential of NLP to address environmental challenges. Our findings can also be used in other similar NLP tasks related to multi-label text classification.

## 2 Related Work

Modern approaches to multi-label text classification are mainly based on the use of encoder-only PLMs. Existing research often utilizes Bidirectional Encoder Representations from Transformers (BERT) (Devlin et al., 2019) and other transformer-based models. In particular, BERT-based approaches to multi-label text classification were used by Zahera et al. (2019); Chalkidis et al. (2020); Yarullin and Serdyukov (2021). Chalkidis et al. (2021) were the first to use the T5 model (Raffel et al., 2020) for multi-label classification. However, their approach utilized only the encoder component of the model, omitting the use of the model's decoder.

To date, there are several studies that used the encoder-decoder models fine-tuned for multi-label text classification in a generative manner. Kementchedjhieva and Chalkidis (2023) analyzed four methods for multi-label classification based on T5 and evaluated several types of label descriptors. Savci and Das (2024) compared multi-label BART (Lewis et al., 2020) and BERT; however, the results of BART were lower.

Up to now, there are only several approaches to perform multi-label text classification using decoder-only models. Peña et al. (2023); Siddiqui et al. (2024) performed fine-tuning of a pre-trained GPT2-model (Radford et al., 2019) with different prompt formats. Peskine et al. (2023) analyzed the performance of GPT-3 (Brown et al., 2020) for fine-grained multi-label tweet classification using zero-shot labeling. Vithanage et al. (2024) revealed that few-shot learning consistently outperforms zero-shot learning.

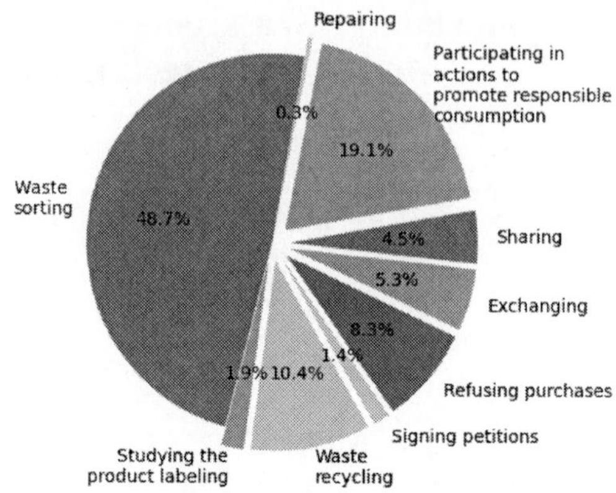


Figure 1: The distribution of mentions of green waste practices in GreenRu.

## 3 Data

This study uses the GreenRu[1] dataset (Zakharova and Glazkova, 2024) for detecting mentions of green waste practices in Russian social media texts. GreenRu consists of 1,326 posts in the Russian language with an average length of 880 symbols collected from online green communities. The posts have a sentence-level multi-label markup indicating green waste practices mentioned in them. The average length of a sentence is 110 symbols. Nine types of green waste practices (Zakharova et al., 2022) were used for the annotation of GreenRu: 1) **waste sorting**, i.e. separating waste by its type; 2) **studying the product labeling** to indicate product packaging as a type of waste; 3) **waste recycling**, i.e. transforming waste materials into reusable resources for future production.; 4) **signing petitions** to influence the authorities; 5) **refusing purchases** to reduce consumption and environmental footprint; 6) **exchanging** an unnecessary item or service for a desired one; 7) **sharing** things with other people for a fee or free of charge; 8) **participating in actions to promote responsible consumption**, including workshops, festivals, lessons, etc.; 9) **repairing** things as an alternative to throwing them away. The distribution of mentions of green waste practices in the dataset is presented in Figure 1. GreenRu is pre-split into training and test sets, with their characteristics presented in Table 1.

[1] https://github.com/green-solutions-lab/GreenRu

| Characteristic | | Training set | Test set |
|---|---|---|---|
| Total number of posts | | 913 | 413 |
| Total number of sentences with multi-label markup | | 2442 | 1058 |
| **Distribution of green practice mentions** | | | |
| 1 | Waste sorting | 1275 | 560 |
| 2 | Studying the product labeling | 55 | 17 |
| 3 | Waste recycling | 272 | 121 |
| 4 | Signing petitions | 22 | 31 |
| 5 | Refusing purchases | 236 | 75 |
| 6 | Exchanging | 146 | 52 |
| 7 | Sharing | 109 | 62 |
| 8 | Participating in actions to promote responsible consumption | 510 | 209 |
| 9 | Repairing | 10 | 3 |

Table 1: The statistics of GreenRu.

## 4 Models

In this study, we compared several approaches to multi-label text classification to detect mentions of green waste practices in social media. Alongside encoder-only PLMs, which are traditionally used for multi-label text classification, we also employed encoder-decoder and decoder-only models. All transformer-based PLMs were implemented using the Simple Transformers[2] and Transformers (Wolf et al., 2020) libraries. The overview of models is shown in Table 2. In addition to fine-tuned PLMs, we evaluated the effectiveness of prompt-based learning and two traditional machine learning baselines.

### 4.1 Encoder-only Models

- ruBERT, a version of BERT (Devlin et al., 2019) for the Russian language. We used two versions of this model, namely **ruBERT-base**[3] (Kuratov and Arkhipov, 2019) and **ruBERT-large**[4] (Zmitrovich et al., 2024).

- ruELECTRA (Zmitrovich et al., 2024), a model is based on the ELECTRA architecture (Clark et al., 2020). In this study, **ruELECTRA-base**[5] and **ruELECTRA-large**[6] were utilized.

[2]https://simpletransformers.ai/

[3]https://huggingface.co/DeepPavlov/rubert-base-cased

[4]https://huggingface.co/ai-forever/ruBert-large

[5]https://huggingface.co/ai-forever/ruElectra-base

[6]https://huggingface.co/ai-forever/ruElectra-large

All encoder-only PLMs were fine-tuned for five epochs using the AdamW optimizer, a learning rate of 4e-5, a batch size of eight, and a maximum sequence length of 256 tokens. The fine-tuning procedure was performed in a multi-label setting, with a transformer-based classifier outputting $n$ binary labels. This study used $n$ equal to nine in accordance with the number of green waste practices in the dataset.

### 4.2 Encoder-decoder Models

- **ruT5**[7] (Zmitrovich et al., 2024), a text-to-text transformer pre-trained only on Russian-language textual data and designed analogically to T5 (Raffel et al., 2020).

- **mBART**[8] (Tang et al., 2021), a sequence-to-sequence machine translation model built on the baseline architecture of BART (Lewis et al., 2020). It was pre-trained on more than 50 languages using a combination of span masking and sentence shuffling techniques.

ruT5 and mBART were fine-tuned for 20 epochs. We explored several alternative forms of label descriptors, some of which were previously introduced in (Kementchedjhieva and Chalkidis, 2023), while others were proposed for the first time in this study. The following descriptors were used: **original** label descriptors in the Russian language; **simplified** one-word versions of original label descriptors; **numbers** assigned to green

[7]https://huggingface.co/ai-forever/ruT5-base

[8]https://huggingface.co/facebook/mbart-large-50

| Model | Version | Architecture | Params | Data source |
|---|---|---|---|---|
| ruBERT | rubert-base-cased | encoder-only | 180M | Wikipedia, news texts |
| | rubert-large | | 427M | Wikipedia, news texts, Librusec, C4, OpenSubtitles |
| ruELECTRA | ruelectra-medium | | 85M | |
| | ruelectra-large | | 427M | |
| ruT5 | rut5-base | encoder-decoder | 222M | |
| mBART | mbart-large-50 | | 680M | Common Crawl (CC25), monolingual data from XLMR |
| ruGPT | rugpt-3-medium | decoder-only | 355M | Wikipedia, news texts, Librusec, C4, OpenSubtitles |
| T-lite | t-lite-instruct-0.1 | | 8B | Open Source English-language datasets, translations of English-language datasets, synthetic grounded QA contexts |

Table 2: Overview of transformer-based models.

waste practices according to Table 1; **special tokens** added to the model and corresponding to green waste practices; **one-hot** label presentation. Since mBART is a multi-lingual model designed for machine translation, we also evaluated original and simplified label descriptors translated into the English language (**original-Eng**, **simplified-Eng**) for the mBART model. The examples of label descriptors are given in Table 3.

### 4.3 Decoder-only Models

- **ruGPT**[9] (Zmitrovich et al., 2024), a Russian equivalent of GPT-3, uses its architecture (Brown et al., 2020) and the GPT-2 code base from the Transformers library (Radford et al., 2019; Wolf et al., 2020).

- **T-lite**[10], an open-source instruction-based LLM with 85% of its pre-training data in Russian. For text generation, a temperature value was set to 1.

ruGPT was fine-tuned with a causal language modeling objective with a maximum sequence length of 1024 tokens for ten epochs. The input text was presented as follows: *text* + "Категории: " (*"Categories: "*) + *label descriptors*. The same list of label descriptors was used for ruGPT as for ruT5.

For T-lite, prompt-based learning was implemented using the Transformers library (Wolf et al., 2020). The models were tasked with analyzing the text, identifying mentions of green waste practices, and selecting one or more categories from the list of labels. Then, ten examples of texts and their corresponding labels were provided. We used two variations of a few-shot prompt. In the first case, the list of labels was provided without explanations. In the second case, each label was accompanied by a description (for example, Перерабатывать отходы: преобразование отходов в перерабатываемые материалы для дальнейшего использования в производстве, *Waste recycling: converting waste materials into reusable materials for further use in the production of something*).

### 4.4 Baselines

- K-nearest Neighbors classifier (**KNN**) with a number of neighbors equal to three and the weight points obtained by the inverse of their distance.

- Multi-layer Perceptron (**MLP**), a feed-forward neural network with a single hidden layer of size 100 and a hyperbolic tangent (tanh) activation function.

Both models were implemented using Scikit-Learn (Pedregosa et al., 2011) and the paraphrase-multilingual-MiniLM-L12-v2 model (Reimers and Gurevych, 2020) as a sentence embedder.

### 4.5 Evaluation Metric

The multi-label F1-score was used as an evaluation metric. This metric was calculated by determining the F1-score for each class individually and then averaging the results.

[9] `https://huggingface.co/ai-forever/rugpt3medium_based_on_gpt2`

[10] `https://huggingface.co/AnatoliiPotapov/T-lite-instruct-0.1`

| Label descriptor | Example |
|---|---|
| Text: Мой муж возит меня на сортировку с мешками вторсырья и не ворчит, неидентифицируемую упаковку складывает кучкой в кухне (*My husband takes me to the waste sorting center with the bags of recyclables without complaining and neatly stacks unidentifiable packaging in a corner of the kitchen*) | |
| Original | сортировать отходы, изучать маркировку товаров |
| Simplified | сортировка, маркировка |
| Numbers | 1, 2 |
| Special tokens | P1, P2 |
| One-hot | 110000000 |
| Original-Eng | waste sorting, studying the product labeling |
| Simplified-Eng | sorting, labeling |

Table 3: Label descriptors.

## 5 Results and Discussion

The results are presented in Table 4. The scores of baselines were 43.03% and 59.75% in terms of the multi-label F1-score for KNN and MLP respectively. The scores that outperform both baselines are underlined. The dotted line underlines the scores that surpass the KNN baseline. The highest value of the multi-label F1-score is shown in bold.

Encoder-only PLMs demonstrated relatively high results. All four PLMs outperformed baselines. The highest result of 67.88% in terms of the multi-label F1-score was shown by ruBERT-large.

Encoder-decoder PLMs mostly achieved the results above baselines. The best scores for ruT5 were obtained using simplified and original label descriptors (62.51% and 60.54% respectively). The use of the numbers, special tokens, and one-hot label descriptors did not increase the MLP results. The one-hot label descriptors did not even surpass KNN (34. 95%), indicating that the ruT5 model struggles to interpret this method of label representation. mBART demonstrated the highest score using simplified label descriptors (69.76%). The second and third highest scores were obtained with the original and simplified-Eng labels descriptors (69.49% and 69%). The use of the numbers and original-Eng label descriptors also improved the results of encoder-only PLMs (68.91% and 68.53%). The one-hot and special token label descriptors demonstrated the multi-label F1-score of 67.12% and 65.71% respectively which did not surpass ruBERT-large but outperformed baselines.

| Model | F1-score, % |
|---|---|
| Encoder-only models | |
| ruBERT-base | 66.53 |
| ruBERT-large | 67.88 |
| ruELECTRA-base | 65.28 |
| ruELECTRA-large | 65.69 |
| Encoder-decoder models | |
| ruT5 + original | 60.54 |
| ruT5 + simplified | 62.51 |
| ruT5 + numbers | 59.16 |
| ruT5 + special tokens | 52.60 |
| ruT5 + one-hot | 34.95 |
| mBART + original | 69.49 |
| mBART + simplified | **69.76** |
| mBART + numbers | 68.91 |
| mBART + special tokens | 65.71 |
| mBART + one-hot | 67.12 |
| mBART + original-Eng | 68.53 |
| mBART + simplified-Eng | 69.00 |
| Decoder-only models | |
| ruGPT + original | 46.66 |
| ruGPT + simplified | 51.08 |
| ruGPT + numbers | 33.07 |
| ruGPT + special tokens | 38.96 |
| ruGPT + one-hot | 41.29 |
| T-lite$_{few-shot}$ | 42.04 |
| T-lite$_{few-shot+explanations}$ | 47.77 |
| Baselines | |
| KNN | 43.03 |
| MLP | 59.75 |

Table 4: Results.

In general, decoder-only PLMs demonstrated

the lowest results in comparison to encoder-only and encoder-decoder PLMs. The highest result of ruGPT was obtained using the simplified label descriptors (51.08%). The use of the numbers, special tokens, and one-hot label descriptors showed the results below the KNN baseline. The instruction-based T-lite model also did not demonstrate high results. The use of prompt-based learning obtained 42.04% and 47.77% in terms of the multi-label F1-score. Despite the fact that incorporating explanations of green waste practices led to a more than 5% improvement in performance, T-lite failed to outperform the MLP baseline.

Figure 2 shows the performance growth using different label descriptors in comparison to the MLP baseline. The figure reveals that the labels descriptors based on text representation (original, simplified, original-Eng, and simplified-Eng) show higher results than the labels descriptors based on numerical and special token representation. For all three models (ruT5, mBART, ruGPT) the best results were achieved using the simplified label descriptors.

The RQs were aimed to evaluate the effectiveness of PLMs in detecting mentions of green waste practices on social media and to determine which transformer-based model architectures are the most effective for this task. Our experiments demonstrated that the performance of PLMs varies depending on their architecture and model type. Encoder-only models achieved the multilabel F1 score values between 65.28% and 67.88%, showing consistent and relatively strong performance. This supports their common use in multi-label classification tasks. However, the best result in our experiments was achieved by the mBART model (69.76%), highlighting the strong potential of encoder-decoder models for multi-label classification. Label descriptors greatly affect encoder-decoder models; for example, ruT5 results vary from 34.95% to 62.51%. Decoder-only models, including instruction-based ones, showed the poorest performance in our experiments. However, the results indicate that incorporating explanations into the prompt can enhance the performance of instruction-based models.

## 6 Conclusion

In this work, we explored the efficiency of PLMs for detecting mentions of green waste practices in social media. To address RQs, we compared encoder-only, encoder-decoder, and decoder-only PLMs. Our findings showed that encoder-only and encoder-decoder models generally outperformed decoder-only models. mBART achieved the best performance and revealed the most suitable label descriptors for generative PLMs in the multi-label text classification task.

This current study is limited by the use of only one data set to detect green waste practices. This is due to the fact that, to the best of the authors' knowledge, GreenRu is currently the only freely available dataset specifically annotated for this task. A potential future direction for this research could involve applying transfer learning techniques and generating texts to train models for other languages. Another possible limitation of this study is the use of general-domain models. Further research can investigate the role of in-domain pre-training for this task. Future research directions can additionally include exploring additional multilingual models beyond mBART and the MLP baseline to expand comparative insights. Investigating models with billion-scale parameters while incorporating PEFT (Parameter-Efficient Fine-Tuning) approaches could also enhance performance and efficiency.

The results obtained in this study allowed us to identify the most effective models for searching for green waste practices on social networks. Using these models, the following management tasks can be solved:

1. The prevalence of green waste practices in the text of posts from individual communities can be used to identify the specific activities of a particular community and select the most appropriate solutions when organizing companies to combat plastic pollution or solve the problem of food waste by organizing food sharing.

2. The most popular practices can be found in formalizing this activity through the form of standards for organizing green waste practices and their subsequent replication through training and information for eco-activists. For example, organizing separate waste collection in the yards of apartment blocks.

3. The least popular practices include organizing support for these practices, if they are seen as important behavioral changes to reduce anthropogenic climate impacts. For ex-

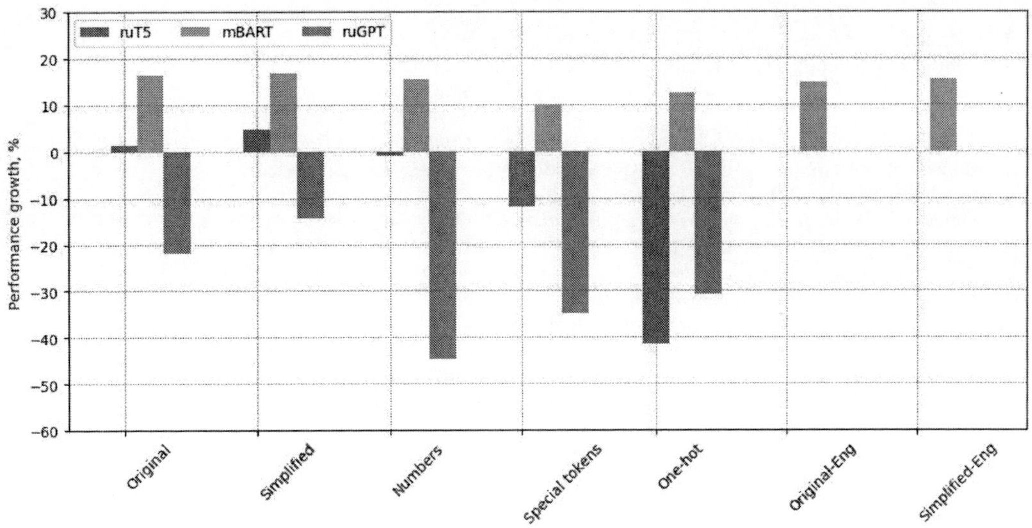


Figure 2: The performance growth using different label descriptors in comparison to the MLP baseline.

ample, organizing enlightening lectures on sustainable fashion.

4. The dynamics of mentions of each green practice can be studied to further explore the ways in which it is scaled up or the factors influencing green social innovation.

5. Communities can be found that do not position themselves as green, but organize eco-friendly activities to develop interactions between activists and provide mutual support for promoting green waste practices.

The information obtained through PLMs can be used by authorities, eco-businesses, and activists to promote behavioral change, support green innovation and promote sustainable social practices. The models for automatically detecting mentions of green waste practices make researching these practices easier and cheaper as they replace experts in dealing with textual information. Additionally, these methods allow processing large amounts of textual data that are not accessible to expert analysis.

## Acknowledgment


This study was supported by the Ministry of Science and Higher Education of the Russian Federation within the framework of the Carbon Measurement Test Area in Tyumen' Region (FEWZ-2024-0016).

We are grateful to Nadezhda Zhuravleva (Center for Academic Writing "Impulse", University of Tyumen) for her assistance with the English language.


## References


Tom Brown, Benjamin Mann, Nick Ryder, Melanie Subbiah, Jared D Kaplan, Prafulla Dhariwal, Arvind Neelakantan, Pranav Shyam, Girish Sastry, Amanda Askell, Sandhini Agarwal, Ariel Herbert-Voss, Gretchen Krueger, Tom Henighan, Rewon Child, Aditya Ramesh, Daniel Ziegler, Jeffrey Wu, Clemens Winter, Chris Hesse, Mark Chen, Eric Sigler, Mateusz Litwin, Scott Gray, Benjamin Chess, Jack Clark, Christopher Berner, Sam McCandlish, Alec Radford, Ilya Sutskever, and Dario Amodei. 2020. Language models are few-shot learners. In *Advances in Neural Information Processing Systems*, volume 33, pages 1877–1901. Curran Associates, Inc.

Ilias Chalkidis, Manos Fergadiotis, and Ion Androutsopoulos. 2021. MultiEURLEX-A multi-lingual and multi-label legal document classification dataset for zero-shot cross-lingual transfer. In *Proceedings of the 2021 Conference on Empirical Methods in Natural Language Processing*, pages 6974–6996.

Ilias Chalkidis, Manos Fergadiotis, Sotiris Kotitsas, Prodromos Malakasiotis, Nikolaos Aletras, and Ion Androutsopoulos. 2020. An empirical study on large-scale multi-label text classification including few and zero-shot labels. In *Proceedings of the 2020 Conference on Empirical Methods in Natural Language Processing (EMNLP)*, pages 7503–7515.

Kevin Clark, Minh-Thang Luong, Quoc V. Le, and Christopher D. Manning. 2020. ELECTRA: Pre-training text encoders as discriminators rather than generators. In *ICLR*.

Jacob Devlin, Ming-Wei Chang, Kenton Lee, and Kristina Toutanova. 2019. BERT: Pre-training of deep bidirectional transformers for language understanding. In *2019 Conference of the North American Chapter of the Association for Computational Linguistics: Human Language Technologies, Volume 1 (Long and Short Papers)*, pages 4171–4186, Minneapolis, Minnesota. Association for Computational Linguistics.

Anthony Giddens. 1984. The constitution of society: Outline of the theory of structuration. *Polity*.

Shelley Haines, Omar H Fares, Myuri Mohan, and Seung Hwan Lee. 2023. Social media fashion influencer eWOM communications: understanding the trajectory of sustainable fashion conversations on YouTube fashion haul videos. *Journal of Fashion Marketing and Management: An International Journal*, 27(6):1027–1046.

Yova Kementchedjhieva and Ilias Chalkidis. 2023. An exploration of encoder-decoder approaches to multi-label classification for legal and biomedical text. In *Findings of the Association for Computational Linguistics: ACL 2023*, pages 5828–5843.

Yuri Kuratov and Mikhail Arkhipov. 2019. Adaptation of deep bidirectional multilingual transformers for Russian language. In *Komp'juternaja Lingvistika i Intellektual'nye Tehnologii*, pages 333–339.

Jenna A Lamphere and Jon Shefner. 2018. How to green: Institutional influence in three us cities. *Critical Sociology*, 44(2):303–322.

Mike Lewis, Yinhan Liu, Naman Goyal, Marjan Ghazvininejad, Abdelrahman Mohamed, Omer Levy, Veselin Stoyanov, and Luke Zettlemoyer. 2020. BART: Denoising sequence-to-sequence pre-training for natural language generation, translation, and comprehension. In *Proceedings of the 58th Annual Meeting of the Association for Computational Linguistics*, pages 7871–7880.

Marion van Lunenburg, Karin Geuijen, and Albert Meijer. 2020. How and why do social and sustainable initiatives scale? a systematic review of the literature on social entrepreneurship and grassroots innovation. *VOLUNTAS: International Journal of Voluntary and Nonprofit Organizations*, 31(5):1013–1024.

Fabian Pedregosa, Gaël Varoquaux, Alexandre Gramfort, Vincent Michel, Bertrand Thirion, Olivier Grisel, Mathieu Blondel, Peter Prettenhofer, Ron Weiss, Vincent Dubourg, et al. 2011. Scikit-learn: Machine learning in Python. *the Journal of machine Learning research*, 12:2825–2830.

Alejandro Peña, Aythami Morales, Julian Fierrez, Ignacio Serna, Javier Ortega-Garcia, Iñigo Puente, Jorge Cordova, and Gonzalo Cordova. 2023. Leveraging large language models for topic classification in the domain of public affairs. In *International Conference on Document Analysis and Recognition*, pages 20–33. Springer.

Youri Peskine, Damir Korenčić, Ivan Grubisic, Paolo Papotti, Raphael Troncy, and Paolo Rosso. 2023. Definitions matter: Guiding GPT for multi-label classification. In *Findings of the Association for Computational Linguistics: EMNLP 2023*, pages 4054–4063, Singapore. Association for Computational Linguistics.

Alec Radford, Jeffrey Wu, Rewon Child, David Luan, Dario Amodei, and Ilya Sutskever. 2019. Language models are unsupervised multitask learners. *OpenAI*. Accessed: 2024-11-15.

Colin Raffel, Noam Shazeer, Adam Roberts, Katherine Lee, Sharan Narang, Michael Matena, Yanqi Zhou, Wei Li, and Peter J Liu. 2020. Exploring the limits of transfer learning with a unified text-to-text transformer. *Journal of machine learning research*, 21(140):1–67.

Nils Reimers and Iryna Gurevych. 2020. Making monolingual sentence embeddings multilingual using knowledge distillation. In *Proceedings of the 2020 Conference on Empirical Methods in Natural Language Processing*. Association for Computational Linguistics.

Pinar Savci and Bihter Das. 2024. Multi-label classification in text data: An examination on innovative technologies. In *2024 12th International Symposium on Digital Forensics and Security (ISDFS)*, pages 1–4. IEEE.

Muhammad Hammad Fahim Siddiqui, Diana Inkpen, and Alexander Gelbukh. 2024. Instruction Tuning of LLMs for Multi-label EmotionClassification in Social Media Content. *Proceedings of the Canadian Conference on Artificial Intelligence*. Https://caiac.pubpub.org/pub/lezimqvm.

Uthayasankar Sivarajah, Zahir Irani, Suraksha Gupta, and Kamran Mahroof. 2020. Role of big data and social media analytics for business to business sustainability: A participatory web context. *Industrial Marketing Management*, 86:163–179.

Yuqing Tang, Chau Tran, Xian Li, Peng-Jen Chen, Naman Goyal, Vishrav Chaudhary, Jiatao Gu, and Angela Fan. 2021. Multilingual translation from denoising pre-training. In *Findings of the Association for Computational Linguistics: ACL-IJCNLP 2021*, pages 3450–3466, Online. Association for Computational Linguistics.

Dinithi Vithanage, Chao Deng, Lei Wang, Mengyang Yin, Mohammad Alkhalaf, Zhenyu Zhang, Yunshu Zhu, Alan Christy Soewargo, and Ping Yu. 2024.

Evaluating approaches of training a generative large language model for multi-label classification of unstructured electronic health records. *medRxiv*, pages 2024–06.

Thomas Wolf, Lysandre Debut, Victor Sanh, Julien Chaumond, Clement Delangue, Anthony Moi, Pierric Cistac, Tim Rault, Rémi Louf, Morgan Funtowicz, et al. 2020. Transformers: State-of-the-art natural language processing. In *Proceedings of the 2020 conference on empirical methods in natural language processing: system demonstrations*, pages 38–45.

Ramil Yarullin and Pavel Serdyukov. 2021. BERT for sequence-to-sequence multi-label text classification. In *Analysis of Images, Social Networks and Texts*, pages 187–198, Cham. Springer International Publishing.

Hamada M Zahera, Ibrahim A Elgendy, Rricha Jalota, Mohamed Ahmed Sherif, and E Voorhees. 2019. Fine-tuned BERT model for multi-label tweets classification. In *TREC*, pages 1–7.

Olga Zakharova and Anna Glazkova. 2024. GreenRu: A Russian dataset for detecting mentions of green practices in social media posts. *Applied Sciences*, 14(11):4466.

Olga Zakharova, Anna Glazkova, and Lyudmila Suvorova. 2023. Online equipment repair community in Russia: Searching for environmental discourse. *Sustainability*, 15(17):12990.

Olga V Zakharova, Anna V Glazkova, Irina N Pupysheva, and Natalia V Kuznetsova. 2022. The importance of green practices to reduce consumption. *Changing Societies & Personalities. 2022. Vol. 6. Iss. 4*, pages 884–905.

Olga V Zakharova, Tatiana I Payusova, Irina D Akhmedova, and Lyudmila G Suvorova. 2021. Green practices: Approaches to investigation. *Sotsiologicheskie issledovaniya*, (4):25–36.

Dmitry Zmitrovich, Aleksandr Abramov, Andrey Kalmykov, Vitaly Kadulin, Maria Tikhonova, Ekaterina Taktasheva, Danil Astafurov, Mark Baushenko, Artem Snegirev, Tatiana Shavrina, et al. 2024. A family of pretrained transformer language models for Russian. In *Proceedings of the 2024 Joint International Conference on Computational Linguistics, Language Resources and Evaluation (LREC-COLING 2024)*, pages 507–524.

# Perspectives on Forests and Forestry in Finnish Online Discussions - A Topic Modeling Approach to Suomi24

**Telma Peura, Attila Krizsán, Salla-Riikka Kuusalu and Veronika Laippala**
School of Languages and Translation studies,
University of Turku
tejpeu, attila.krizsan, srkbos, mavela
@utu.fi

## Abstract

This paper explores how forests and forest industry are perceived on the largest online discussion forum in Finland, Suomi24 ('Finland24'). Using 30,636 posts published in 2014–2020, we investigate what kind of topics and perspectives towards forest management can be found. We use BERTopic as our topic modeling approach and evaluate the results of its different modular combinations. As the dataset is not labeled, we demonstrate the validity of our best model through illustrating some of the topics about forest use. The results show that a combination of UMAP and K-means leads to the best topic quality. Our exploratory qualitative analysis indicates that the posts reflect polarized discourses between the forest industry and forest conservation adherents.

## 1 Introduction

The importance of forests as carbon sinks has been globally recognized as part of climate change mitigation (IPCC, 2023). In Finland, where forests have a significant socio-economic role, the issue has received increased attention and created tensions across different economic and political views (Makkonen et al., 2015; Kellokumpu, 2022; Blattert et al., 2023). In fact, around 75% of Finnish land area is covered by forests of which only 12.9% is partially or totally conserved from industrial forest management (Ministry of Agriculture and Forestry, 2024).

Perspectives of the forest industry have also been prominent in the media. Analyses of Finnish newspapers show that despite emerging multi-objective discourses, the positive framing of the forest industry still seems to dominate (Näyhä and Wallius; Takala et al.). However, computational approaches to forest discourses have not, to our knowledge, been applied.

While analyzing the representation of forests in the mainstream media is valuable, the voices of common citizens cannot be overlooked. In fact, around 60% of Finnish forests are owned by private individuals (Karppinen et al., 2020). The right of public access and the high percentage of private forest ownership make public opinion critical to understanding how forest-related issues are perceived and debated.

To set light on the perspective of forest owners and users and understand their attitudes towards forest management, we used data from Suomi24 (translated as 'Finland24'). Suomi24 is the oldest and largest online forum in Finland and has been called a pool of Finnish public opinions (Ylisiurua, 2024).

We applied topic modeling to cluster documents and to identify forest-related themes in our dataset. Recent advances in machine learning and large language models have led to the development of new topic modeling tools (Abdelrazek et al., 2023). In particular, Bidirectional Encoder Representations from Transformers (BERT) have been found to be powerful in many NLP tasks (Wijanto et al., 2024; Devlin et al., 2019). BERTopic presented by Grootendorst (2022) has proved to perform well in many topic modeling tasks and was also adopted in our work. The modular approach of BERTopic allowed us to build several different models. The different combinations were compared through computational and qualitative measures.

In this paper, our first aim is to evaluate the performance of different BERTopic models and demonstrate how topic modeling can be used to identify relevant topics about the use of forests in Finland. Second, we aim at characterizing how forest management and industry are discussed in our Suomi24 dataset.



*Proceedings of the 1st Workshop on Ecology, Environment, and Natural Language Processing (NLP4Ecology2025)*, pages 10–15
March 2, 2025 

The model evaluation results showed that there was great variance in the model quality. However, a comparison of topic keywords showed that all of them captured similar topics that can give valuable insights into Finnish forest discourse. The qualitative exploration suggested that pro-forestry discourses dominate over pro-nature discourses, but the distinction between these two is not always clear. Finally, we briefly discuss how this analysis can be extended in the future.

## 2 Data and Methods

Our methodology combined quantitative exploration and closer qualitative analysis of selected topics. The design allowed to compare the performance of different topic models on unlabeled data. The steps of the workflow are described in this section.

### 2.1 Dataset Preparation

The Suomi24 corpus was gathered and made openly available by the Language Bank of Finland[1] (Lagus et al., 2016). Overall, it contains discussions from 2001 to 2020, amounting to over 480,000,000 tokens (City Digital Group, 2021). In our study, we use posts beginning from year 2014, when the Forest Act providing a legislative framework for forest management in Finland was amended (Ministry of Agriculture and Forestry, n.d.). Following Lehti et al. (2020), we curated a list of search words to collect posts that were potentially relevant for our study. The list contained terms related to forest industry, forest conservation and the recreational use of forests. In addition, Word2Vec was applied to expand the list with semantically similar words in the same corpus[2]. This was done to reduce the subjectivity of the search words and to make the resulting dataset more comprehensive. Next, we removed duplicates and filtered out short documents (under 7 tokens). Upper-case words were lowercased. The final dataset consisted of 30,636 documents, when 10% of the total data was retained as a test set for later use.

### 2.2 Topic Modeling

We selected BERTopic (Grootendorst, 2022) as our topic modeling approach. Based on pre-trained language models, BERT can generate contextual vector embeddings of text documents (Wijanto et al., 2024). BERTopic relies on the assumption that semantically similar documents have similar embeddings, and the pipeline consists of the following steps: First, documents are converted into BERT embeddings with a pre-trained language model. In our experiment, we compared the performance of a multilingual sentence transformer, 'paraphrase-xlm-r-multilingual-v1' (Reimers and Gurevych, 2019), and the Cased Finnish Sentence BERT model, specifically trained for Finnish language [3]. Next, to optimize the clustering performance, the dimensionality of the embeddings is reduced. By default, the framework employs UMAP (McInnes et al., 2020), but some experiments have obtained superior results with principal component analysis (PCA) (Wijanto et al., 2024). Thus, both algorithms were tested.

For topic creation, we used two different clustering algorithms, HDBSCAN, and K-Means. The advantage of HDBSCAN is that it assigns the label -1 to documents considered noise (Grootendorst, 2022), and it can automatically determine the number of topics (McInnes et al., 2017). In contrast, the number of topics for K-Means has to be predetermined. To estimate an optimal number of topics, the elbow method (Cui, 2020) and silhouette scores (Shutaywi and Kachouie, 2021) were used.

Finally, BERTopic uses a class-based variant of term frequency-inverse document frequency (c-TF-IDF) to produce topic representations from the clusters. Instead of a classical TF-IDF that extracts words important for a document, the proposed c-TF-IDF procedure extracts words that have importance for the whole topic (Grootendorst, 2022).

### 2.3 Evaluation Methods and Qualitative Analysis

We evaluated the models in two ways. As a computed metric, we chose the coherence score $C_v$ that has been found to correlate well with human ratings (Röder et al., 2015). Moreover, a member of the research team reviewed the topic keywords (20 per topic) of all models and rated their quality as good, satisfactory or unsatisfactory. For a good topic, all keywords had to be co-

[1] https://www.kielipankki.fi/corpora/suomi24/

[2] The similarity was calculated using http://epsilon-it.utu.fi/wv_demo/]

[3] For documentation, see https://turkunlp.org/paraphrase.html

| Embedding model | Dimensionality reduction | Clustering | Topics | Coherence score, $C_v$ | Avg. topic size (nr of -1 docs) | Quality topics |
|---|---|---|---|---|---|---|
| Finnish | UMAP | HDBSCAN | 175 | 0.49 | 52 (21 623) | |
| | PCA | HDBSCAN | 35 | 0.45 | 18 (30 013) | |
| | UMAP | K-means | 175 | 0.47 | 175 | **99** |
| | PCA | K-means | 200 | **0.54** | 153 | 52 |
| Multilingual | UMAP | HDBSCAN | 175 | 0.49 | 60 (20 145) | |
| | PCA | HDBSCAN | 32 | 0.48 | 32 (29 659) | |
| | UMAP | K-means | 175 | 0.47 | 175 | 93 |
| | PCA | K-means | 150 | 0.50 | 204 | 41 |

Table 1: An overview of trained models and evaluation results. For the models using HDBSCAN, the size of the 'noise' cluster (nr of -1 docs) is reported along with the average topic size.

herent, the label 'satisfactory' allowed for 2-3 outliers, and the label 'unsatisfactory' was used for mixed or incomprehensible keywords. The number of good-quality topics was used as an indicator of model performance. Only good-quality topics (represented as 'Quality topics' in Table 1) were considered in the further qualitative analysis.

Since K-means forces all documents into some clusters, the documents with a low topic probability were filtered out. A good threshold was found experimentally to be at $M_{topic}$ - $SD_{topic}$ where *M* is the mean probability of the assigned topic and *SD* the respective standard deviation per topic cluster.

After this, relevant topics were identified on the basis of topic keywords. The relevance was determined by the following criteria: the topic was of good quality and the keywords were related to forestry and forest management. Consequently, e.g. recreational forest activities such as berry-picking and hiking, were not considered in this paper. A member of the research team read a sample of 20 documents from each potentially relevant topic to validate the selection.

The relevant documents were grouped into broader thematic categories, and posts from these thematic categories were used in the preliminary close reading analysis.

## 3 Results and Analysis

The combinations of different algorithms and the evaluation results are shown in Table 1. The results point to a discrepancy between the computational and human-annotated measures of topic coherence, as the columns 'Coherence score, $C_v$' and 'Quality topics' show. While the amount of good-quality topics was highest for the models using UMAP and K-means, the models with PCA yielded a better coherence score. It indicates that the coherence measure $C_v$ is not well adapted for BERTopic.

Moreover, the HDBSCAN algorithm labeled most of the documents as 'noise', while a closer look at the discarded documents showed that many of them were relevant to forest discussion, and the 'noise' category keywords contained several forest-related terms. Due to this, the HDBSCAN models were not included in further evaluation of topic quality and qualitative analysis.

Although the performance of the models varied, we observed that all of them produced topics with similar keywords. This reinforced our confidence in the reliability of the generated topics.

The Finnish sentence embedding model performed slightly better than the multilingual one, but the choice of the dimensionality reduction and clustering algorithms had a greater effect on the result. Overall, UMAP was the most suitable dimensionality reduction algorithm for our dataset and K-means functioned well for topic clustering.

As Table 1 shows, the combination of Finnish BERT model, UMAP and K-means yielded the highest amount of good-quality topics. Since the difference from the multilingual model was relatively small, we analyzed the hierarchical topic structure[4] of these two models and inspected a sample of 10 documents from 15 randomly selected topics. This check confirmed that the Finnish model performed best with our data, and it was selected for further analysis[5].

[4]The hierarchy was produced with BERTopic's in-built hierarchical topic modeling function.

[5]The topic assignments are provided on: `https://github.com/TurkuNLP/forest-in-s24`.

| Topics | Example keywords | Theme | Nr of posts |
|---|---|---|---|
| 30, 80, 99, 112, 136, 141 | kasvatus ('forestry'), raivaus ('clearing'), taimikko ('seedling stand'), omistaja ('owner'), kemera ('a forestry funding'), metsuri ('logger') | Forestry | 1,185 |
| 2, 10, 43, 72, 173 | luonnonsuojelija ('environmentalist'), linkola (a Finnish ecologist and nature activist, Pentti Linkola), vihreät ('The Greens'), luonnonsuojelu-alue ('nature reserve'), biologia ('biology') | Nature conservation, environmentalists | 1,111 |
| 42, 73, 106, 133 | ostaja ('purchaser'), hinta ('price'), $m^3$, pystykauppa ('stumpage sale'), kuitupuu ('pulp-wood'), osake ('share'), hakkuukone ('harvester') | Forest and timber trade | 1,017 |
| 24, 88, 151 | Avohakkuu ('clearcutting'), puupelto ('forest field'), päätehakkuu ('regeneration felling'), metsä ('for-est'), puu ('wood') | Clearcutting | 678 |
| 34, 64, 79, 127 | $CO_2$, ilmasto ('climate'), turve ('peat'), hiilinielu ('carbon sink'), päästöt ('emissions'), energiantuotanto ('energy production') | Climate change | 662 |
| 120, 165 | metsänhoitoyhdistys, mhy ('Forestry management association, FMA'), jäsenyys ('membership'), palvelu ('service') | Forestry management associations | 508 |

Table 2: A table of relevant topics with example keywords and topic size.

The topic annotation and evaluation showed that various forest-related themes were discussed, and 41 of the quality topics were considered relevant from the perspective of forestry and forest industry. The most prominent of these are listed in Table 2. All translations to English are done by the authors. A comparison of topic sizes indicates that topics related to forest management and trade (2 880 posts) dominate over topics about forest conservation and climate change (1 773 posts).

However, the distinction between the themes is not always clear. For instance, the proponents (example 1) and opponents (example 2) of clearcutting both appeal to the health of the forest:

> (1) In Finland, forest management aims to ensure that forests only have healthy growing trees. No thickets or rotten wood.

> (2) Forest fields and pine trees struggling along ditched banks are not forests. Forests exist only in nature reserves and among the few landowners who think with their own brains.

The term 'forest field' is frequently evoked by the opponents. Example 2 also shows how the intelligence of the forest owners is questioned. Similarly, the proponents of clearcutting rely on their expertise and criticize their opponents for not knowing the field. A typical view is shown in example 3.

> (3) Finland has university-level forestry education and, even on a global scale, Finland is one of the most competent and professional forestry countries. It is sad and stupid to see how eagerly people who live in cities and know almost nothing about forests discuss forest management and take strict positions on, for example, this issue of clearcutting.

Overall, the exploratory close reading suggested that the issue of clearcuttings is polarized with few negotiating voices in the discussions.

## 4 Discussion and Future Work

In this paper, we presented a framework that combined topic modeling and qualitative exploration to investigate how forest-related issues are addressed in a Finnish online forum, Suomi24. We compared different BERTopic models, and the evaluation results showed that its default clustering algorithm, HDBSCAN, did not function well with our data. Based on our observations, numerous relevant posts were discarded by these models.

Best results were obtained by combining Finnish sentence BERT, UMAP, and K-means.

As Abdelrazek et al. (2023) point out, the parameters of a neural topic model are often difficult to interpret and hence it is hard to diagnose why the HDBSCAN model did not work. K-means was found to produce topics of better quality, but as the method forces all texts into some clusters, we needed to filter the resulting topics to discard irrelevant documents.

Even the best models contained several topics of low quality, which is due to several reasons. First, we collected the dataset from the Suomi24 corpus using a list of search words, which means that it potentially contained several texts not related to the themes of interest. Misspellings and colloquial language in the posts introduced noise in the data, leading to suboptimal sentence embeddings and reduced model accuracy. While the Finnish sentence transformer outperformed the multilingual one, Finnish is still a lower-resource language, which may show in the performance of the models.

The best model could be improved by changing the number of topics. In addition, we did not test different hyperparameters for the used algorithms, so our final model could be improved through finetuning the UMAP and K-means modules.

We noted a striking difference in the computational and human annotated results of quality evaluation. Moreover, the coherence measure $C_v$ is usually used with LDA models, and it measures coherence based on the co-occurrence of the given topic keywords in a corpus. Since BERTopic generates topics through embeddings, not words, this approach does not fully capture the semantic coherence of the generated topics. These observations remind us that quality in topic modeling is dependent on several aspects (Abdelrazek et al., 2023) and computational performance measures can be misleading. Thus, human evaluation is crucial when the resulting topics are used for qualitative analysis. Overall, the evaluation of neural topic models calls for new measures.

Many topics shared a common broader theme, and this overlap suggests that the number of topics could be further reduced. However, close reading the posts showed that different topics offered diverse viewpoints and reflected distinct discourses on the same theme. For instance, the theme related to nature conservation and environmentalists could have been further divided into political, activist, and other perspectives on the theme. Although the scope of this paper did not allow us to delve deeper into these differences, it was an interesting observation for future studies.

The exploratory qualitative analysis showed that opinions on forestry and forest management tend to be polarized. In the future, we aim to expand the analysis of such polarization by studying texts in selected topics (e.g., clearcuttings) by applying methods of 'making strange', close-reading (Gasper, 2022) and analyses of topic chains following Li (2004) and Li and Thompson (1981).

## Acknowledgments

This work has been supported by Kone Foundation, grant number 202302300 for *Seedling*.

## References

Aly Abdelrazek, Yomna Eid, Eman Gawish, Walaa Medhat, and Ahmed Hassan. 2023. Topic modeling algorithms and applications: A survey. *Information Systems*, 112:102131.

Clemens Blattert, Mikko Mönkkönen, Daniel Burgas, Fulvio Di Fulvio, Astor Toraño Caicoya, Marta Vergarechea, Julian Klein, Markus Hartikainen, Clara Antón-Fernández, Rasmus Astrup, Michael Emmerich, Nicklas Forsell, Jani Lukkarinen, Johanna Lundström, Samuli Pitzén, Werner Poschenrieder, Eeva Primmer, Tord Snäll, and Kyle Eyvindson. 2023. Climate targets in european timber-producing countries conflict with goals on forest ecosystem services and biodiversity. *Communications Earth Environment*, 4(1):1–12.

City Digital Group. 2021. Suomi24-korpus 2001-2020, VRT-versio.

Mengyao Cui. 2020. Introduction to the k-means clustering algorithm based on the elbow method. *Accounting, Auditing and Finance*, 1(1):5–8.

Jacob Devlin, Ming-Wei Chang, Kenton Lee, and Kristina Toutanova. 2019. Bert: Pre-training of deep bidirectional transformers for language understanding. (arXiv:1810.04805).

Des Gasper. 2022. 'making strange': Discourse analysis tools for teaching critical development studies. *Progress in Development Studies*, 22(3):288–304.

Maarten Grootendorst. 2022. Bertopic: Neural topic modeling with a class-based tf-idf procedure.

IPCC. 2023. Summary for policymakers. In *Climate Change 2023: Synthesis Report. Contribution of Working Groups I, II and III to the Sixth Assessment Report of the Intergovernmental Panel on Climate Change*, pages 1–34. IPCC.

Heimo Karppinen, Harri Hänninen, and Paula Horne. 2020. *Suomalainen metsänomistaja 2020*. Luonnonvarakeskus.

Ville Kellokumpu. 2022. The bioeconomy, carbon sinks, and depoliticization in finnish forest politics. 5(3):1164–1183. Publisher: SAGE Publications Ltd STM.

Krista Hannele Lagus, Minna Susanna Ruckenstein, Mika Pantzar, and Marjoriikka Jelena Ylisiurua. 2016. Suomi24: muodonantoa aineistolle.

Lotta Lehti, Milla Luodonpää-Manni, Jarmo Harri Jantunen, Aki-Juhani Kyröläinen, Aleksi Vesanto, and Veronika Lappala. 2020. Commenting on poverty online : A corpus-assisted discourse study of the suomi24 forum. 37. Accepted: 2021-03-05T10:02:31Z Publisher: Suomen kielitieteellinen yhdistys.

Charles N Li and Sandra A Thompson. 1981. *Mandarin Chinese: A Functional Reference Grammar*. University of California Press.

Wendan Li. 2004. Topic chains in chinese discourse. *Discourse Processes*, 37(1):25–45.

Marika Makkonen, Suvi Huttunen, Eeva Primmer, Anna Repo, and Mikael Hildén. 2015. Policy coherence in climate change mitigation: An ecosystem service approach to forests as carbon sinks and bioenergy sources. 50:153–162.

Leland McInnes, John Healy, Steve Astels, et al. 2017. hdbscan: Hierarchical density based clustering. *J. Open Source Softw.*, 2(11):205.

Leland McInnes, John Healy, and James Melville. 2020. Umap: Uniform manifold approximation and projection for dimension reduction. (arXiv:1802.03426). ArXiv:1802.03426 [stat].

Ministry of Agriculture and Forestry. 2024. Forest resources in finland.

Ministry of Agriculture and Forestry. n.d. Forest act.

Annukka Näyhä and Venla Wallius. Actors, discourses and relations in the finnish newspapers' forest discussion: Enabling or constraining the sustainability transition? 169:103331.

Nils Reimers and Iryna Gurevych. 2019. Sentence-bert: Sentence embeddings using siamese bert-networks. In *Proceedings of the 2019 Conference on Empirical Methods in Natural Language Processing*. Association for Computational Linguistics.

Michael Röder, Andreas Both, and Alexander Hinneburg. 2015. Exploring the space of topic coherence measures. In *Proceedings of the eighth ACM international conference on Web search and data mining*, pages 399–408.

Meshal Shutaywi and Nezamoddin N. Kachouie. 2021. Silhouette analysis for performance evaluation in machine learning with applications to clustering. *Entropy*, 23(66):759.

Tuomo Takala, Ari Lehtinen, Minna Tanskanen, Teppo Hujala, and Jukka Tikkanen. The rise of multi-objective forestry paradigm in the finnish print media. 106:101973.

Maresha Caroline Wijanto, Ika Widiastuti, and Hwan-Seung Yong. 2024. Topic modeling for scientific articles: Exploring optimal hyperparameter tuning in bert. *International Journal on Advanced Science, Engineering Information Technology*, 14(3).

Marjoriikka Ylisiurua. 2024. *Online swarm dynamics at Suomi24 discussion: Turning points and their stimulation*. Ph.D. thesis, Helsingin yliopisto.

# Mining for Species, Locations, Habitats, and Ecosystems from Scientific Papers in Invasion Biology: A Large-Scale Exploratory Study with Large Language Models

**Jennifer D'Souza**[1], **Zachary Laubach**[2], **Tarek Al Mustafa**[3], **Sina Zarrieß**[4], **Robert Frühstückl**[5], **Phyllis Illari**[6]
[1]TIB Leibniz Information Centre for Science and Technology,
[2]University of Colorado Boulder, [3]Friedrich Schiller University Jena, [4,5]Bielefeld University,
[6]University College London
jennifer.dsouza@tib.eu

## Abstract

This study explores the use of large language models (LLMs), specifically GPT-4o, to extract key ecological entities—species, locations, habitats, and ecosystems—from invasion biology literature. This information is critical for understanding species spread, predicting future invasions, and informing conservation efforts. Without domain-specific fine-tuning, we assess the potential and limitations of GPT-4o, out-of-the-box, for this task, highlighting the role of LLMs in advancing automated knowledge extraction for ecological research and management.

## 1 Introduction

Human population growth and expansion drive the intentional and unintentional movement of species beyond their historic ranges, leading to significant ecological impacts (Roy et al., 2023). Invasion biology seeks to understand these impacts across ecological scales to conserve native species and maintain functional ecosystems that provide essential services (Cassey et al., 2018; Jeschke and Heger, 2018). However, alien species introductions occur at an accelerating pace globally, making it increasingly difficult for researchers to systematically track and categorize species, their locations, and relationships. This paper explores the potential of recent NLP technologies, specifically Information Extraction (IE) approaches based on Large Language Models (LLMs) (Amatriain et al., 2023; Jennifer D'Souza, 2025), as tools for predicting future invasions and their consequences.

The extraction and categorization of information from scientific publications is a well-known NLP task (Augenstein et al., 2017; Gábor et al., 2018; Luan et al., 2018; Brack et al., 2020; Dessì et al., 2020; D'Souza et al., 2021; Liu et al., 2021; Kabongo et al., 2021; D'Souza and Auer, 2022; D'Souza, 2024; Shamsabadi et al., 2024; D'Souza et al., 2024). While Named Entity Recognition (NER) and Relation Extraction (RE) have been extensively applied in the biomedical domain for network biology (Zhou et al., 2014), gene prioritization (Aerts et al., 2006), drug repositioning (Wang and Zhang, 2013), and curated database creation (Li et al., 2015), their application in invasion biology remains underexplored. To the best of our knowledge, the small-scale INAS dataset (Brinner et al., 2022) is the only invasion biology-specific resource with annotated hypotheses for scientific abstracts.

This paper investigates information extraction (IE) in invasion biology, encompassing both named entity recognition (NER) and relation extraction (RE). We simultaneously build on studies showing that jointly learning NER and RE can enhance overall performance (Giorgi et al., 2019) and on recent LLMs which may open new opportunities for IE. Thus, our central question is whether LLMs, with their advanced pattern recognition capabilities, can be effectively applied to a new domain to simultaneously identify entities and infer their relationships. We prompt LLMs to extract four key entities—species, location, habitat, and ecosystem—and qualitatively evaluate results by addressing: (i) the relevance of extracted entities and interactions, (ii) the types of inferred relationships, and (iii) the benefits of LLM workflows for large-scale data mining. This work makes two key contributions: (i) the release of a text data mining corpus of over 10,000 invasion biology papers, including full text for nearly 2,000, with structured information extracted by GPT-4o (`https://doi.org/10.5281/zenodo.13956882`); and (ii) a systematic workflow for schema discovery in IE tasks, broadly applicable for leveraging LLMs in open-ended IE objectives.



*Proceedings of the 1st Workshop on Ecology, Environment, and Natural Language Processing (NLP4Ecology2025)*, pages 16–23
March 2, 2025 ©2025 University of Tartu Library

## 2 Our Text Data Mining Corpus

As a first step, we compiled a literature corpus as the unstructured source of scientific information. Starting with the Invasion Biology Corpus (Mietchen et al., 2024), which catalogs metadata for 49,438 papers in Wikidata. Using their DOIs, we queried the ORKG ASK search engine's API to retrieve abstracts and full texts, leveraging ASK's broad coverage of over 80 million papers (Knoth et al., 2023). Of the 49,438 queried papers, 12,636 were available in ASK—9,802 with abstracts only and 2,834 with both abstracts and full texts—highlighting the challenge of limited open-access availability. Bibliometric analysis of these abstracts shows papers spanning 52 years (since 1950), with full texts available from 1990 onward. A snapshot of the past 20 years (Figure 1) shows 2016 as the peak year for abstracts (1,183) and 2017 for full texts (294). Figure 2 presents the distribution across the top ten publishers, with further details in our online repository.

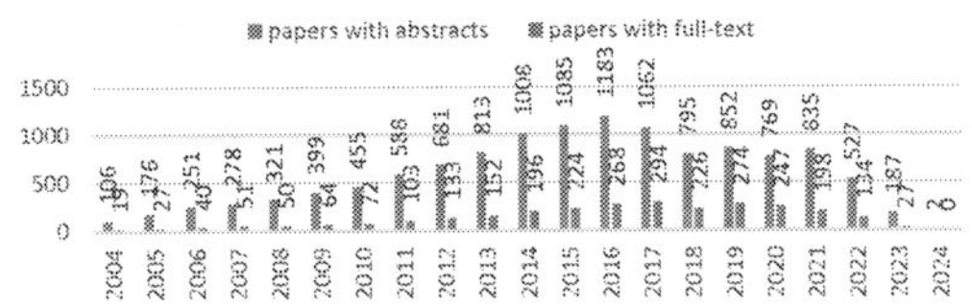


Figure 1: Distribution of papers in our corpus over the past 20 years.

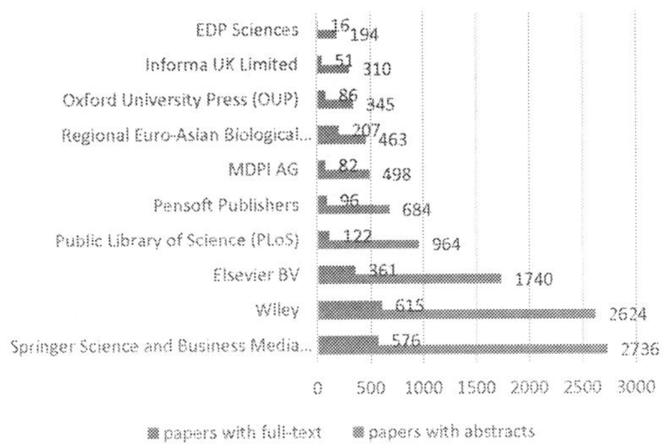


Figure 2: Distribution of papers in our corpus across the top ten publishers.

## 3 Information Extraction with LLMs

An IE task requires two prerequisites: 1) a collection of papers for processing, and 2) a schema defining the extraction targets.

### 3.1 Schema Discovery

Schema discovery is central to our approach, aiming to define a standardized semantic structure for IE from scientific papers. Without a predefined set of relations, our schema must flexibly capture extracted entities and their relationships. We achieve this in two stages: **specialize** and **generalize.** In the **specialize** stage, the LLM generates a schema for each paper in a given small sample, positing specialized extraction targets on four entities—*species*, *location*, *habitat*, and *ecosystem*. In the **generalize** stage, the LLM synthesizes a unified schema from multiple specialized schema instances, providing a flexible framework for relation extraction across all papers.

#### 3.1.1 Stage Specialize: Schemas per Paper

The LLM operates in *completion* mode, guided by a SYSTEM PROMPT that defines its role as a "research assistant in invasion biology," tasked with extracting entity relationships. Initially, the prompt lacked precise entity definitions, but expert feedback led to refinements incorporating formal definitions, improving consistency (Table 1). The final system prompt aims to align the LLM for more accurate structured IE. The USER PROMPT then supplies each paper's title and abstract.

**Results.** Ten randomly selected papers were processed, with the resulting schemas available in our repository. Nine were true positives, while one was an outlier, indicating potential false positives in dataset filtering. Early schemas, such as Schema 1, employed basic entity categorization, whereas later schemas, like Schema 8, introduced more nuanced relationships by incorporating ecological and anthropogenic interactions. This evolution improved granularity and contextual relevance, capturing species dynamics within environmental conditions. Recurring patterns and study-specific distinctions emerged, with common themes—e.g., invasion biology, pollination networks, and anthropogenic impacts—highlighting research priorities. Standardized fields such as *species* and *location* ensured consistency, while tailored relationships, including "most effective pollinators" in Schema 2 and "competitive replacement" in Schema 5, provided contextual specificity. Integrating spatial and environmental parameters further reinforced the significance of habitats and ecosystems in ecological interactions.

| Entity | Description |
|---|---|
| **Species** | Includes specific named species (e.g., Asterias amurensis) and broader categories (e.g., demersal fish, aquatic invertebrates), covering plants, animals, fungi, or microbes introduced to new environments where they establish, spread, and cause ecological or economic impacts. Higher-level taxonomic or functional groups are included when specific species are not identified, but generic terms like "invasive species" are excluded. |
| **Location** | Refers to study sites, from specific locations (e.g., "Port Phillip Bay, southern Australia") to broader regions (e.g., southern Australia, Amazon rainforest). Includes natural features (rivers, bays, mountains) and administrative areas (cities, states, countries). |
| **Ecosystem** | A system of interacting biological and abiotic components, often spanning multiple locations (e.g., the savannah ecosystem across Kenya and Tanzania). |
| **Habitat** | A specific part of an ecosystem where an organism lives, such as crocodiles in freshwater habitats (e.g., rivers) within the savannah ecosystem. |

Table 1: Definitions of the four entities that encompass the information extraction (IE) aim of this paper.

#### 3.1.2 Stage Generalize: Generic Schema

The goal of this stage was to develop a standardized schema in JSON format, capturing relationships among the four entities. The system prompt, similar to the specialize stage, defined the LLM's role as both a research assistant and an expert in semantic modeling. Inspired by prior schema discovery research (Baazizi et al., 2017, 2020), the LLM reviewed all individual schemas and proposed a unified structure. Since LLM outputs vary across runs, we prompted the model three times with: "Read the nine schema instances and generate a standardized schema in JSON format."

**Results.** The three generated JSON schema variants structured entity relationships with slight variations. Schema 1 emphasized geospatial precision, incorporating coordinates and linking habitats to ecosystems. Schema 2 detailed species roles (native, invasive) and introduced broader biological, physical, and anthropogenic interactions. Schema 3 focused on taxonomy, physiographic attributes, and habitat specificity. Despite minor differences, all schemas captured essential relations.

From these insights, we finalized a standardized schema, organizing data around species, locations, ecosystems, habitats, and relationships, each with structured properties tailored to ecological contexts. For instance, species include roles (e.g., invasive, native) and taxonomic classification, while locations integrate geopolitical and environmental details. Ecosystems and habitats are linked hierarchically, and relationships are classified by type (e.g., biological, ecological) and directionality. This schema enhances ecological network mapping, providing structured insights into species interactions across datasets. Table 2 presents a detailed breakdown.

### 3.2 Information Extraction

With a standardized semantic structure for extracting information from each paper, enabling easier downstream processing, the LLM-based IE task was conducted.

#### 3.2.1 Stage Extract: Populate Schema

This stage now fulfills the main objective of this work, i.e. to extract information from a large-scale corpus (12,636 in our case) with an LLM to mine species, location, habitat, and ecosystem entities and their relations. The system prompt in this stage was close to the **specialize** stage system prompt where the role specified for the LLM was "research assistant in invasion biology or ecology tasked with reading and understanding scientific papers *to* extract relevant information *per the given predefined schema*."

### 3.3 Technical Details

The proprietary OpenAI GPT-4o model was used for all tasks in this paper. Schema generation in the **specialize** (Section 3.1.1) and **generalize** (Section 3.1.2) stages took only a few seconds per schema. The full extraction task in the **extract** stage (Section 3.2.1), applied to 12,636 papers, required approximately three days. The total cost was $1,000.

### 3.4 Results and Discussion

Of the 12,636 papers, the LLM classified 1,740 as outside invasion biology ("N/A"), leaving 10,896 for IE. This section summarizes the results.

| Extraction Target | Extracted Item | Extracted Item Properties |
|---|---|---|
| **Species** | `name`: species_name | `role`: native/introduced/alien/invasive<br>`taxonomy_level`: species/genus/family |
| **Location** | `name`: location_name | `category`: natural/administrative<br>`geopolitical_info`: country/region/city<br>`additional_details`: climatic/physiographic |
| **Ecosystem** | `name`: ecosystem_name | `type`: aquatic/terrestrial/marine<br>`scope`: local/regional/global |
| **Habitat** | `name`: habitat_name | `type`: aquatic/terrestrial/marine<br>`subcomponent_of`: ecosystem_name<br>`specifics`: e.g., benthic, litoral |
| **Relationships** | `related_entities`: [entity1, entity2, ...] | `name`: relationship_name<br>`type`: biological/physical/ecological/anthropogenic<br>`directionality`: unidirectional/bidirectional<br>`context`: relationship_contextual_description |

Table 2: Standardized information extraction (IE) schema for four ecological entities, their relationships, and associated properties, pertinent to structure information from invasion biology scientific papers.

The extracted species roles reflect diverse ecological functions, origins, behaviors, and impacts in invasion biology. Broad categories include **native**, **alien**, **introduced**, **invasive**, and **naturalized**, alongside specific roles such as **agricultural weeds**, **biological control agents**, **pathogens**, **mutualists**, and **ecosystem engineers**. Some roles emphasize origins (**indigenous**, **non-native**, **cryptogenic**), behaviors (**colonizer**, **expanding**), or ecological functions (**symbiont**, **facilitator**, **pioneer**). Others capture ecosystem interactions (**co-introduced species**, **specialist herbivores**, **cryptic invaders**) or relate to conservation and management (**natural enemies**, **candidate biological control agents**, **quarantine pests**). This complexity underscores species' dynamic roles, informing biodiversity patterns, ecosystem impacts, and management strategies (full list here). A finer-grained analysis highlights **invasive species** as the most cited, including *Procambarus clarkii* (76 mentions), *Harmonia axyridis* (73), and *Rhinella marina* (68). **Native species** such as *Austropotamobius pallipes* and *Phragmites australis* (24 mentions each) appeared less frequently, while **introduced species** like *Oncorhynchus mykiss* and *Crassostrea gigas* showed varying ecological impacts. However, extraction also included generic terms (e.g., "native species," "native plants"), introducing noise due to the unsupervised nature of the task, highlighting the need for post-filtering (full list here).

The dataset highlights key **geopolitical locations**, with the most frequent countries being Australia (406), South Africa (248), New Zealand (236), Italy (187), and France (168). Regions include Europe (601), North America (348), the Mediterranean (117), Asia (112), and South America (98). Cities like Sydney (8), Hong Kong (7), and Rome (6) appear less frequently. The prominence of Europe and North America reflects their strong representation, while frequent mentions of Australia, South Africa, and New Zealand suggest a focus on biodiversity hotspots. The dataset spans continents, regions, countries, and cities, emphasizing a global perspective.

The extracted data provides a comprehensive view of **terrestrial, marine, and aquatic ecosystems**, highlighting their ecological diversity. Terrestrial ecosystems (93) dominate, with grasslands (42), forests (45), and agricultural landscapes (47) being the most cited. Mediterranean (37) and tropical ecosystems (26) reflect climate-specific regions, while urban ecosystems (46) underscore human-nature interactions. Marine ecosystems feature prominently, with the Mediterranean Sea (71) leading, followed by coral reefs (8) and the Baltic Sea (12). Aquatic ecosystems, especially freshwater systems (199), are well-represented, including lake (59), riverine (36), and wetland (40) ecosystems. Transitional zones such as estuarine (35) and coastal wetlands (10) further bridge freshwater and marine systems (full list here). Additionally, the dataset captures **habitat-ecosystem relationships**, showcasing their ecological complexity. In aquatic systems, *pelagic zones* align with lake ecosystems, while *ballast water* links to marine environments. Marine habitats like *kelp beds* and *mussel beds* are associated with rocky subtidal and intertidal ecosystems, respectively. Human-modified environments, such as *artificial coastal defenses* linked to *biogenic reefs*, emphasize anthropogenic influences. Terrestrial systems highlight relationships like *forest habitats* in forest ecosystems, *soybean fields* in agricultural settings, and *urban areas* tied to urban ecosystems, underscoring the impact of land use. These insights illustrate the dataset's detailed representation of ecological interactions across environments.

The extracted information in our invasion biology corpus reveals diverse relation types, reflecting the field's interdisciplinary nature. **Ecological relations** dominate, with **invasion** (814), **competition** (429), **impact** (349), and **predation** (301) highlighting key species interactions and environmental changes. Other notable relations include **colonization** (179), **distribution** (179), and **habitat preference** (123), emphasizing species spread and habitat use. **Biological relations** such as **parasitism** (151), **hybridization** (74), and **pollination** (25) capture specific ecological interactions. **Physical relations** like **location**, **transport**, and **introduction location** focus on spatial and movement dynamics. **Anthropogenic relations**, including **introduction** (157) and **introduction pathway** (45), underscore the role of human activities in species dispersal. These relations collectively show the complexity of invasion biology.

The fully unsupervised IE task demonstrates the immense potential of LLMs as powerful tools for ecological research, assisting with tasks like systematic and scoping reviews. The insights presented here represent only a fraction of what can be derived from our corpus of over 10,000 papers, which we have made publicly available (`https://doi.org/10.5281/zenodo.13956882`). This work aligns with open information extraction (OIE) (Etzioni et al., 2008; Fader et al., 2011; Etzioni et al., 2011), traditionally reliant on syntactic patterns. However, LLMs surpass these methods by leveraging advanced semantic comprehension, enabling more effective analysis of complex relationships in large-scale corpora.

## 4 Recommendations for Future Work

Future work should explore integrating ontologies with LLMs to enhance information extraction (IE) and linked data creation, addressing key research questions: how LLMs can assist in ontology and knowledge graph construction (Kommineni et al., 2024), improve question answering through ontology support (Allemang and Sequeda, 2024), enable ontology learning from text (Babaei Giglou et al., 2023, 2024), and enhance representation learning (Ronzano and Nanavati, 2024). Ontologies, as *formal specifications of shared conceptualizations* (Studer et al., 1998), enable structured knowledge representation, yet their adoption is hindered by expertise barriers. Future research should investigate schema-driven IE, optimizing the information provided to LLMs, refining structured guidance (Caufield et al., 2024), and assessing how LLM-derived knowledge aligns with expert consensus. Ontologies can improve LLMs by supplying domain-specific definitions, guiding semantic modeling, enhancing entity and relation extraction, and integrating with retrieval-augmented generation (RAG) to reduce hallucinations (Soman et al., 2024). However, constraints must be considered in rapidly evolving fields, where rigid ontological structures may limit adaptability to emerging knowledge. Balancing structured knowledge integration with flexibility will be crucial for leveraging LLMs effectively across diverse domains.

## 5 Conclusion

This study highlights the potential of LLMs for advancing IE in invasion biology by extracting species, locations, habitats, and ecosystems from scientific literature. Through a standardized semantic schema, we demonstrated how LLMs can structure complex ecological data, enhancing research workflows. Our two-stage approach first extracts detailed, context-specific structures (specialize stage) and then integrates them into a flexible schema (generalize stage) balancing specificity and generality. This method enables structured representation of ecological complexity. The released dataset and schema support refining extraction methods, integrating ontologies, and broader ecological applications, underscoring LLMs' role in bridging unstructured data and structured knowledge in ecology.

## Acknowledgments

The experiments reported in this paper using the OpenAI models were supported by the SCINEXT project grant (BMBF, German Federal Ministry of Education and Research, Grant ID: 01IS22070) and by the TIB Leibniz Information Centre for Science and Technology, Hannover, Germany. This work is also conducted in the context of the ZiF interdisciplinary research group "Mapping Evidence to Theory in Ecology," hosted at Bielefeld University.

## Limitations

While this study highlights the potential of LLMs for IE in invasion biology, certain limitations remain. The extracted entities and relations were not evaluated against a gold-standard dataset, making it difficult to quantify precision and recall. A future inter-annotator agreement (IAA) study on a subset of the corpus (e.g., 20%) or a qualitative error analysis could enhance its reliability for researchers. Our approach also relies solely on OpenAI GPT-4o, without comparing alternative LLMs or prompting strategies, such as chain-of-thought prompting, which may improve extraction accuracy. Additionally, potential data contamination (Ranaldi et al., 2024) remains a concern, as LLMs may reproduce information seen during pre-training rather than extracting it anew. A systematic comparison against pre-training corpora would help assess this effect.

## References

Stein Aerts, Diether Lambrechts, Sunit Maity, Peter Van Loo, Bert Coessens, Frederik De Smet, Leon-Charles Tranchevent, Bart De Moor, Peter Marynen, Bassem Hassan, et al. 2006. Gene prioritization through genomic data fusion. *Nature biotechnology*, 24(5):537–544.

Dean Allemang and Juan Sequeda. 2024. Increasing the llm accuracy for question answering: Ontologies to the rescue! *arXiv preprint arXiv:2405.11706*.

Xavier Amatriain, Ananth Sankar, Jie Bing, Praveen Kumar Bodigutla, Timothy J Hazen, and Michaeel Kazi. 2023. Transformer models: an introduction and catalog. *arXiv preprint arXiv:2302.07730*.

Isabelle Augenstein, Mrinal Das, Sebastian Riedel, Lakshmi Vikraman, and Andrew Mccallum. 2017. Semeval 2017 task 10: Scienceie-extracting keyphrases and relations from scientific publications. In *Proceedings of the 11th SemEval (SemEval-2017)*, pages 546–555.

Mohamed-Amine Baazizi, Clément Berti, Dario Colazzo, Giorgio Ghelli, and Carlo Sartiani. 2020. Human-in-the-loop schema inference for massive json datasets. In *EDBT 2020-23nd International Conference on Extending Database Technology*, pages 635–638. OpenProceedings. org.

Mohamed-Amine Baazizi, Houssem Ben Lahmar, Dario Colazzo, Giorgio Ghelli, and Carlo Sartiani. 2017. Schema inference for massive json datasets. In *Extending Database Technology (EDBT)*.

Hamed Babaei Giglou, Jennifer D'Souza, and Sören Auer. 2023. Llms4ol: Large language models for ontology learning. In *International Semantic Web Conference*, pages 408–427. Springer.

Hamed Babaei Giglou, Jennifer D'Souza, and Sören Auer. 2024. Preface for llms4ol 2024: The 1st large language models for ontology learning challenge at the 23rd iswc. *Open Conference Proceedings*, 4:1–2.

Arthur Brack, Jennifer D'Souza, Anett Hoppe, Sören Auer, and Ralph Ewerth. 2020. Domain-independent extraction of scientific concepts from research articles. In *European Conference on Information Retrieval*, pages 251–266. Springer.

Marc Brinner, Tina Heger, and Sina Zarriess. 2022. Linking a hypothesis network from the domain of invasion biology to a corpus of scientific abstracts: The INAS dataset. In *Proceedings of the first Workshop on Information Extraction from Scientific Publications*, pages 32–42, Online. ACL.

Phillip Cassey, Pablo García-Díaz, Julie L Lockwood, and Tim M Blackburn. 2018. Invasion biology: searching for predictions and prevention, and avoiding lost causes. In *Invasion biology: hypotheses and evidence*, pages 3–13. CAB International Wallingford UK.

J Harry Caufield, Harshad Hegde, Vincent Emonet, Nomi L Harris, Marcin P Joachimiak, Nicolas Matentzoglu, HyeongSik Kim, Sierra Moxon, Justin T Reese, Melissa A Haendel, et al. 2024. Structured prompt interrogation and recursive extraction of semantics (spires): A method for populating knowledge bases using zero-shot learning. *Bioinformatics*, 40(3):btae104.

Danilo Dessì, Francesco Osborne, Diego Reforgiato Recupero, Davide Buscaldi, Enrico Motta, and Harald Sack. 2020. Ai-kg: an automatically generated knowledge graph of artificial intelligence. In *The Semantic Web–ISWC 2020: 19th International Semantic Web Conference, Athens, Greece, November 2–6, 2020, Proceedings, Part II 19*, pages 127–143. Springer.

Jennifer D'Souza, Sören Auer, and Ted Pedersen. 2021. SemEval-2021 task 11: NLPContributionGraph - structuring scholarly NLP contributions for a research knowledge graph. In *Proceedings of the 15th International Workshop on Semantic Evaluation (SemEval-2021)*, pages 364–376, Online. Association for Computational Linguistics.

Jennifer D'Souza. 2024. Agriculture named entity recognition—towards fair, reusable scholarly contributions in agriculture. *Knowledge*, 4(1):1–26.

Jennifer D'Souza and Sören Auer. 2022. Computer science named entity recognition in the open research knowledge graph. In *International Conference on Asian Digital Libraries*, pages 35–45. Springer.

Jennifer D'Souza, Salomon Kabongo, Hamed Babaei Giglou, and Yue Zhang. 2024. Overview of the clef 2024 simpletext task 4: Sota? tracking the state-of-the-art in scholarly publications. In *Working Notes of the Conference and Labs of the Evaluation Forum (CLEF 2024)*, pages 3163–3173.

Oren Etzioni, Michele Banko, Stephen Soderland, and Daniel S Weld. 2008. Open information extraction from the web. *Communications of the ACM*, 51(12):68–74.

Oren Etzioni, Anthony Fader, Janara Christensen, Stephen Soderland, et al. 2011. Open information extraction: The second generation. In *Twenty-Second International Joint Conference on Artificial Intelligence*. Citeseer.

Anthony Fader, Stephen Soderland, and Oren Etzioni. 2011. Identifying relations for open information extraction. In *Proceedings of the 2011 conference on empirical methods in natural language processing*, pages 1535–1545.

Kata Gábor, Davide Buscaldi, Anne-Kathrin Schumann, Behrang QasemiZadeh, Haïfa Zargayouna, and Thierry Charnois. 2018. SemEval-2018 task 7: Semantic relation extraction and classification in scientific papers. In *Proceedings of the 12th International Workshop on Semantic Evaluation*, pages 679–688, New Orleans, Louisiana. Association for Computational Linguistics.

John Giorgi, Xindi Wang, Nicola Sahar, Won Young Shin, Gary D Bader, and Bo Wang. 2019. End-to-end named entity recognition and relation extraction using pre-trained language models. *arXiv preprint arXiv:1912.13415*.

Jennifer D'Souza. 2025. A catalog of transformer models.

Jonathan M Jeschke and Tina Heger. 2018. *Invasion biology: hypotheses and evidence*. CAB International.

Salomon Kabongo, Jennifer D'Souza, and Sören Auer. 2021. Automated mining of leaderboards for empirical ai research. In *International Conference on Asian Digital Libraries*, pages 453–470.

Petr Knoth, Drahomira Herrmannova, Matteo Cancellieri, Lucas Anastasiou, Nancy Pontika, Samuel Pearce, Bikash Gyawali, and David Pride. 2023. Core: a global aggregation service for open access papers. *Scientific Data*, 10(1):366.

Vamsi Krishna Kommineni, Birgitta König-Ries, and Sheeba Samuel. 2024. From human experts to machines: An llm supported approach to ontology and knowledge graph construction. *arXiv preprint arXiv:2403.08345*.

Gang Li, Karen E Ross, Cecilia N Arighi, Yifan Peng, Cathy H Wu, and K Vijay-Shanker. 2015. mirtex: a text mining system for mirna-gene relation extraction. *PLoS computational biology*, 11(9):e1004391.

Haoyang Liu, M Janina Sarol, and Halil Kilicoglu. 2021. Uiuc_bionlp at semeval-2021 task 11: A cascade of neural models for structuring scholarly nlp contributions. *arXiv preprint arXiv:2105.05435*.

Yi Luan, Luheng He, Mari Ostendorf, and Hannaneh Hajishirzi. 2018. Multi-task identification of entities, relations, and coreference for scientific knowledge graph construction. In *Proceedings of the 2018 EMNLP*, pages 3219–3232.

Daniel Mietchen, Jonathan M. Jeschke, Maud Bernard-Verdier, Tina Heger, Camille Musseau, and Steph Tyszka. 2024. Invasion biology corpus 2024-07.

Federico Ranaldi, Elena Sofia Ruzzetti, Dario Onorati, Leonardo Ranaldi, Cristina Giannone, Andrea Favalli, Raniero Romagnoli, and Fabio Massimo Zanzotto. 2024. Investigating the impact of data contamination of large language models in text-to-SQL translation. In *Findings of ACL*, pages 13909–13920, Bangkok, Thailand. ACL.

Francesco Ronzano and Jay Nanavati. 2024. Towards ontology-enhanced representation learning for large language models. *arXiv preprint arXiv:2405.20527*.

Helen E Roy, Aníbal Pauchard, Peter Stoett, Tanara Renard Truong, Sven Bacher, Bella S Galil, Philip E Hulme, Tohru Ikeda, Kavileveettil Sankaran, Melodie A McGeoch, et al. 2023. Ipbes invasive alien species assessment: summary for policymakers. *IPBES*.

Mahsa Shamsabadi, Jennifer D'Souza, and Sören Auer. 2024. Large language models for scientific information extraction: An empirical study for virology. In *Findings of the Association for Computational Linguistics: EACL 2024*, pages 374–392, St. Julian's, Malta. Association for Computational Linguistics.

Karthik Soman, Peter W Rose, John H Morris, Rabia E Akbas, Brett Smith, Braian Peetoom, Catalina Villouta-Reyes, Gabriel Cerono, Yongmei Shi, Angela Rizk-Jackson, et al. 2024. Biomedical knowledge graph-optimized prompt generation for large language models. *Bioinformatics*, 40(9):btae560.

Rudi Studer, V Richard Benjamins, and Dieter Fensel. 1998. Knowledge engineering: Principles and methods. *Data & knowledge engineering*, 25(1-2):161–197.

Zhong-Yi Wang and Hong-Yu Zhang. 2013. Rational drug repositioning by medical genetics. *Nature biotechnology*, 31(12):1080–1082.

XueZhong Zhou, Jörg Menche, Albert-László Barabási, and Amitabh Sharma. 2014. Human symptoms–disease network. *Nature communications*, 5(1):4212.

# Large Language Models as Annotators of Named Entities in Climate Change and Biodiversity: A Preliminary Study

**Elena Volkanovska**
Technische Universität Darmstadt / Residenzschloss 1, 64283 Darmstadt, Germany
elena.volkanovska@tu-darmstadt.de

## Abstract

This paper examines whether few-shot techniques for Named Entity Recognition (NER) utilising existing large language models (LLMs) as their backbone can be used to reliably annotate named entities (NEs) in scientific texts on climate change and biodiversity. A series of experiments aim to assess whether LLMs can be integrated into an end-to-end pipeline that could generate token- or sentence-level NE annotations; the former being an ideal-case scenario that allows for seamless integration of existing with new token-level features in a single annotation pipeline. Experiments are run on four LLMs, two NER datasets, two input and output data formats, and ten and nine prompt versions per dataset. The results show that few-shot methods are far from being a silver bullet for NER in highly specialised domains, although improvement in LLM performance is observed for some prompt designs and some NE classes. Few-shot methods would find better use in a human-in-the-loop scenario, where an LLM's output is verified by a domain expert.

## 1 Introduction

Analysing the language of climate change is an important step in following and understanding ongoing debates in this field. In a corpus linguistics setting, an important precondition for performing such an analysis is the access to corpora that have been annotated with morpho-syntactic and semantic features at the token level. Named entities (NEs) belong to the latter category and constitute an important part of linguistic analysis: Glaser et al. (2022) underline that linguistic choices in terms of decisions to explicitly name or leave out a certain entity or concept is an important notion in analysing political speeches. This line of thinking can easily apply to texts of various genres from the climate change domain, too.

In many instances, available corpora for corpus linguistics research, such as those hosted on English-Corpora.org,[1] rarely offer token-level annotations that extend beyond lemma and part-of-speech (POS) tags, and eventually syntactic dependency tags. These corpora can be obtained as pre-tokenized data; preserving existing token-level features and enriching them with custom NE annotations is contingent upon having (a) an annotation tool capable of processing tokenized input, and (b) having sufficient data to train a custom NER component within the tool. Depending on the annotation tool, such training data must usually be annotated in the IOB or BIOES/BILOU format[2] or contain character span information about the NE instance.

Challenge (a) is alleviated by the fact that (1) some known annotation tools, such as stanza (Qi et al., 2020) and trankit (Nguyen et al., 2021), can accept pre-tokenized input, and (2) obtaining high-quality morpho-syntactic features by re-annotating the corpus is generally unproblematic.[3] Challenge (b) is more complex, especially concerning the annotation of specialised corpora. In the context of adding climate-change-related token-level NE annotations that would be relevant to analysing the scientific climate change discourse, which could involve NE categories such as *greenhouse-gases* or *climate-datasets*, the first step would be to define a set of relevant categories, and the second to obtain a high-quality annotated corpus of sufficient size to train an NER compo-

[1] https://www.english-corpora.org/

[2] "IOB" stands for "inside, outside, beginning", while "BIOES/BILOU" stands for "beginning, inside, outside, end/last, single (element)/unit (element)"

[3] This would not be an ideal solution if the goal is to preserve the original token-level features.



*Proceedings of the 1st Workshop on Ecology, Environment, and Natural Language Processing (NLP4Ecology2025)*, pages 24–33
March 2, 2025 

nent of a tool for linguistic annotation. Creating richly annotated specialised corpora is thus a time- and resource-intensive activity.

Meanwhile, large language models (LLMs) have been seen as possible "destabilizers" of "inequalities of academic research", as they might allow moderately-funded labs to perform analyses that were previously accessible to well-funded institutes only (Törnberg, 2024, p.17). Motivated by the positive results in LLM-powered few-shot NER for specialised domains reported in Ashok and Lipton (2023), this paper employs a number of few-shot experiments to investigate whether this "destabilization effect" also transfers onto the annotation of NEs in scientific literature on climate change and biodiversity. Experiments undertaken in the scope of this study should answer two questions: (Q1) *Can LLMs be used as reliable "annotators" of named entities at the token and sentence levels in the domains of climate change and biodiversity?* and (Q2) *Does providing tokenized input affect an LLM's performance when identifying named entities in these domains?* Descriptive information about the datasets used in the study and extensive supplementary materials related to the experiments and the results are available in a dedicated GitHub repository.[4] Finally, an effort is made to refrain from using anthropomorphic language when disucssing LLMs (Inie et al., 2024), as long as this does not hinder the description of LLM-based systems, methodologies and functionalities.

## 2 Related work

Jehangir et al. (2023) distinguish between three types of NER techniques: a rule-based approach, unsupervised learning, and supervised learning. A rule-based approach entails the careful crafting of domain-specific rules to extract and classify patterns representing NEs of interest. Unsupervised learning is used in data-poor contexts, but can yield results that are difficult to evaluate. Supervised learning utilizes manually annotated data to learn representations of relevant NE categories. Corpus annotation libraries, such as CoreNLP (Manning et al., 2014), spaCy, stanza, and trankit, have incorporated supervised learning in a modular pipeline design, allowing researchers to train their own NER component provided that they have sufficient data.

The advent of Transformer-based LMs has put the limelight on transfer learning and fine-tuning, methodologies that demonstrate robust results with fewer manually labelled training examples. In fine-tuning, the architecture of an LM is modified in line with the task requirements: Wang et al. (2022) present a methodology for learning an LM to understand language structure, and then test its performance on downstream tasks including NER. Many of the tools developed in this way, such as BiodivBERT (Abdelmageed et al., 2023), are models that have been developed for an NER task only and merging their output with the morpho-syntactic token-level features obtained from a linguistic annotation library is not always a seamless process due to variations in tokenization approaches.[5]

The increased availability of open-source and paid text-generation and question-answering models, alongside reports of pre-trained LLMs performing well on NLP tasks in zero- and few-shot settings in data-poor contexts (Brown et al., 2020), have fuelled the interest in experimenting with zero-shot and few-shot NER approaches. In most instances, this means that NER is defined as a question-answering task, where the LLM is expected to generate an answer based on a prompt sent to the system. Epure and Hennequin (2022) perform zero-shot and few-shot NER using GPT-2. Before prompting the model, they ensure a low ambiguity level between NE categories by merging possibly confusing NE labels into a single, unambiguous label. They also simplify the task by prompting the model to recognise one NE category at a time. Wang et al. (2023) ensure that the input sequence from which the model is expected to extract NEs is semantically similar to the example sequence in the prompt template by retrieving the *k* nearest neighbour of the input sequence. They also prompt the model to enclose the NE into special tokens, which should allow for span retrieval. Ashok and Lipton (2023) have presented an intuitive approach to NER, where they propose a prompt template that can easily be customized to any project using own NE categories and definitions. Their approach has been implemented in

[4] `https://github.com/volkanovska/NER-annotation-with-LLMs`

[5] A "token" can be a unit at the word- or punctuation-, character-, or sub-word level. Discussing tokenization approaches is beyond the scope of this study; however, it is worth mentioning that LMs using transformer architecture (Vaswani et al., 2017) mostly rely on sub-word units.

spacy-llm's NE annotation pipeline, where users can define NE categories on the fly and annotate their data with an LM of their choice.[6]

This study builds on existing work in the field of few-shot NER and conducts experiments using different prompt templates and a varying number of task examples. It differs from previous methods in (1) the format of the input given to the model and the requested output, and (2) the use of highly-specialised NER datasets, which, to the best of my knowledge, have not been used in a few-shot NER setting previously.

## 3 Data

Basic descriptive information about the two NER datasets that are used in the experiments described in Section 4 is provided below; a comprehensive dataset description involving definitions of each NE class, information about the distribution of NE instances per category and per data split, descriptive statistical sentence- and token-level information, as well as the ten most and least frequent NE instances per each NE class, are provided in the dataset documentation available in the dedicated GitHub repository referred to in Section 1.

**Climate-Change-NER** is a publicly-available dataset[7] for English-language NER in scientific texts on climate change, developed in an IBM Research AI[8]-led initiative, involving NASA[9] (Bhattacharjee et al., 2024) among other organisations. The dataset has 13 climate-specific NE classes, which originate from complex taxonomies used in climate-related literature. These are: *climate-assets*, *climate-datasets*, *climate-greenhouse-gases*, *climate-hazards*, *climate-impacts*, *climate-mitigations*, *climate-models*, *climate-nature*, *climate-observations*, *climate-organisms*, *climate-organizations*, *climate-problem-origins*, and *climate-properties*. Seed keywords, such as *wildfire* and *floods*, had been used to collect a total of 534 abstracts from the Semantic Scholar Academic Graph (Kinney et al., 2023), which were then manually annotated with the IOB tagging scheme, with the help of a set of class-specific dictionaries (Pfitzmann, 2024). The train and test data splits, which are used in the experiments of this paper, contain 985 and 177 sentences and 3029 and 555 NE instances respectively.

**BiodivNER** is a publicly-available dataset[10] for English-language NER in the biodiversity domain (Abdelmageed et al., 2022). The dataset has 6 biodiversity-related NE classes: *organism*, *phenomena*, *matter*, *environment*, *quality*, and *location*. The annotated corpus comprises of abstracts, tables, and metadata files collected by using a set of keywords from Semedico,[11] BEF-China,[12] and data.world[13] and manually annotated with the IOB tagging scheme. BiodivNER's train and test data splits contain 1828 and 229 sentences and 6709 and 1277 NE instances respectively.

## 4 Methodology

This section presents the steps taken to preprocess the data, the prompt design, the LLMs used in the experiments, the evaluation approach, and the baseline against which the LLMs' performance is compared.

### 4.1 Data preprocessing

The NER data is used in two settings: (1) to train a custom NER component in spaCy, and (2) to design prompts for few-shot learning. Use case (1) requires span information about each NE instance, while for use case (2) each sentence needs to be saved as a Python list, with each token index and token saved as sublists and as a string. To achieve (1) and guarantee compatibility between each dataset's and spaCy's tokenization, all sentences were re-tokenized and only those that were identical to the tokenized sentences in the original datasets were taken into account. All re-tokenized sentences for Climate-Change-NER were identical; from BiodivNER, 90 re-tokenized sentences from the train file, and 11 from the development and test file each were not identical.

### 4.2 Prompt design

To explore whether the task input-output format influences a model's performance, the study adopts a custom prompt design that differs from the few-shot prompt design suggested by Ashok and Lipton (2023) in the following features: (1) the definition of each NE class is followed by

[6] *spacy-llm* is spaCy's LLM-supporting package, available at `https://github.com/explosion/spacy-llm`.

[7] `https://huggingface.co/datasets/ibm/Climate-Change-NER`

[8] International Business Machines Corporation

[9] National Aeronautics and Space Administration

[10] `https://zenodo.org/records/6575865`

[11] A semantic search engine for the life sciences.

[12] `https://bef-china.com/`

[13] `https://data.world/`

several real-world instances of the respective NE class; (2) the task examples (TEs) include sentences presented either as a Python string or a Python list of tokens and token indices, hereinafter referred to as *string-based* and *token-based* input-output, and an answer section containing the expected output from the model; (3) the format of the task input sentence corresponds to the format of the task examples described in (2) i.e. is either a Python list or a string; (4) the LLM is not prompted to emulate "reasoning" for its decision; (5) only true NE instances are provided as examples of correct answers. The features (4) and (5) were implemented after the preliminary tests showed that they did not contribute to consistent improvement in the results. Each prompt has three sections: (a) a *definitions-and-instances* section, where real-world instances of the NE class accompany its definition, (b) a *task example* section, which includes an *n* number of examples of the task the model is expected to complete, and (c) a *task* section, where the model is "asked" to annotate a sentence and return its output in a specific format. Figure 1 provides an overview of the prompt design.

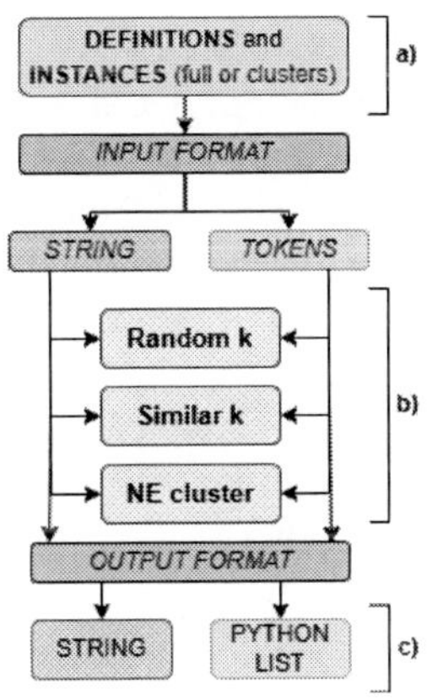


Figure 1: Blueprint for prompt design. The *string-based* input-output format refers to the task of identifying NEs at the sentence level, while a *token-based* format involves identifying NEs at the token level.

Section (a) remains unchanged in each prompt of the prompt versions described below. For BiodivNER, the definitions of the NE categories included in section (a) have been obtained from the description of the dataset creation and annotation process, available in Abdelmageed et al. (2022). The definitions of the NE classes contained in Climate-Change-NER are available in the dataset card on Hugging Face, referred to in the dataset description in Section 3. Sections (b) and (c) are created by applying two formats for the input-output requirements as described in prompt features (2) and (3), and by introducing three different selection criteria for examples included in the task-example (TE) pairs of section (b).[14]

**Prompt version one: random k-examples** A *k* number of random TEs is extracted from the train data split, where *k* can be 3, 4, or 5 TE pairs, and section (b) is populated with the selected TE pairs. This prompt version, where a *k* number of randomly chosen sentences is used in the TE section, follows the prompt design adopted in the work of Ashok and Lipton (2023).

**Prompt version two: semantically similar k-examples** Motivated by the prompt design presented in Wang et al. (2023), each sentence of the test split of both datasets is paired with five sentences of the train data split, which have the highest similarity score with the test sentence. Semantic text similarity is calculated with the library sentence-transformers[15] (Reimers and Gurevych, 2019) and the model *sentence-transformers/stsb-distilroberta-base-v2*. The idea is to investigate whether LLMs' performance can be improved by including in the TE pairs sentences that have a degree of similarity to the sentence the model is expected to process. Section (b) of the prompt is populated with *k* number of semantically similar TE pairs, where *k* can be 3, 4, or 5.

**Prompt version three: clustered NE classes** To simplify the task at hand, clusters of NE classes within each dataset are created on the basis of the classes' perceived relatedness. The idea behind this prompt design choice is to (1) frame the models' output into a narrower, topic-related semantic field and (2) rather than collapse NE categories that bear a perceived degree of similarity, test if LLMs can differentiate between them. Four NE class clusters are created for Climate-Change-NER and three for BiodivNER. Prompt sections (a) and (b) are pop-

[14]A limitation of a maximum number of 60 tokens was introduced for TE pairs from BiodivNER's training data, due to the observation that the data contained tokenized sentences whose length varied from 3 to 1053 tokens. Such a limitation was not necessary for Climate-Change-NER training samples, as the length of sentences varied between 32 and 115 tokens.

[15]`https://sbert.net/`

ulated with definitions and four randomly selected TE pairs pertaining only to the cluster's classes. The NE clusters for Climate-Change-NER are: (1) *climate-hazards, climate-problem-origins, climate-greenhouse-gases*; (2) *climate-impacts, climate-assets, climate-nature, climate-organisms*; (3) *climate-datasets, climate-models, climate-observations, climate-properties*, and (4) *climate-mitigations, climate-organisations*. For BiodivNER, the three clusters are: (1) *environment, location*; (2) *organism, matter*, and (3) *phenomena, quality*.

**Input-output format** For **string-based** input, the TEs include a string and the correct NE instances and their categories in parenthesis. The model is expected to generate the correct NE instance and its category in parentheses, but not the token indices pertaining to the tokens within the span. For **token-based** input, the TEs include tokenized sentences containing a token and a token index. The model is expected to identify the NE instance, its category, and the start- and end-token indices. Ideally, the token-based output should allow for simple integration of a model's annotation with existing token-level features.

| Prompt version | $k$=3 | $k$=4 | $k$=5 |
|---|---|---|---|
| Random $k$ | 177 | 177 | 177 |
| Similar $k$ | 177 | 177 | 177 |
| NE cluster 1 | 0 | 177 | 0 |
| NE cluster 2 | 0 | 177 | 0 |
| NE cluster 3 | 0 | 177 | 0 |
| NE cluster 4 | 0 | 177 | 0 |
| Prompts, per input type | **354** | **1062** | **354** |
| Prompts, both input types | **708** | **2124** | **708** |

Table 1: Number of prompts for test sentences of Climate-Change-NER for each prompt version and input type (token/string based).

### 4.3 Language models

The choice of LLMs was guided by two factors: previous successful deployment in similar tasks and cost. Two models of OpenAI's GPT family, gpt-4o-2024-05-13 (hereinafter: gpt-4o) and gpt-4o-mini,[16] were run using OpenAI's API. OpenAI's models were chosen over other proprietary models of similar performance and price range due to their previous successful deployment in a similar setting (Ashok and Lipton, 2023). The experiments are also run on two open-source models: Meta-Llama-3.1-70B-Instruct (hereinafter: Llama-70B) and Meta-Llama-3.1-405B-Instruct (hereinafter: Llama-405B), both developed by Meta and run through an API of Nebius AI Studio.[17] The total cost of the experiments is reported in Section 7.

| Prompt version | $k$=3 | $k$=4 | $k$=5 |
|---|---|---|---|
| Random $k$ | 229 | 229 | 229 |
| Similar $k$ | 229 | 229 | 229 |
| NE cluster 1 | 0 | 229 | 0 |
| NE cluster 2 | 0 | 229 | 0 |
| NE cluster 3 | 0 | 229 | 0 |
| Prompts, per input type | **458** | **1145** | **458** |
| Prompts, both input types | **916** | **2290** | **916** |

Table 2: Number of prompts for test sentences of Climate-Change-NER for each prompt version and input type (token/string based).

### 4.4 Evaluation

**Baseline** The performance of the four models on the BiodivNER dataset is compared against the results of BiodivBERT (Abdelmageed et al., 2023), an LM pre-trained and fine-tuned specifically for an NER task in the biodiversity domain, with a reported F1 score of **0.87**. For Climate-Change-NER, the baseline is that of the model INDUSBASE (Bhattacharjee et al., 2024), an LM pre-trained and fine-tuned on relevant scientific data, with a reported F1 score of **0.64**.

**Custom NER components within tools for linguistic annotation** To measure how the number of NE instances per category affects the performance of a custom NER component within an annotation tool, custom NER components were trained on each dataset using spaCy and the model en_core_web_lg[18] as a base model. SpaCy's NER tagger achieves an F1 score of 0.73 on BiodivNER's test data, and 0.43 on the Climate-Change-NER's test data.

**Token-based prompts** Micro F1 score is calculated and reported in accordance with the standard CoNLL metric (Sang and De Meulder, 2003), as well as simple span-and-category matches (Chinchor and Sundheim, 1993). The former refer to

[16] `https://platform.openai.com/docs/models`

[17] `https://studio.nebius.ai/`.

[18] https://spacy.io/models/en_core_web_lg

a complete match in NE instance, label, and NE span boundaries (start- and end-token), while the latter takes into account only the NE instance and label, but not token indices. Reporting simple span-and-category matches serves as a point of comparison with the results of the string-based prompts.

**String-based prompts** For these prompts, the goal is to identify NEs at the sentence level, the F1 score is based on span-and-category matches, with strict span boundaries. Partial span matches are not considered true positives.

## 5 Results and analysis

Tables 3 and 4 summarize the F1 scores for experiments conducted on the test data split of Climate-Change-NER and BiodivNER involving the prompts described in Section 4.2. One iteration was performed on each prompt set and on each model. In the tables, *k* stands for the number of TE pairs included in the prompt. Prior to calculating the results, each model's output was cleaned from misspelled or non-existing categories (e.g. *organsim* instead of *organism*).

Tables 5 and 6 present the percentage of span-and-category matches between a model's predicted NEs and the gold standard. *Span-and-category matches* measure instances where the model correctly identifies the span of an NE instance and the NE class. For token-based input and output, this means that the token indices are not taken into account when calculating the percentage of span-and-category matches, while for string-based input and output, the model is not expected to generate token indices at all. Therefore, these two tables allow one to gauge the degree to which a model is affected by the input-output format.

### 5.1 Quantitative analysis

Even the best-performing all-class token-based prompt & model combinations substantially lag behind the baseline NER models for the datasets, more so in the case of BiodivNER, where the baseline F1 score is 0.87 and spaCy's NER classifier F1 score is 0.73. For Climate-Change-NER, which has a baseline score of 0.64, the best-performing all-class prompt & model combination achieve an F1 score of 0.44, which is similar to spaCy's score of 0.43.

**Model performance** The average F1 scores for all prompts achieved by the tested LLMs is within the 0.24 to 0.43 range for both datasets. Per prompt type, the highest F1 score of 0.53 is achieved by gpt-4o on the token-based NE class cluster 1 of Climate-Change-NER and the lowest F1 score of 0.16 by Llama-70B on the string-based NE class cluster 4 of the same corpus. For **token-based** prompts, gpt-4o has the highest average score, followed by Llama-405B; gpt-4o-mini and Llama-70B come third and achieve equal performance. For **string-based** prompts, Llama-405B performs slightly better on Climate-Change-NER, followed by gpt-4o and the two smaller models; for BiodivNER, it is a tie between gpt-4o and Llama-405B.

In terms of overall model ranking, gpt-4o seems to be the best performer, closely followed by Llama-405B. Llama-70B comes third due to its slightly better performance on the BiodivNER dataset relative to gpt-4o-mini, the latter coming in fourth.

**Prompt performance** As expected, prompt design can affect the quality of the output. In general, including more TE pairs in the prompt yields better results for both random and similar TEs, with a few exceptions that were mostly noticed in the output of Meta's models for the random-k prompt version in BiodivNER; the number of TEs also seems to be more important than TEs' similarity to the task sentence. Task simplification by grouping NE classes showed benefits only in NE class cluster 1 of Climate-Change-NER; in all other instances, this step did not lead to better performance.

The impact of the input-output format is measured by calculating the simple **span-and-category matches** of the output with the gold standard in the test data split. For token-based prompts, this is the percentage of correctly predicted NEs when the token indices are not considered. Tables 5 and 6 show that the models handle token-based input well - in fact, token-based prompts achieve better average results on both datasets. Llama-405B ranks first in this performance measure on the Climate-Change-NER dataset, while gpt-4o outperforms the other three models on the BiodivNER dataset.

**Per-class performance** Given that token-based prompts outperformed string-based prompts, an analysis of per-class performance of **token-based** prompts was done on the two datasets. Per **dataset**, the best-performing and worst-

| Prompt version | k | Total instances | gpt-4o-mini | | gpt-4o-2024-05-13 | | Meta-Llama-3,1-70B-Instruct | | Meta-Llama-3,1-405B-Instruct | | Average, all models | Average, all models |
|---|---|---|---|---|---|---|---|---|---|---|---|---|
| | | | Tokens | Strings | Tokens | Strings | Tokens | Strings | Tokens | Strings | Tokens | Strings |
| NE class cluster 1 | 4 | 85 | **0,39** | **0,39** | **0,53** | **0,5** | 0,33 | **0,25** | **0,47** | **0,41** | **0,43** | **0,39** |
| NE class cluster 2 | 4 | 176 | 0,23 | 0,19 | 0,33 | 0,34 | 0,28 | 0,24 | 0,22 | 0,26 | 0,27 | 0,26 |
| NE class cluster 3 | 4 | 226 | 0,33 | 0,29 | 0,43 | 0,23 | **0,38** | 0,23 | 0,42 | 0,31 | 0,39 | 0,27 |
| NE class cluster 4 | 4 | 68 | 0,17 | 0,28 | 0,38 | 0,35 | 0,21 | 0,16 | 0,4 | 0,25 | 0,29 | 0,26 |
| Random k examples | 3 | 555 | 0,32 | 0,28 | 0,38 | 0,29 | 0,35 | 0,36 | **0,42** | 0,39 | 0,37 | 0,33 |
| Random k examples | 4 | 555 | 0,33 | 0,29 | 0,41 | 0,3 | **0,37** | 0,37 | 0,4 | 0,41 | 0,38 | 0,34 |
| Random k examples | 5 | 555 | **0,36** | **0,32** | **0,44** | **0,32** | 0,36 | **0,39** | 0,39 | **0,42** | **0,39** | **0,36** |
| Similar k examples | 3 | 555 | 0,33 | 0,33 | 0,38 | 0,38 | **0,36** | 0,4 | 0,38 | 0,43 | 0,36 | 0,39 |
| Similar k examples | 4 | 555 | **0,36** | 0,32 | 0,4 | 0,41 | 0,28 | 0,4 | 0,42 | 0,43 | **0,37** | 0,39 |
| Similar k examples | 5 | 555 | **0,36** | **0,38** | **0,42** | **0,43** | 0,3 | 0,4 | **0,39** | **0,44** | **0,37** | **0,41** |
| Average F1 score (all prompts) | | | 0,32 | 0,32 | **0,41** | 0,36 | 0,32 | 0,32 | 0,39 | **0,38** | 0,36 | 0,35 |

Table 3: Climate-Change-NER results: F1 scores for all versions of token- and string-based input-output prompts.

| Prompt version | k | Total instances | gpt-4o-mini | | gpt-4o-2024-05-13 | | Meta-Llama-3,1-70B-Instruct | | Meta-Llama-3,1-405B-Instruct | | Average, all models | Average, all models |
|---|---|---|---|---|---|---|---|---|---|---|---|---|
| | | | Tokens | Strings | Tokens | Strings | Tokens | Strings | Tokens | Strings | Tokens | Strings |
| NE class cluster 1 | 4 | 186 | 0,21 | **0,28** | 0,34 | **0,28** | 0,2 | 0,16 | 0,22 | **0,29** | 0,24 | **0,25** |
| NE class cluster 2 | 4 | 573 | **0,26** | 0,24 | **0,42** | 0,2 | **0,27** | **0,25** | **0,33** | 0,28 | **0,32** | 0,24 |
| NE class cluster 3 | 4 | 518 | 0,21 | 0,25 | 0,35 | 0,22 | 0,24 | 0,23 | 0,23 | 0,28 | 0,26 | **0,25** |
| Random k examples | 3 | 1277 | 0,23 | 0,26 | 0,32 | 0,29 | **0,28** | **0,27** | **0,31** | **0,33** | **0,29** | 0,29 |
| Random k examples | 4 | 1277 | **0,25** | 0,27 | **0,33** | **0,39** | 0,25 | 0,26 | 0,3 | **0,33** | **0,29** | **0,31** |
| Random k examples | 5 | 1277 | **0,25** | **0,29** | 0,31 | **0,39** | 0,27 | **0,27** | 0,26 | 0,3 | 0,27 | **0,31** |
| Similar k examples | 3 | 1277 | 0,34 | 0,36 | 0,4 | **0,46** | 0,34 | 0,33 | 0,35 | 0,37 | 0,36 | **0,38** |
| Similar k examples | 4 | 1277 | 0,34 | 0,36 | **0,46** | 0,38 | 0,35 | **0,36** | 0,35 | **0,39** | **0,38** | 0,37 |
| Similar k examples | 5 | 1277 | **0,35** | **0,38** | 0,37 | 0,38 | **0,38** | **0,36** | **0,38** | 0,4 | 0,37 | **0,38** |
| Average F1 score (all prompts) | | | 0,27 | 0,3 | **0,37** | **0,33** | 0,29 | 0,28 | 0,3 | **0,33** | 0,31 | 0,31 |

Table 4: BiodivNER results: F1 scores for all versions of token- and string-based input-output prompts.

performing classes for Climate-Change-NER are *climate-organizations* (0.59)[19] and *climate-assets* (0.23) respectively. For BiodivNER, the best and worst performing classes are *organism* (0.48) and *matter* (0.18). Per **model**, for Climate-Change-NER, gpt-4o-mini and Llama-70B perform best on *climate-organizations* (0.63 and 0.51), while gpt-4o and Llama-405B on *climate-greenhouse-gases* (0.62 and 0.74). For BiodivNER, all models perform best on the class *organism* (score range of 0.43 to 0.52) and worst on *mater* (0.15 to 0.19).

## 5.2 Qualitative analysis

The two worst-performing classes in the output of the highest-F1 score models for all-class token-based prompts were further investigated. For Climate-Change-NER, this is the model gpt-4o with a prompt containing 5 random TEs, while for BiodivNER this is the same model with a prompt containing 4 similar TEs.

**Climate-Change-NER** The two worst-performing classes are *climate-assets* and *climate-problem-origins*. When annotating instances of *climate-assets*, defined as "objects or services of value to humans that can get destroyed or diminished by climate-hazards", the model tends to prefer the longest-span option: it annotates the span *pavement structure*, instead of *pavement*, *bioclimatic skyscrapers* instead of *skyscrapers*, *livestock industry* instead of just *livestock*. The model does not delineate well between *climate-assets*, *climate-nature*, and *climate-mitigations*. The model annotates as *climate-problem-origins*, defined as "problems that describe why the climate is changing", instances such as *global warming*, considered non-entity in the test split of the gold dataset. It also fails to annotate *emissions* as an entity of this class only when it is used in the context of climate change. Sources of energy, including *hydropower*, are also annotated with this class.[20]

**BiodivNER** The two lowest-scoring classes in this instance are *matter* (F1 of 0.18) and *location* (0.25). Instances incorrectly annotated with the class *matter*, defined as "chemical and biological compounds, and natural elements", usually involve cases when the model only annotates

[19] Average F1 score from all prompts and all models.

[20] In the gold dataset, *hydropower* is annotated with the class *climate-mitigations*.

| Prompt version | k | Total instances | gpt-4o-mini | | gpt-4o-2024-05-13 | | Meta-Llama-3,1-70B-Instruct | | Meta-Llama-3,1-405B-Instruct | | Average, all models | Average, all models |
|---|---|---|---|---|---|---|---|---|---|---|---|---|
| | | | Tokens | Strings | Tokens | Strings | Tokens | Strings | Tokens | Strings | Tokens | Strings |
| NE class cluster 1 | 4 | 85 | **0,61** | **0,38** | **0,75** | **0,54** | **0,68** | **0,51** | **0,74** | 0,47 | **0,7** | **0,48** |
| NE class cluster 2 | 4 | 176 | 0,38 | 0,34 | 0,47 | 0,46 | 0,48 | 0,38 | 0,4 | **0,53** | 0,43 | 0,43 |
| NE class cluster 3 | 4 | 226 | 0,46 | 0,31 | 0,42 | 0,2 | 0,49 | 0,31 | 0,49 | 0,37 | 0,47 | 0,3 |
| NE class cluster 4 | 4 | 68 | 0,34 | 0,22 | 0,56 | 0,35 | 0,5 | 0,35 | 0,5 | 0,34 | 0,48 | 0,3 |
| Random k examples | 3 | 555 | 0,35 | 0,29 | 0,36 | 0,3 | 0,34 | 0,35 | **0,45** | 0,39 | 0,38 | 0,33 |
| Random k examples | 4 | 555 | 0,39 | 0,31 | 0,4 | 0,31 | **0,38** | **0,37** | 0,44 | **0,43** | **0,4** | 0,36 |
| Random k examples | 5 | 555 | **0,41** | **0,35** | **0,45** | **0,33** | **0,38** | 0,4 | 0,42 | **0,43** | **0,4** | **0,38** |
| Similar k examples | 3 | 555 | 0,36 | **0,35** | 0,35 | 0,37 | **0,34** | 0,39 | 0,42 | **0,45** | **0,38** | 0,39 |
| Similar k examples | 4 | 555 | **0,39** | 0,34 | 0,38 | 0,41 | 0,26 | **0,4** | **0,45** | 0,44 | 0,37 | 0,4 |
| Similar k examples | 5 | 555 | **0,39** | 0,41 | **0,39** | **0,45** | 0,29 | **0,4** | 0,44 | **0,45** | **0,38** | **0,43** |
| Average simple span score | | | 0,41 | 0,33 | 0,45 | 0,37 | 0,41 | 0,39 | **0,48** | **0,43** | 0,44 | 0,38 |

Table 5: Climate-Change-NER: Span-and-category matches for token- and string-based input-output prompts. The values are given as percentages of total instances.

| Prompt version | k | Total instances | gpt-4o-mini | | gpt-4o-2024-05-13 | | Meta-Llama-3,1-70B-Instruct | | Meta-Llama-3,1-405B-Instruct | | Average, all models | Average, all models |
|---|---|---|---|---|---|---|---|---|---|---|---|---|
| | | | Tokens | Strings | Tokens | Strings | Tokens | Strings | Tokens | Strings | Tokens | Strings |
| NE class cluster 1 | 4 | 186 | 0,21 | 0,23 | 0,41 | 0,24 | 0,33 | 0,21 | **0,47** | 0,28 | 0,36 | 0,24 |
| NE class cluster 2 | 4 | 573 | **0,26** | 0,22 | **0,57** | 0,31 | 0,29 | 0,24 | 0,43 | 0,26 | **0,39** | 0,26 |
| NE class cluster 3 | 4 | 518 | 0,21 | **0,36** | 0,46 | **0,44** | **0,36** | **0,36** | 0,38 | **0,37** | 0,35 | **0,38** |
| Random k examples | 3 | 1277 | 0,23 | **0,28** | 0,34 | 0,38 | 0,31 | 0,27 | **0,31** | **0,34** | 0,3 | 0,32 |
| Random k examples | 4 | 1277 | **0,25** | 0,27 | **0,36** | **0,41** | **0,34** | 0,26 | 0,3 | **0,34** | **0,31** | 0,32 |
| Random k examples | 5 | 1277 | **0,25** | **0,28** | 0,32 | 0,4 | 0,27 | **0,29** | 0,26 | 0,29 | 0,28 | 0,32 |
| Similar k examples | 3 | 1277 | **0,34** | 0,36 | 0,39 | 0,46 | 0,37 | 0,32 | 0,28 | 0,35 | 0,35 | 0,38 |
| Similar k examples | 4 | 1277 | **0,34** | 0,37 | **0,49** | 0,46 | **0,42** | **0,34** | 0,26 | 0,37 | **0,38** | **0,39** |
| Similar k examples | 5 | 1277 | 0,35 | **0,38** | 0,34 | 0,46 | 0,39 | **0,34** | **0,37** | **0,38** | 0,36 | **0,39** |
| Average simple span score | | | 0,27 | 0,31 | **0,41** | **0,40** | 0,34 | 0,29 | 0,34 | 0,33 | 0,34 | 0,33 |

Table 6: BiodivNER: Span-and-category matches for token- and string-based input-output prompts. The values are given as percentages of total instances.

a nested span, which can function as an NE instance on its own and within a longer span (capturing only *woody debris* instead of *woody debris item*). The wrongly-annotated instances of *location*, defined as a "geographic location, such as China", are interesting, as they reveal plausible NE candidates that have not been included in the gold dataset, such as *Turkey*, *Papua New Guinea* and *tropical South America*.

## 6 Discussion and future work

The experiments reveal that few-shot NER methods are not a turnkey solution for highly-specialised NE annotation at token- and sentence-level, which answers Q1 and further highlights the importance of reflecting on and reporting LLMs' limitations on domain-specific tasks, especially at a time of benchmark-centric research. Nevertheless, the results also reveal possible use cases for LLMs in the context of NER, which include testing the robustness of datasets and further simplifying the task by focusing on isolated NE classes and extensive task descriptions; both of these are discussed in subsection 6.1.

Regarding the **input-output format** investigated within Q2, the experiments show that LLMs achieved slightly better performance on token-based than on string-based input. A plausible explanation for this might be that repeated NE instances in a single sentence are more likely to be identified with a token-based approach, as the LLM processes each token individually. In future iterations, it would be useful to investigate whether the prompt for string-based processing could benefit by including an instruction for the LLM to extract repeated occurrences of the same NE instance. Since LLMs' performance could improve with more context, it would be worthwhile investigating whether redefining the string-based prompt as a document-level NER task would yield better performance. Finally, it was noticed that the BiodivNER dataset contained many tokens that were remnants of PDF parsing, which might also have affected the LLMs' output for string-based prompts.

In many cases, there was an overlap in the classes on which the LLMs performed well or poorly. The experiment results seem to hint that the **complexity** of the task could be rooted in the LLMs not having been exposed to sufficient data about the specialised domains. It would be interesting to test this approach on a domain-specific LLM developed for climate change question-answering, such as models belonging to the ClimateGPT family (Thulke et al., 2024). Unfortunately, this was not realistic for this study due to infrastructure constraints.

### 6.1 Possible use-cases

**Testing robustness of datasets** While LLMs cannot be considered reliable "annotators" in an end-to-end pipeline for corpus annotation, they could be valuable assets in testing the definitions and labels of an existing NER dataset. This is corroborated by the fact that in BiodivNER, the models identified valid NE candidates of the category *location*. This experimental setup would be an affordable way of probing NE definitions and categories prior to embarking on manual annotation. Such "probing" could also uncover class ambiguities, where an instance could make a plausible NE candidate of two or more classes.

**Focusing on isolated NE classes** While LLMs were not capable of capturing NEs in the same way a dedicated NE classifier would do, their performance on certain categories, such as *climate-greenhouse-gases* and *climate-organisations*, was acceptable. It would be interesting to explore how the models would perform in a single-class scenario with a more extensive task description.

## 7 Ethical considerations

This study uses publicly available datasets. The experiments do not require specialised infrastructure and can be reproduced using an API and the prompts provided in the dedicated GitHub repository. The costs for all experiments, per language model family are: ca. 40 EUR for OpenAI's GPT4 models, and ca. 20 EUR for Llama's 3.1 models.

## Limitations

The experiments use text generation in an LLM-as-a-service setup, which makes them vulnerable to non-responsive APIs. Given that an LLM may not yield the same result twice even when prompted with the same text, it is impossible to guarantee 100% reproducibility. Guardrails against bias and offensive content are recommended before real-world deployment. Information considered confidential or sensitive should not be sent in API calls.


## Funding

The research presented in this paper was conducted within the research project InsightsNet (`https://insightsnet.org/`), which is funded by the Federal Ministry of Education and Research (BMBF) under grant no. 01UG2130A. The funder had no role in study design, data collection and analysis, decision to publish, or preparation of the manuscript.

## Acknowledgments

The author would like to thank the anonymous reviewers for their helpful feedback.


## References


Nora Abdelmageed, Felicitas Löffler, Leila Feddoul, Alsayed Algergawy, Sheeba Samuel, Jitendra Gaikwad, Anahita Kazem, and Birgitta König-Ries. 2022. Biodivnere: Gold standard corpora for named entity recognition and relation extraction in the biodiversity domain. *Biodiversity Data Journal*, 10.

Nora Abdelmageed, Felicitas Löffler, and Birgitta König-Ries. 2023. Biodivbert: a pre-trained language model for the biodiversity domain. *CEUR-WS. org*, pages 62–71.

Dhananjay Ashok and Zachary Chase Lipton. 2023. Promptner: Prompting for named entity recognition. *ArXiv*, abs/2305.15444.

Bishwaranjan Bhattacharjee, Aashka Trivedi, Masayasu Muraoka, Muthukumaran Ramasubramanian, Takuma Udagawa, Iksha Gurung, Rong Zhang, Bharath Dandala, Rahul Ramachandran, Manil Maskey, et al. 2024. Indus: Effective and efficient language models for scientific applications. *arXiv preprint arXiv:2405.10725*.

Tom Brown, Benjamin Mann, Nick Ryder, Melanie Subbiah, Jared D Kaplan, Prafulla Dhariwal, Arvind Neelakantan, Pranav Shyam, Girish Sastry, Amanda Askell, et al. 2020. Language models are few-shot learners. *Advances in neural information processing systems*, 33:1877–1901.

Nancy Chinchor and Beth Sundheim. 1993. MUC-5 evaluation metrics. In *Fifth Message Understanding Conference (MUC-5): Proceedings of a Conference Held in Baltimore, Maryland, August 25-27, 1993*.

Elena V. Epure and Romain Hennequin. 2022. Probing pre-trained auto-regressive language models for named entity typing and recognition. In *Proceedings of the Thirteenth Language Resources and*

*Evaluation Conference*, pages 1408–1417, Marseille, France. European Language Resources Association.

Luis Glaser, Ronny Patz, and Manfred Stede. 2022. Unsc-ne: A named entity extension to the un security council debates corpus. *Journal for Language Technology and Computational Linguistics*, 35(2):51–67.

Nanna Inie, Stefania Druga, Peter Zukerman, and Emily M Bender. 2024. From" ai" to probabilistic automation: How does anthropomorphization of technical systems descriptions influence trust? In *The 2024 ACM Conference on Fairness, Accountability, and Transparency*, pages 2322–2347.

Basra Jehangir, Saravanan Radhakrishnan, and Rahul Agarwal. 2023. A survey on named entity recognition—datasets, tools, and methodologies. *Natural Language Processing Journal*, 3:100017.

Rodney Kinney, Chloe Anastasiades, Russell Authur, Iz Beltagy, Jonathan Bragg, Alexandra Buraczynski, Isabel Cachola, Stefan Candra, Yoganand Chandrasekhar, Arman Cohan, et al. 2023. The semantic scholar open data platform. *arXiv preprint arXiv:2301.10140*.

Christopher D Manning, Mihai Surdeanu, John Bauer, Jenny Rose Finkel, Steven Bethard, and David McClosky. 2014. The stanford corenlp natural language processing toolkit. In *Proceedings of 52nd annual meeting of the association for computational linguistics: system demonstrations*, pages 55–60.

Minh Van Nguyen, Viet Dac Lai, Amir Pouran Ben Veyseh, and Thien Huu Nguyen. 2021. Trankit: A light-weight transformer-based toolkit for multilingual natural language processing. In *Proceedings of the 16th Conference of the European Chapter of the Association for Computational Linguistics: System Demonstrations*.

Birgit Pfitzmann. 2024. Personal correspondence. Personal correspondence with Birgit Pfitzmann on 2 September 2024.

Peng Qi, Yuhao Zhang, Yuhui Zhang, Jason Bolton, and Christopher D Manning. 2020. Stanza: A python natural language processing toolkit for many human languages. *arXiv preprint arXiv:2003.07082*.

Nils Reimers and Iryna Gurevych. 2019. Sentence-bert: Sentence embeddings using siamese bert-networks. In *Proceedings of the 2019 Conference on Empirical Methods in Natural Language Processing*. Association for Computational Linguistics.

Erik F Sang and Fien De Meulder. 2003. Introduction to the conll-2003 shared task: Language-independent named entity recognition. *arXiv preprint cs/0306050*.

David Thulke, Yingbo Gao, Petrus Pelser, Rein Brune, Rricha Jalota, Floris Fok, Michael Ramos, Ian van Wyk, Abdallah Nasir, Hayden Goldstein, et al. 2024. Climategpt: Towards ai synthesizing interdisciplinary research on climate change. *arXiv preprint arXiv:2401.09646*.

Petter Törnberg. 2024. Best practices for text annotation with large language models. *arXiv preprint arXiv:2402.05129*.

Ashish Vaswani, Noam Shazeer, Niki Parmar, Jakob Uszkoreit, Llion Jones, Aidan N Gomez, Łukasz Kaiser, and Illia Polosukhin. 2017. Attention is all you need. *Advances in neural information processing systems*, 30.

Chenguang Wang, Xiao Liu, Zui Chen, Haoyun Hong, Jie Tang, and Dawn Song. 2022. DeepStruct: Pretraining of language models for structure prediction. In *Findings of the Association for Computational Linguistics: ACL 2022*, pages 803–823, Dublin, Ireland. Association for Computational Linguistics.

Shuhe Wang, Xiaofei Sun, Xiaoya Li, Rongbin Ouyang, Fei Wu, Tianwei Zhang, Jiwei Li, and Guoyin Wang. 2023. Gpt-ner: Named entity recognition via large language models. *arXiv preprint arXiv:2304.10428*.

# Communicating urgency to prevent environmental damage: insights from a linguistic analysis of the WWF24 multilingual corpus

**Cristina Bosco**
Dipartimento di Informatica
Università di Torino
Torino (Italy)
cristina.bosco@unito.it

**Adriana Silvina Pagano**
Università di Torino /
Universidade Federal de Minas Gerais
Belo Horizonte (Brazil)
apagano@ufmg.br

**Elisa Chierchiello**
Dipartimento di Informatica
Università di Torino
Torino (Italy)
elisa.chierchiello@unito.it

## Abstract

Contemporary environmental discourse focuses on effectively communicating ecological vulnerability to raise public awareness and encourage positive actions. Hence there is a need for studies to support accurate and adequate discourse production, both by humans and computers. Two main challenges need to be tackled. On the one hand, the language used to communicate about environment issues can be very complex for human and automatic analysis, there being few resources to train and test NLP tools. On the other hand, in the current international scenario, most texts are written in multiple languages or translated from a major to minor language, resulting in different meanings in different languages and cultural contexts.

This paper presents a novel parallel corpus comprising the text of World Wide Fund (WWF) 2024 Annual Report in English and its translations into Italian and Brazilian Portuguese, and analyses their linguistic features.

## 1 Introduction

Environmental issues, such as biodiversity loss, global climate and sustainability, have an important social relevance today and are increasingly debated in all countries, in a variety of communication channels and media.

Nevertheless, notwithstanding the great amount of dissemination and communication about environmental matters, the recent literature has problematized the effectiveness of such discourse due to the complexity in the content of this kind of texts. For instance, Italian dissemination texts discussing issues related to the environment, published by the European Agency and journals, have been evaluated as posing readability challenges for people who do not have at least a high school degree (Bosco et al., 2023).

Moreover, in the current international scenario in which disseminating clear and homogeneous messages about the environmental crisis is crucial, texts are often written in multiple languages or translated from a major (in most of cases English) to minor languages, resulting in the construal of different meanings in different countries.

Governmental entities have also detected this kind of difficulty and are trying to address it. For example, in 2020 the European Commission published a study showing that more than half of the environmental claims examined in the European countries were vague, misleading or unfounded, while 40% were completely unfounded. To promote more accurate and timely information, in March 2023, the European Parliament published the *Green Claims Directive*[1].

In countries especially involved in the environmental crisis, such as Brazil, a large variety of educational and informative initiatives are promoted to foster the correct dissemination of information (see, among other, *Climate Change and Public Perception in Brazil*[2], a project for measuring knowledge and concern of Brazilians on climate change and the yearly forest fires in the country.

The studies and political interventions above reported clearly point to the importance of language in raising public awareness to save the planet. In addition to the life sciences, disciplines such as computational linguistics are also expected to address the challenges posed by environmental discourse from the perspective of their theoretical and methodological approaches and applying different strategies that can impact on discourse and, ultimately, on societal moves towards sustainability. By providing a fine-grained analysis of the

[1] https://environment.ec.europa.eu/topics/circular-economy/green-claims_en

[2] https://en.percepcaoclimatica.com.br/



*Proceedings of the 1st Workshop on Ecology, Environment, and Natural Language Processing (NLP4Ecology2025)*, pages 34–43
March 2, 2025 

language used to communicate environmental issues, computational linguistics can indeed collaborate with crucial information on how individuals, groups of people or entire societies are coping with environmental issues, their attitudes, awareness and willingness to work towards more sustainable life patterns for the planet.

Nonetheless, machines also are facing challenges to analyse texts on environmental discourse, first of all because they use a specialized lexicon even when written with a popularization intent. This motivates the development of pretrained models (Thulke et al., 2024) dedicated to address texts about environmental issues which include specific expressions that general language LMs can not represent accurately (Webersinke et al., 2022) and different languages. But there are other challenges when dealing with environmental texts. For example, the frequent inclusion of infographics, images and tables that integrate the text content can make automatic analysis particularly difficult (Saha et al., 2024; Mishra et al., 2024).
A further and also more serious challenge is the scarcity of available datasets and corpora to train tools for automatic analysis and evaluate their performance on texts about environmental issues. For example, as reported in (Ibrohim et al., 2023), resources for Sentiment Analysis of environmental texts are currently very poor for all languages. Some corpora about environmental topics are available for English and very few for other languages. In general, it is striking that the development of tools and resources to tackle the problem, including by computational linguistics, has not yet involved languages spoken in countries which have long been among key stakeholders in environmental phenomena, as is Brazil, for example.
On top of that, only topics related to climate change seem to have attracted most of the research community interest (probably due to the higher visibility and quantifiability of its effects), while others are less studied in the context of computational linguistics. This is the case of biodiversity loss, one of the most debated environmental topics at present.

In this paper, we introduce a novel multilingual parallel corpus WWF24 comprising texts about biodiversity loss and other environmental issues published within a report in 2024 by the World Wildlife Fund (WWF)[3], and we provide the results of the language analysis we applied to it. In line with the literature, the results reveal differences in the way meanings are construed in each language. They may have significant impact on the ultimate effectiveness in the way meanings are construed to communicate ecological vulnerability and raise public awareness and encourage positive actions accordingly. We have included three languages in the preliminary release of our corpus, namely English, Brazilian Portuguese and Italian, also taking into account issues related to translation and different renditions for the key concepts.
The research questions we want to investigate are therefore as follows:

- Are meanings pertaining to environmental issues construed analogously in different languages?
- What do language patterns show about how the notion of biodiversity and nature is construed in Italian, Portuguese and English?
- What impact does translation have on meaning construal in the Italian and Brazilian texts?

Our main contribution includes the preliminary release of a novel multilingual parallel corpus WWF24 of environmental discourse[4] and the reporting of results of a set of analyses.
Our main goal is to provide data that support the development of LMs especially dedicated to the topics related to biodiversity. Drawing on the premise that our language construes our experience of the world (Halliday and Matthiessen, 2006) examining the language used in environmental discourse allows us, not only to gather insights into how different languages construe different meanings, but also to better characterize the complexity of environmental discourse.

The paper is organized as follows. The next section briefly surveys related work. Section 3 introduces the WWF24 corpus providing the details about the texts compiled. Section 4 and 5 are devoted to describing the analysis performed on the corpus and the results obtained. In Section 6 we

[3]The WWF is the leading wordlwide organization in wildlife conservation and endangered species (https://www.worldwildlife.org/).

[4]The corpus will be made publicly available and downloadable upon paper acceptance

provide a discussion of the results of our analysis, conclusions and envisioned steps for further work.

## 2 Related Work

NLP approaches to the analysis of environmental discourse have mainly focused on Sentiment Analysis.

A systematic survey of the application of Sentiment Analysis on environment related topics is presented in (Ibrohim et al., 2023). The paper shows that few projects on the subject have been carried out, even for major languages such as English, and these have used fairly rough techniques. In (Stede and Patz, 2021), a review is conducted to explore the application of Sentiment Analysis in the debate about climate change. The authors show how different communities (general public, policy-makers and scientists) use different genres, registers, and terminologies to communicate with each other and with other communities about this issue, pointing to the potential of NLP to assist them to assess in which direction the debate may evolve and to respond accordingly.

(Du et al., 2020) explore the use of Sentiment Analysis for examining opinions on several smart city issues like climate change, urban policy, energy, and traffic drawing on social media texts.

(Stede and Patz, 2021) review approaches to the analysis of climate change discourse both from the perspective of NLP studies and social science studies, arguing for potential enhancement of studies if both fields take each other's perspectives into account. Both these surveys, (Stede and Patz, 2021) and (Du et al., 2020) are enlightening in the results reported but do not provide an in-depth exploration of NLP techniques needed to apply Sentiment Analysis on natural environment topics and are restricted to a specific topic, not considering many other topics related to nature and environmental issues.

In the last year, the application of NLP to environmental issues has been more reported on in scientific events and, in particular, in workshops such as ClimateNLP 2024[5] or ICLR 2024 - Tackling Climate Change with Machine Learning[6]. Both events will be held again in 2025.

The development of language models dedicated to climate change topics, such as ClimateBERT (Webersinke et al., 2022) and the above mentioned events underline how climate change is currently raising a specific attention within computational linguistics.

As far as corpora to be used in NLP experiments, a corpus for Italian has been recently published and is described in (Grasso et al., 2024a), while efforts made for building a multilingual corpus including Italian, Indonesian and English are described in (Bosco et al., 2023). Among the most recent corpora for English we can cite (Grasso et al., 2024b), which is focused on issues related to climate change observed from a diachronic perspective.

One of the aims of our contribution is expanding the variety of environment-related topics and number of languages, in this particular paper including Brazilian Portuguese, which is currently under represented.

## 3 Data

This section describes the corpus we collected for the purpose of analysing linguistic features of environmental discourse.

To compile our corpus WWF24, we downloaded the original version of *WWF's 2024 Living Planet Report*, available in English at `https://livingplanet.panda.org/en-US/`. The Brazilian version was downloaded from `https://livingplanet.panda.org/pt-BR/` and the Italian version from `https://www.wwf.it/cosa-facciamo/pubblicazioni/living-planet-report/`. Henceforth the three versions will be referred as WWF24-Eng, WWF24-Ita and WWF24-Bra. They can be considered as a starting point for a resource in which more languages will be included and the same methodology applied.

A comparison of the three versions of *WWF's 2024 Living Planet Report* showed that they all featured the same images and text content. In both the Italian and Brazilian versions, the names of the translators are acknowledged. However, unlike the Brazilian version, in which all infographics are translated, most infographics in the Italian version are partially translated or not translated at all. For the purposes of language analysis, images and infographics were removed and plain text files were created as part of the novel corpus WWF24.

As *WWF's 2024 Living Planet Report* is a technical report, drawing on data and domain termi-

[5] `https://nlp4climate.github.io/climatenlp2024/`

[6] `https://www.climatechange.ai/events/iclr2024`

nology used by WWF in accordance to other major stakeholders and at the same time aiming at a wider readership, we expected the use of technical terms as well as lay explanations, which knowledgeably poses a challenge in translations. An example of one such challenge is the terminology in*WWF's 2024 Living Planet Report*, for instance "tipping point" and "nature-positive" (see section 4), which are used as technical terms in the environmental domain and which need to be clarified to a lay audience.

Our analysis thus began by exploring general characteristics of the texts and finally focused on specific terms. To query the corpus we relied on text analysis software: Sketch Engine[7] and Voyant Tools[8]. For a fine-grained analysis of two particular terms - 'tipping point' and 'nature-positive'- we performed manual alignment of the sentences in which the terms occurred.

The corpus compiled is deemed a valuable contribution for an area in which there are only very few datasets. Moreover, the first release of our corpus compiles data for Italian, Brazilian Portuguese and English, but and expansion is scheduled to include in WWF24 texts from other language families, as is the case of Turkish. Some considerations related to the debate about the environment and languages in general motivated our initial choice of three languages.

**English** is the language in which the WWF's reports are originally written, assumed as a medium of communication and the most spoken language around the world.

**Portuguese** (including European and Brazilian Portuguese) is among the 8 most spoken languages with 264 million speakers, and most of them being in Brazil[9]. Brazil is one of the countries most impacted by environmental phenomena and one of the main stakeholders in environmental discussions with the greatest biodiversity of flora and fauna on the planet. Nevertheless, based on our knowledge, we are not aware of corpora available for this language about the discussion of biodiversity loss.

Finally, **Italian** has been selected because of our expertise and because it underlines a culture that is enough different from those represented by the other two languages.

[7]https://www.sketchengine.eu/

[8]https://voyant-tools.org/

[9]The country for which the report is published by the WWF is Brazil and the language is Brazilian Portuguese.

Linguistic analysis is expected to pave the way for the development of annotation schemes that can be later applied on the data for building, not only LMs, but also benchmarks that are crucial for the evaluation of results provided by LMs.

## 4 Linguistic Analysis

We performed different techniques aimed at extracting the most important lexical and semantic features in a cross language perspective. We computed the number of sentences, words and lemmas in the WWF24-Eng corpus using the text analysis software Sketch Engine. Table 1 shows distributions in our corpus.

| | Eng | Ita | Bra |
|---|---|---|---|
| tokens | 29,996 | 33,437 | 32,914 |
| words | 25,359 | 29,087 | 28,467 |
| different words | 4,344 | 4,977 | 4,866 |
| lemmas | 3,036 | 3,479 | 3,354 |

Table 1: Distribution of tokens, words, different words and lemmas in the three subcorpora of the WWF24 corpus .

As can be seen in Table 1, figures are higher in the Italian and Brazilian Portuguese texts than in the original in English. This may be accounted for by typological features of the languages. Italian and Brazilian Portuguese, for instance, make use of prepositional phrases to realize many noun phrases in English, which adds to the number of tokens. Also, Italian and Brazilian Portuguese make use of more lemmas to realize a single lemma in English. For example, 'to see' is rendered by several lemmas, among them 'vedere' and 'osservare' in Italian and 'ver' e 'observar' in Brazilian Portuguese.

In order to explore lexical characteristics, using Sketch Engine we extracted the most frequent lemmas for nouns in each subcorpus. Table 2 shows similarities and differences between the three languages regarding the 10 **most frequent nouns**. For example, 'nature'/'natura'/'natureza' and 'biodiversity'/'biodiversità'/'biodiversidade' rank among the first most frequent nouns in all three languages. However, 'species' does not rank amid the first ten positions in English (it can be found at the 16th position with 82 occurrences), while unlike in English, 'planet' does not rank in Italian and Brazilian Portuguese (it is in the 70th position with 25 occurrences in Italian and

| English | Italian | Brazilian |
|---|---|---|
| nature (196) | natura (224) | natureza (226) |
| climate (180) | cambiamento (165) | mudança (158) |
| change (150) | specie (124) | espécie (127) |
| food (138) | sistema (117) | ecossistema (116) |
| ecosystem (126) | popolazione (116) | área (115) |
| energy (124) | ecosistema (113) | sistema (113) |
| system (109) | obiettivo (107) | água (102) |
| population (105) | biodiversità (99) | população (100) |
| biodiversity (103) | acqua (94) | biodiversidade (99) |
| planet (103) | persona (91) | energia (98) |

Table 2: 10 most frequent nouns in WWF24-Eng, WWF24-Ita and WWF24-Bra (frequency of each word in brackets).

in the 22th position with 62 occurrences in Brazilian Portuguese).

Comparing the three subcorpora, we can observe that only the following 6 nouns occur in all three of them (with comparable number of occurrences):
'nature'/'natura'/'natureza'
'change'/'cambiamento'/'mudança'
'ecosystem'/'ecosistema'/'ecossistema'
'population'/'popolazione'/'população'
'biodiversity'/'biodiversità'/'biodiversidade'
'system'/'sistema'/'sistema'.

These **6 nouns** were selected in order to examine their **co-occurrence with verbs**. It should be noted that the results of the following analyses (created with the Word Sketch function of Sketch Engine) are not identical for all three languages. Morpho-syntactic annotation tools are available for Italian and English, allowing Sketch Engine to build on its results to obtain accurate information about word behaviour, whereas they are not available for Brazilian Portuguese. This means, for example, that for a noun N, Sketch Engine can distinguish between verbs where N occurs as a subject and those where N occurs as an object complement, whereas for Brazilian Portuguese it can only recognise verbs with which N co-occurs.

In the upper part of the figure 1 we can see some important differences for the noun 'nature'/'natura'/'natureza', i.e. those that occur most frequently in all three languages: In Italian, the most frequently used verbs with 'natura' as object are 'ripristinare' (to restore) and 'proteggere' (to protect); they also occur in the other languages, but the link between the words 'nature' and 'natureza' and these verbs is less strong in the data for English and Brazilian.

In the lower part of the figure 1, the diagrams for the nouns 'biodiversity'/'biodiversità'/'biodiversidade' are shown. We can see that in all languages the concept of biodiversity is linked to the action of preserving ('conserve', 'conservare' and 'conservar'). However, the fact that in Italian biodiversity is in almost all cases the object of active verb forms underlines that the responsibility for its conservation is perceived as the task of a specific person or entity (subject of these verbs). For the other 4 most frequent word groups mentioned above, the analysis is given in the diagrams in the Appendix-A.

We can also observe that different attitudes towards environmental issues emerge from the data if we focus on the **types of verbs** used in their discourses. If we read the lists of verbs used in the three subcorpora of WWF24, we can see a significant difference in the use of modal verbs and thus an underlying expression of a different intention to describe actions as possible and their resolution as obligatory. Modal verbs are used more frequently in the Italian subcorpus than in the other two ones. In WWF24-Ita, among 558 different verbs, the modal verb 'potere' (can) is the second most frequently used (169 occurrences) and 'dovere' (must) the fourth most frequently used (115 occurrences). In WWF24-Bra, over 577 different verbs, 'poder' is the second most used verb (169 occurrences) and 'dever' the ninth (52 occurrences). In WWF24-Eng, modal verbs occur less than ten times in 557 different verbs.

The detection of **keywords**[10] from the three

[10] According to the approach applied by Sketch Engine, keywords are the words that are more frequent in the observed

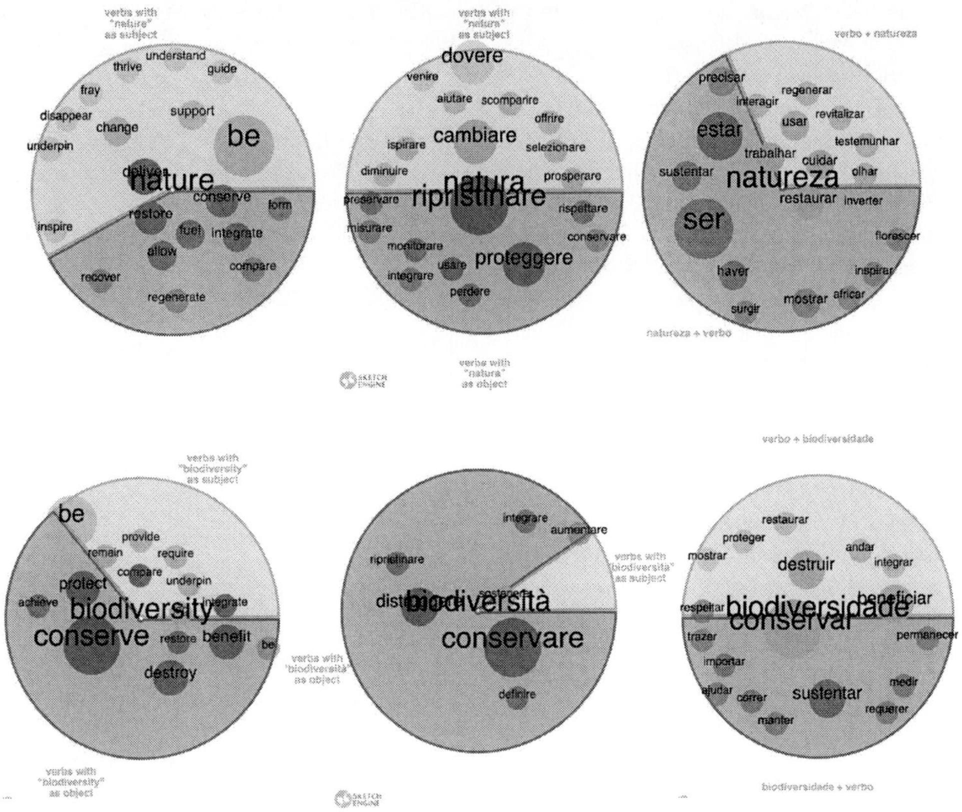


Figure 1: Behavior of 'nature'/'natura'/'natureza' and 'biodiversity'/'biodiversità'/'biodiversidade' with verbs.

subcorpora also shows that there are important differences among them and that the focus of the discourse is not exactly the same in the three versions of the WWF's report.

We started from the list of the ten more characteristic keywords extracted from WWF24-Eng, i.e. 'wwf', 'lip', 'nature-positive', 'nature-based', 'overexploitation', 'ipbes', biodiversity', 'gbf', 'oecm', 'deforestation'. Then we observed whether the corresponding keywords occur also in the lists for Italian and Brazilian Portuguese respectively drawn from WWF24-Ita and WWF24-Bra. Only six of the ten keywords occur in the three subcorpora, but only four with comparable weight (rank in the list). It must be noted that among these four, three are acronyms which are not translatable expressions, i.e. 'lpi' (living planet index), 'ipbes' (Intergovernmental Science-Policy Platform on Biodiversity and Ecosystem Services) and 'gdf' (global diversity framework), while the remaining one is 'biodiversity'/'biodiversidade'/'biodiversità'.

The keywords related to 'overexploitation' ('superexploração' and 'sovrasfruttamento') are similarly ranked in the three subcorpora. It is particularly striking that 'deforestation', the keyword ranking as tenth in the list from WWF24-Eng and as sixth in the list from WWF24-Ita, does not appear in the list from WWF24-Bra.

With regard to **technical terms**, some of which are likely candidates to multi-word expressions[11], two in particular were explored in our analysis. The first one is 'tipping point', a term which is pivotal in the report and which is amply used and defined in several websites [12]. The original 'tipping point' has 74 occurrences in the WWF24-

corpus with respect to a very large reference corpus for the same language. The reference corpora used in our analysis of keywords are: enTenTen21 for English, itTenTen20 for Italian and ptTenTen23 for Portuguese.

[11]For a definition of MWE, see (Bhatia et al., 2024).

[12]https://www.reteclima.it/tipping-points-ambientali-e-riscaldamento-climatico/

Eng. The Italian version introduces the term in quotes and provides a translation: "'tipping point' o punto critico di non ritorno" (lit.: critical point of no return). Subsequently, it alternates between the term in English (41 occurrences) and its Italian translation (13 occurrences). Unlike the Italian text, the Brazilian version uses only 'ponto de não retorno' (73 occurrences).
The term 'tipping point' is actually a concept developed originally from a physics perspective, which later came to be adopted in other domains and introduced to the lay public through science journalism.[13] A quick query in online publications shows that academic publications in Italian and Portuguese use the English term.

The second term is 'nature-positive', technically defined in some websites[14] and which poses a challenge to translations into Italian and Brazilian Portuguese as in English is used mostly attributively in pre-modifying position, i.e. as an attribute to a noun, requiring renditions by qualifiers in post-modifying position. There are 20 occurrences of 'nature-positive' in the WWF24-Eng, collocating with 'production'(7), 'food systems'(4), 'practices' (3), 'businesses and enterprises' (2), 'future' (2), 'food production' (1), and 'energy transformation' (1).
The WWF24-Ita uses different renditions to translate 'nature-positive', namely, qualifiers such as 'rispettose della natura' (lit.: respectful of nature), 'positivo per la natura' ((lit.: positive for nature), 'nature-positive' as a borrowed term operating as a qualifying adjective 'pratiche nature-positive' (lit.: practice nature-positive); and a few adjectival clauses such as 'che rispettano la natura' (lit.: which respect nature).
Finally, the WWF24-Bra uses 'nature-positive' as a noun in prepositional phrases qualifying another noun, e.g., 'produção de natureza-positiva' (lit.: production of nature-positive); 'focado em natureza-positiva' (lit.: focused on nature-positive); and qualifiers such as 'positivo para a natureza' (lit.: positive for nature).

In environmental organizations webpages in Italian (cf. `https://www.reteclima.it/nature-positive-un-mondo-equo-a-zero-emissioni-e-a-favore-della-natura/`), the concept of "nature-positive" is presented as a term borrowed from English and is used in English. So is the case in publications by WWF Italy (cf. `https://www.wwf.it/cosa-facciamo/pubblicazioni/biodiversita-fragile-maneggiare-con-cura/`). In publications by WWF Brazil, the concept is used in Portuguese as "natureza positiva" (lit.: nature positive).

## 5 Sentiment Analysis and Topic Modeling of the WWF24 Corpus

The availability of tools and models for general language allowed us to apply two types of semantics oriented analysis to the English data. The application of the same analyis is scheduled for the other sections of the WWWF.
To **analyze the sentiment** of the WWF24-Eng, we employed the pre-trained BERT-based model *'distilbert-base-uncased-finetuned-sst-2-english'* (Sanh et al., 2019). This model, optimized for sentiment classification, categorizes text into Positive, Negative, or Neutral. Given the corpus's length (25,359 words) and the BERT token limit (512 tokens per input), the text was divided into overlapping chunks of 510 tokens, with a stride of 50 tokens to maintain contextual continuity. Each segment was individually analyzed and the results were aggregated. The analysis revealed the aggregated distribution in figure 2 and more precisely:

- Positive Chunks: 63
- Negative Chunks: 103
- Neutral Chunks: 0

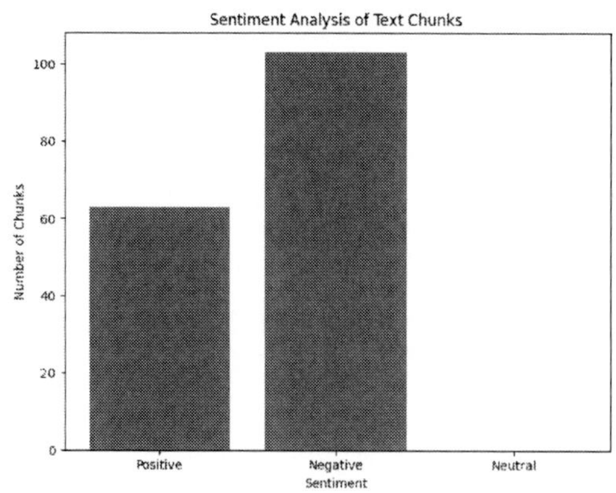


Figure 2: Sentiment distribution across text chunks in the WWF24 Corpus.

[13]cf. (Blaustein, 2015)

[14]`https://blog.3bee.com/guida-al-concetto-di-nature-positive/`

These findings indicate a predominance of negative sentiment throughout the corpus, suggesting a focus on challenges, critical issues or alarming environmental concerns. Positive sentiment, while present, appears significantly less frequent and no neutral segments were detected.

To uncover key themes within the WWF24-Eng, according to **topic modeling** approach, we employed the BERTopic algorithm (Grootendorst, 2022), a technique that uses transformer-based embeddings and clustering. The text was preprocessed to remove stop-words, non-alphanumeric characters and excessive white spaces. Then it was divided into manageable chunks of approximately 200 words to ensure compatibility with the model input size requirements. The resulting blocks were analyzed using BERTopic, generating topic clusters based on semantic similarities.
The analysis revealed three main clusters:

- Topic -1: outliers or segments not clearly assignable to a specific theme. Keywords: *tipping, points, change, energy.*
- Topic 0: global environmental challenges. Keywords: *nature, climate, energy, global, finance.*
- Topic 1: biodiversity and species conservation. Keywords: *species, populations, decline, index, change.*

These topics reflect a strong emphasis on global environmental challenges, energy sustainability and biodiversity conservation. Nevertheless, reporting the results of these analyses we are conscious that pre-training on general language works very well for common language, but its results are not as reliable for particular domain languages, such as texts about environment and we will work in the development of novel resources for it.

## 6 Discussion, Conclusions and Future Work

This paper presents the first release of the novel multilingual corpus WWF24. It compiles texts published in 2024 by the WWF for reporting on the evolution of environmental crisis all around the world and focuses on three languages, i.e. English, Brazilian and Italian.
Both the data and analyses provided in this paper are under several respects preliminary, but useful for drawing the methodology we will apply in the future development of the resource.
Our preliminary analysis points to some interesting avenues for studying diversity in approaches to environmental issues, in particular how meanings are construed in different languages regarding basic notions in the debate about the environment, such as biodiversity and nature. The expression of different intents and attitudes towards the crisis emerge instead from the different verbs used in the three subcorpora we observed. By contrast, the use of technical terms highlights that the language used in the WWF reports is featured by a certain degree of complexity and may be challenging for a significant part of the readers, as terms used to refer to technical concepts, such as 'tipping point' and 'nature-positive' have varied renditions in Italian and Portuguese, which runs counter the univocality of technical terms. However, the choice of varied renditions may be accounted for by the characteristics of the WWF report referred to in our Introduction, namely, the need to present technical information to a lay audience.

Our observations may be seen as the starting point for future work since they help us in formulating hypotheses to be validated (or refuted) following several possible directions. First of all, the availability of the WWF's reports for several other languages will allows us to expand our corpus by including more languages and comparing a larger set of different cultures.
As mentioned above, like most documents for the dissemination and public discussion of environmental issues, the reports published by the WWF also include pictures and infographics that integrate the textual content. By extending the analysis to multimodal information we will be able to collect more insights into the debate about the environmental crisis.

Finally, other forms of analysis, such as sentiment analysis and topic modelling (which we applied only on English data but will be applied on the other languages when more resources will be available for them also), but also frame extraction, can be helpful for collecting the different facets of the ongoing debate and how it varies across different cultures and countries.

## Acknowledgments

The work of E. Chierchiello is funded by the International project *CN-HPC-Spoke1-Future HPC & Big Data, PNRR MUR-M4C2*. A. S. Pagano has a grant from FAPEMIG (Minas Gerais State Agency for Research and Development), Brazil, to develop research at Dipartimento di Informatica, Università di Torino, Italy.

## References

Archna Bhatia, Gosse Bouma, A. Seza Doğruöz, Kilian Evang, Marcos Garcia, Voula Giouli, Lifeng Han, Joakim Nivre, and Alexandre Rademaker, editors. 2024. *Proceedings of the Joint Workshop on Multiword Expressions and Universal Dependencies (MWE-UD) @ LREC-COLING 2024*. ELRA and ICCL, Torino, Italia.

Richard Blaustein. 2015. Predicting tipping points. *World Policy Journal*, 32(1):32–41.

Cristina Bosco, Muhammad Okky Ibrohim, Valerio Basile, and Indra Budi. 2023. How green is sentiment analysis? environmental topics in corpora at the University of Turin. In *Proceedings of the 9th Italian Conference on Computational Linguistics (CLiC-it 2023)*, Venice, Italy. CEUR.

Xu Du, Matthew Kowalski, Aparna S. Varde, Gerard de Melo, and Robert W. Taylor. 2020. Public opinion matters: mining social media text for environmental management. *SIGWEB Newsl.*, 2019(Autumn).

Francesca Grasso, Stefano Locci, Giovanni Siragusa, and Luigi Di Caro. 2024a. Ecoverse: An annotated twitter dataset for eco-relevance classification, environmental impact analysis, and stance detection. In *Proceedings of the 2024 Joint International Conference on Computational Linguistics, Language Resources and Evaluation, LREC/COLING 2024*, pages 5461–5472. ELRA and ICCL.

Francesca Grasso, Ronny Patz, and Manfred Stede. 2024b. NYTAC-CC: A climate change subcorpus based on new york times articles. In *Proceedings of the Tenth Italian Conference on Computational Linguistics (CLiC-it 2024)*, Pisa (Italy). CEUR.

Maarten Grootendorst. 2022. Bertopic: Neural topic modeling with a class-based tf-idf procedure. *arXiv preprint arXiv:2203.05794*.

M.A.K. Halliday and C. Matthiessen. 2006. *Construing Experience Through Meaning: A Language-Based Approach to Cognition*. Open linguistics series. Bloomsbury Academic.

Muhammad Okky Ibrohim, Cristina Bosco, and Valerio Basile. 2023. Sentiment analysis for the natural environment: A systematic review. *ACM Computing Surveys*, 56(4).

Lokesh Mishra, Sohayl Dhibi, Yusik Kim, Cesar Berrospi Ramis, Shubham Gupta, Michele Dolfi, and Peter Staar. 2024. Statements: Universal information extraction from tables with large language models for ESG KPIs. In *Proceedings of the 1st Workshop on Natural Language Processing Meets Climate Change (ClimateNLP 2024)@ACL2024*, pages 193–214, Bangkok, Thailand. ACL.

Diya Saha, Manjira Sinha, and Tirthankar Dasgupta. 2024. EnClaim: A style augmented transformer architecture for environmental claim detection. In *Proceedings of the 1st Workshop on Natural Language Processing Meets Climate Change (ClimateNLP 2024)@ACL2024*, pages 123–132, Bangkok, Thailand. ACL.

Victor Sanh, Lysandre Debut, Julien Chaumond, and Thomas Wolf. 2019. Distilbert, a distilled version of bert: smaller, faster, cheaper and lighter. *arXiv preprint arXiv:1910.01108*.

Manfred Stede and Ronny Patz. 2021. The climate change debate and natural language processing. In *Proceedings of the 1st Workshop on NLP for Positive Impact@ACL-IJCNLP 2021*, pages 8–18, Online. ACL.

David Thulke, Yingbo Gao, Petrus Pelser, Rein Brune, Rricha Jalota, Floris Fok, Michael Ramos, Ian van Wyk, Abdallah Nasir, Hayden Goldstein, Taylor Tragemann, Katie Nguyen, Ariana Fowler, Andrew Stanco, Jon Gabriel, Jordan Taylor, Dean Moro, Evgenii Tsymbalov, Juliette de Waal, Evgeny Matusov, Mudar Yaghi, Mohammad Shihadah, Hermann Ney, Christian Dugast, Jonathan Dotan, and Daniel Erasmus. 2024. ClimateGPT: towards AI synthetizing interdisciplinary research on climate change. *arXiv preprint arXiv:2401.09646*.

Nicolas Webersinke, Mathias Kraus, Julia Anna Bingler, and Markus Leippold. 2022. ClimateBert: A pretrained language model for climate-related text. *ArXiv*, abs/2110.12010.

## Appendix-A: Behavior of the Most Frequent Nouns with Verbs

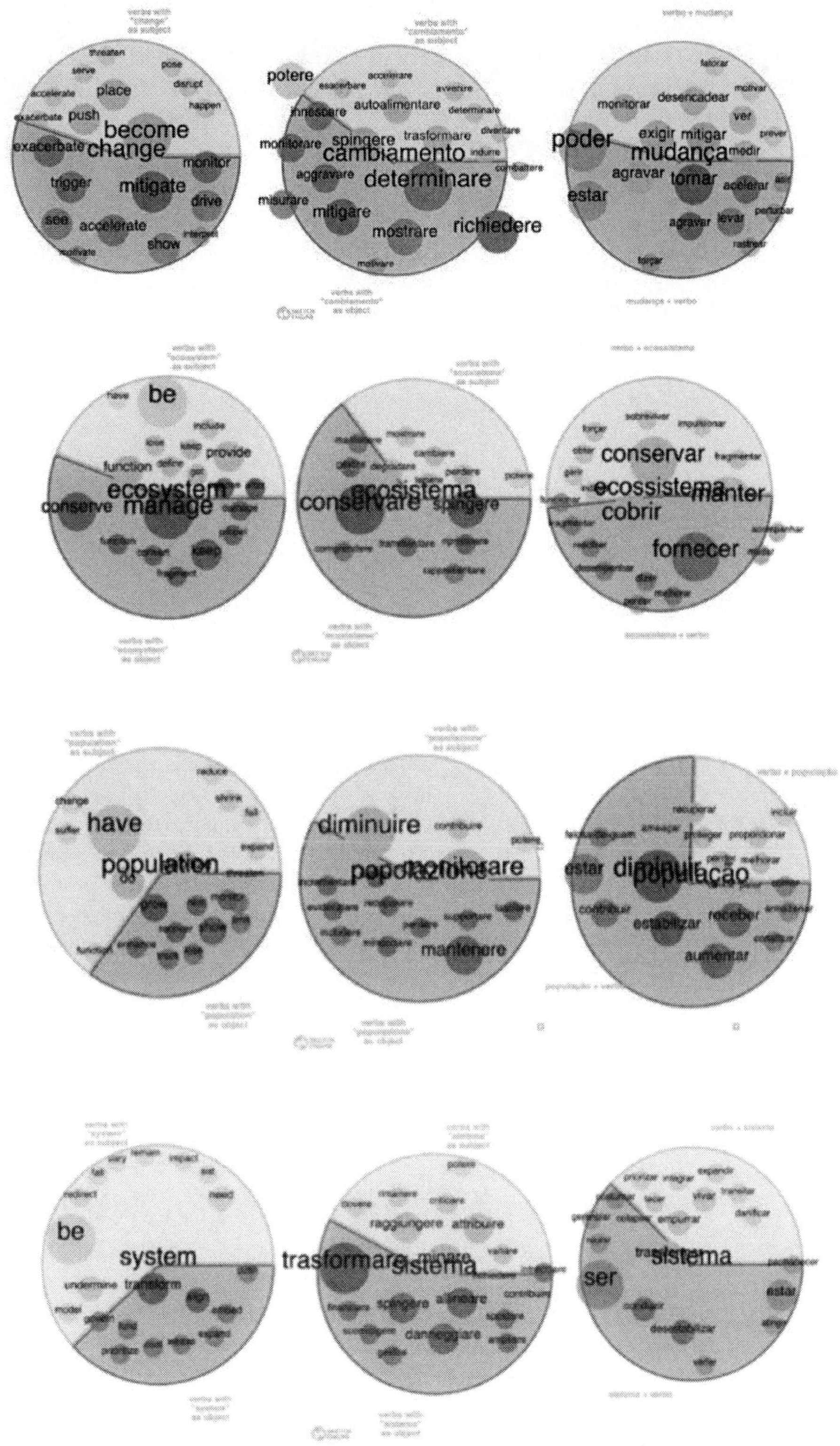

# Thematic Categorization on Pineapple Production in Costa Rica: An Exploratory Analysis through Topic Modeling.

**Valentina Tretti-Beckles**
Potsdam University
Potsdam, Germany
tretti@uni-potsdam.de

**Adrián Vergara-Heidke**
University of Costa Rica
San Jose, Costa Rica
adrian.vergara@ucr.ac.cr

## Abstract

Costa Rica is one of the largest producers and exporters of pineapple in the world. This status has encouraged multinational companies to use plantations in this Central American country for experimentation and the cultivation of new varieties, such as the Pinkglow pineapple. However, pineapple monoculture has significant socio-environmental impacts on the regions where it is cultivated. In this exploratory study, we aimed to analyze how pineapple production is portrayed on the Internet. To achieve this, we collected a corpus of texts in Spanish and English from online sources in two phases: using the BootCaT [1] toolkit and manual search on newspaper websites. The Hierarchical Dirichlet Process (HDP) topic model was then applied to identify dominant topics within the corpus. These topics were subsequently classified into thematic categories, and the texts were categorized accordingly. The findings indicate that environmental issues related to pineapple cultivation are underrepresented on the Internet, particularly in comparison to the extensive focus on topics related to pineapple production and marketing.

## 1 Introduction

Pineapples are widely available in supermarkets across Europe, Japan, and the United States. This tropical fruit is cultivated in several countries, with Costa Rica ranking as one of the leading producers and exporters (FAO, 2024). While pineapple production has generated significant revenue for companies in Costa Rica, it has also raised concerns regarding its impact on labor rights (Rodríguez and Prunier, 2020; Salgado and Acuña, 2021; León and Montoya, 2021) and the environment.

Numerous academic and NGO studies have documented the environmental and health damage caused by pineapple monocultures in Costa Rica. The adverse environmental effects stem primarily from the use of pesticides, which contaminate water and soil, thereby affecting humans, animals, and plants (Valverde and Chaves, 2020; Carazo and Aravena, 2016). Additionally, these effects result from the excessive use of water for irrigation, which depletes wetlands and underground water reserves (Carazo and Aravena, 2016). Finally, monoculture practices leave the land over-exploited and depleted of essential nutrients (Carazo and Aravena, 2016; Obando, 2020). These issues are emblematic of the current geological epoch: the Anthropocene (de Cózar, 2019).

A notable example of the Anthropocene is the creation of the pink pineapple (known as Pinkglow) in Costa Rica. This new variety was developed in the laboratories of the Del Monte company, which holds the patent for it (Del Monte, 2020). The distinctive pink coloration serves purely aesthetic purposes, catering to a market heavily driven by visual appeal. Due to its high market value, the pink pineapple is exclusively marketed outside of Costa Rica (Riviera, 2024), where it is promoted as an exotic product from a tropical country.

In this context, an interdisciplinary group initiated a study on the relationship between pineapple plantations and the territory, as well as the representation of the pineapple—particularly the Pinkglow variety—as a cultural object. Within this framework, we sought to explore the topics circulating on the Internet about pineapple production

[1] *Bootstrapping Corpora and Terms*: a suite of perl programs implementing an iterative procedure to bootstrap specialized corpora and terms from the web (Baroni and Bernardini, 2004). It is a free toolkit available at: https://bootcat.dipintra.it/



*Proceedings of the 1st Workshop on Ecology, Environment, and Natural Language Processing (NLP4Ecology2025)*, pages 44–55
March 2, 2025 

and Costa Rica and to examine whether there are differences between texts in Spanish and English. To address these goals, we aim to apply advances in Natural Language Processing (NLP), specifically Topic Modeling, to identify the thematic categories present in the corpus of digital texts. Accordingly, the objective of this exploratory research is to identify and categorize, through Topic Modeling, the thematic categories associated with pineapple production in Costa Rica within a corpus comprising diverse textual genres.

Numerous studies have applied Natural Language Processing (NLP) techniques to address environmental issues. Some focus on identifying and geographically mapping the impacts of climate change by analyzing academic papers and scholarly articles (Mallick et al., 2024) or through sentiment analysis (Stede and Patz, 2021; Sham and Mohamed, 2022; Mi and Zhan, 2023; Krishnan and Anoop, 2023), and stance classification in tweets (Mohammad et al., 2016) or news articles (Luo et al., 2020). Additionally, efforts have been made to create datasets related to environmental topics, such as EcoVerse, an English Twitter dataset for eco-relevance classification, stance detection, and environmental impact analysis (Grasso et al., 2024); GERCCT, a German Twitter dataset for argument mining (Schaefer and Stede, 2022); and ClimaText, a dataset for detecting topics related to climate change (Varini et al., 2021).

In addition, several studies have applied topic modeling techniques within the environmental domain. These include research on climate change discussions in social media (Dahal et al., 2019; Al-Rawi et al., 2021; Uthirapathy and Dominic, 2023; Kim and Kim, 2024), correlations between topics and sentiment in news articles (Jiang et al., 2017; Rabitz et al., 2021; Ejaz et al., 2022; McAllister et al., 2024), analyses of Nature and Science editorials (Stede et al., 2023), and targeted journal publications (Kim et al., 2021), as well as research and policy papers (Werneck and Gomes, 2023). Topic modeling has also been applied to election manifestos and parliamentary debates (Navarretta and Hansen, 2023).

Although the aforementioned studies provided a foundation, our exploratory research adopted a distinct thematic and methodological approach. Specifically, we examined pineapple production across various textual genres, compared topics and thematic categories between English and Spanish, and implemented the topic model that yielded the highest coherence score (HDP).

## 2 Method

The method used consists of five phases (see figure 1). First, the corpus was extracted and retrieved through two stages:

1. Extraction using BootCaT involved nine tuples, each consisting of three keywords, with at least one keyword being "pineapple" for English and either "piña" or "piñera" for Spanish.
   (a) English keywords: "pineapple", "pineapple plantation", "pinkglow", "costa rica" and "pink pineapple".
   (b) Spanish keywords: "piñera", "plantación de piñas", "piña rosada", "pinkglow", "costa rica", and "piña".
2. Manual search on newspaper websites using the keywords related to pineapple plantation.
   (a) Costa Rican newspapers: Delfino, La Nación, El Observador, La República, Semanario Universidad, and Diario Extra.
   (b) International newspapers: CNN, The Guardian, The New York Times, and The Times.

Second, a manual corpus analysis was conducted to remove irrelevant texts (e.g., incomplete texts, texts without mentions of pineapples or the Pinkglow variety, and empty texts) and to classify textual genres (see table 3 in *Appendix A*). Next, topic modeling experiments were carried out on both subsets of the data using Latent Dirichlet Allocation (LDA) (Blei et al., 2003), Hierarchical Dirichlet Processes (HDP) (Whye Teh et al., 2006), and Latent Semantic Analysis (LSA) (Landauer and Dumais, 2008). This was followed by the classification of the documents based on their dominant topics. Then, thematic categories were determined according to the dominant topics. Finally, the data documents were classified according to their respective thematic category.

### 2.1 Data

The dataset was collected between November and December 2024 and consists of 221 texts, which

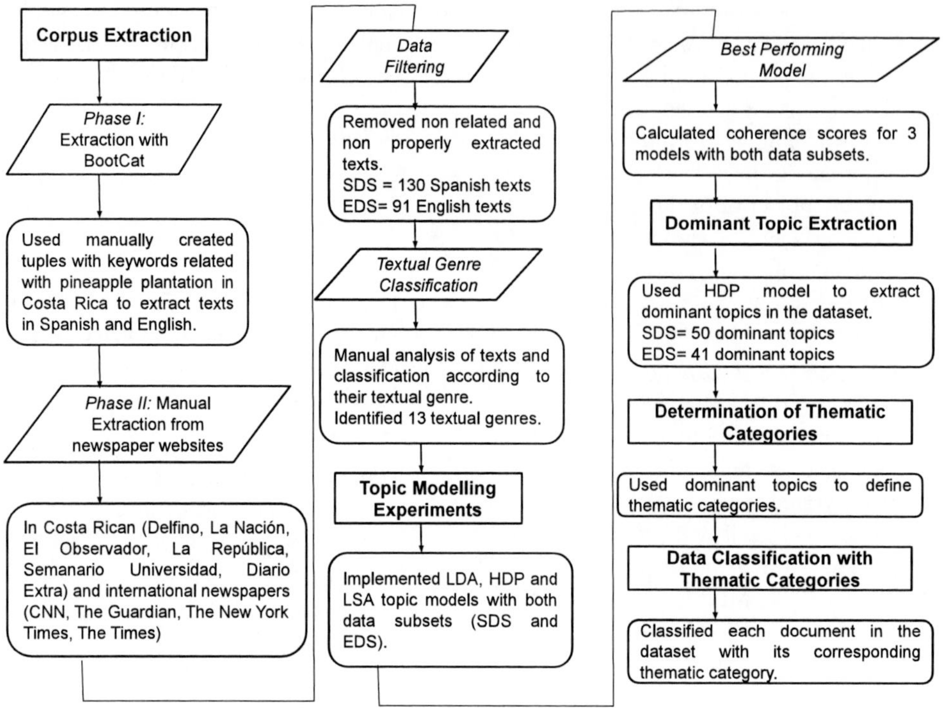


Figure 1: Flowchart with phases followed in the method.

include: blog sites, business websites, news websites, product pages, institutional websites, and documents (e.g., papers, reports, manuals). It comprises a total of 215,241 words. The texts are written in two languages: Spanish (Spanish Data Subset, SDS) and English (English Data Subset, EDS) (see table 1 for more details) and were published between 2001 and 2024. The dataset documents were classified according to their textual genre, with 13 genres identified in total (see table 3 in *Appendix A*). Among these, news articles, divulgative notes, and narrative notes are the most frequent (see figure 2).

| **Data** | **Number of documents** | **Number of words** | **Number of characters** |
|---|---|---|---|
| *Spanish* | 130 | 161,765 | 1,032,436 |
| *English* | 91 | 53,476 | 333,786 |
| **Total** | 221 | 215,241 | 1,366,222 |

Table 1: Data Distribution considering Language, Words and Characters.

### 2.2 Topic Modeling Experiments

As mentioned above, the topic modeling was conducted using three models: Latent Dirichlet Allocation (LDA), Hierarchical Dirichlet Processes (HDP) and Latent Semantic Analysis (LSA) with both SDS and EDS data subsets. The models were evaluated using the topic coherence (TC) score from *Gensim* (Röder et al., 2015). Among these, HDP demonstrated the highest coherence scores for both subsets (see figures 3 and 4) and was consequently selected for further analysis and the development of thematic categories.

Drawing on reference literature (Del Monte, 2020; Riviera, 2024; Carazo and Aravena, 2016; Obando, 2020; Rodríguez and Prunier, 2020; FAO, 2024), we established 13 thematic categories related to pineapple cultivation in Costa Rica, along with an 'other' category for cases that did not fit within a specific category. Subsequently, we classified the dominant topics within these categories. To do this, we considered that at least four out of the ten words in each topic needed to be associated with a thematic category. When a topic contained words corresponding to multiple thematic categories, it was classified under all relevant categories, with a maximum of two assign-

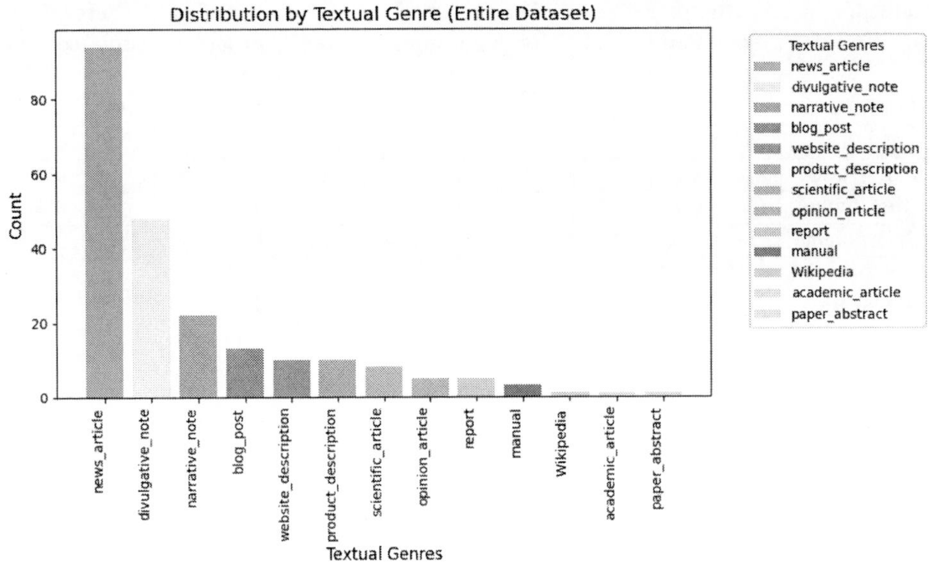


Figure 2: Distribution by Textual Genre (Entire Dataset)

ments per topic. Finally, based on the classification of dominant topics, we analyzed the distribution of texts across thematic categories.

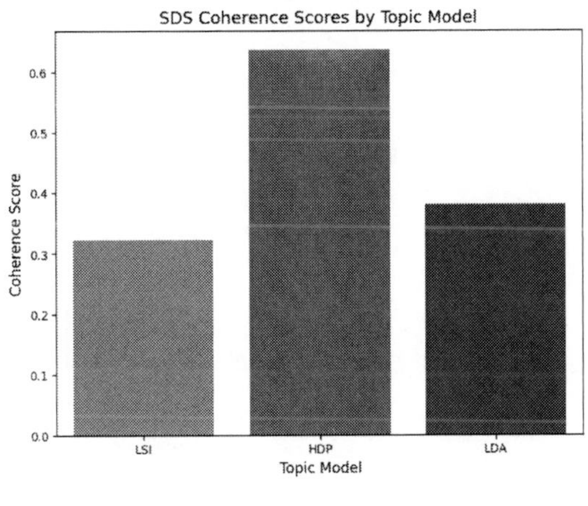


Figure 3: Model's Coherence Score for SDS.

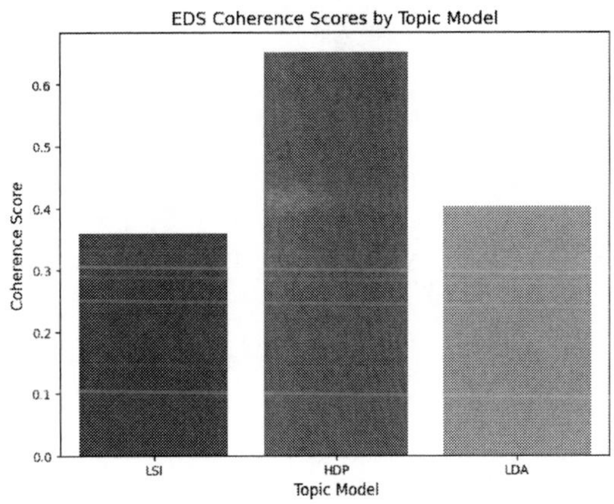


Figure 4: Model's Coherence Score for EDS.

## 3 Analysis

The HDP model dynamically determines the number of topics. For our data, it identified 73 topics for the SDS and 137 topics for the EDS. Of the 73 topics in the SDS, 50 were dominant, while of the 137 topics in the EDS, only 41 were dominant. The dominant topics in both subsets were classified according to pre-established and emerging categories (see figure 2). It is important to note that a single topic could correspond to multiple categories.

The results (figure 5 and table 2) reveal differences in the distribution of the thematic categories between the two subsets. The most notable distinction is found in the categories 'Pineapple production' and 'Consumption food-aesthetic.' In the SDS, 37% of the topics were classified under 'Pineapple production,' whereas only 11% of topics in the EDS were identified with this category. Conversely, 53% of the topics in the EDS fell within the 'Consumption food-aesthetic' category, compared to only 14% in the SDS. These findings suggest that the primary focus of the SDS is on the production and export of pineapples in Costa

| Category | Number of dominant topics SDS | Percentage of dominant topics SDS | Number of dominant topics EDS | Percentage of dominant topics EDS |
|---|---|---|---|---|
| **Contamination** | 1 | 2% | 5 | 10% |
| **Erosion** | 1 | 2% | 1 | 2% |
| **Lack of Water** | 2 | 3% | 0 | 0% |
| **Climate Change** | 1 | 2% | 0 | 0% |
| **Health Problems** | 0 | 0% | 1 | 2% |
| **Labor Shortages** | 2 | 3% | 0 | 0% |
| **Legal Issues** | 3 | 5% | 0 | 0% |
| **Consumption Food-Aesthetic** | 8 | 14% | 25 | 53% |
| **Pineapple Production** | 21 | 37% | 5 | 11% |
| **Health Benefits** | 1 | 2% | 0 | 0% |
| **Sales** | 4 | 7% | 4 | 8,5% |
| **Cultivation** | 4 | 7% | 1 | 2% |
| **Sustainability** | 0 | 0% | 1 | 2% |
| **Other** | 9 | 16% | 4 | 8,5% |
| **Total Topics Classified** | 57 | 100% | 47 | 100% |

Table 2: Distribution of dominant topics in SDS and EDS data subsets.

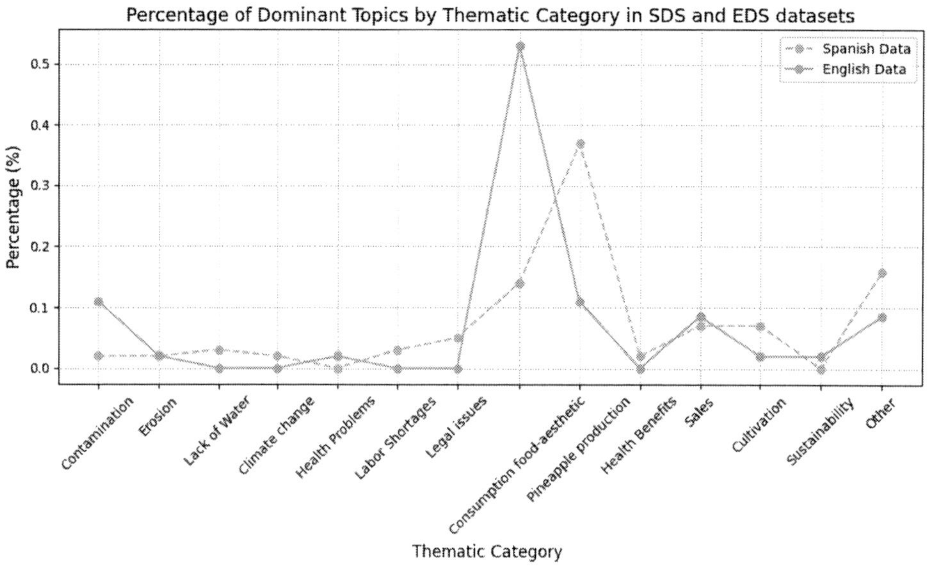


Figure 5: Percentage of Dominant Topics Category by Languages.

Rica, independent of their consumption. In contrast, the results from the EDS indicate a greater emphasis on pineapple consumption, particularly from a food or aesthetic perspective, which may be associated with texts aimed at promoting the international consumption of this fruit, especially the Pinkglow variety.

On the other hand, a greater variety of dominant topics is observed in the SDS compared to the EDS. In the SDS, only two thematic categories lacked a dominant topic, and nine dominant topics could not be classified into any category. In contrast, in the EDS, five thematic categories remained unassigned, and only four dominant topics were unclassified.

The results (figure 6) indicate that the thematic category ‘Pineapple production’ appears in the greatest number of SDS texts, with 61 occurrences, representing 41% of the total occurrences across all thematic categories (149 occurrences). This finding suggests that the majority of the Spanish texts predominantly address aspects of pineapple production. This is somewhat expected, as the majority of the dominant topics (21 topics) were classified under this thematic category. In second place, the thematic category ‘Consumption food-aesthetic’ appeared in 38 texts (26%). Despite being composed of only eight dominant topics, this category’s frequency of occurrence is noteworthy.

On the other hand, in the EDS, the results show that the dominant topics in most texts belong to the thematic category ‘Consumption food-aesthetic’ (50 occurrences, 47%), followed by ‘Pineapple production’ (26 occurrences, 24%). This suggests that the content of most EDS texts focuses on consuming pineapples in general, and Pinkglow in particular. This is consistent with the fact that the majority of the dominant topics (25 topics) were classified under this thematic category. However, it is notable that 24% of texts (26 occurrences) feature dominant topics related to ‘Pineapple production,’ despite being represented by only five topics. Additionally, the category ‘Contamination’ appears in just 10 texts (9%), further emphasizing the thematic focus of the EDS.

Each dominant topic contributes a different percentage within each text. This contribution reflects the extent to which the topic is represented in the text, thereby indicating its importance in terms of coverage or reiteration. For this reason, we chose to examine the percentage contribution of topics within each thematic category across the texts where they were dominant.

Considering the thematic categories with the highest number of texts (‘Pineapple production,’ ‘Other,’ ‘Consumption food-aesthetic,’ and ‘Sales’), the results show that in the SDS, the topics within the ‘Consumption food-aesthetic’ category (80%) contribute the most to the texts when dominant, as their average contribution exceeds that of the other categories (figure 7). This is followed by ‘Sales’ (77%) and ‘Pineapple production’ (75%), while ‘Other’ has the lowest average contribution (65%). These results suggest that when the ‘Consumption food-aesthetic’ category appears, its topics occupy a greater proportion of the text or are repeated more frequently, indicating a stronger presence compared to other topics within the same text. Additionally, the high average (80%) suggests that the primary topics in these texts are more specific in nature.

Finally, the average contribution of the dominant topics in the ‘Other’ thematic category (65%) is the lowest among the four categories with the highest number of texts. It is important to refrain from providing detailed explanations for this result, as the ‘Other’ category encompasses a wide range of topics. As a result, the content of these texts may vary significantly, therefore it would not be advisable to analyze them as a group.

In the EDS (figure 8), two thematic categories clearly group the largest number of texts: ’Pineapple production’ and ’Consumption food-aesthetic.’ The mean for ’Pineapple production’ (75%) suggests that, in the texts where its topics are dominant, there is a greater thematic specialization compared to ‘Consumption food-aesthetic’ (73%). Nevertheless, the topics in both thematic categories contribute over 70% on average in most of the texts in which they are dominant. This substantial contribution indicates a significant presence of these topics, either through their thematic focus or repeated mention within the texts.

## 4 Discussion

The results indicate that in most texts from both subsets, the most frequent categories are ‘Pineapple Production’ and ‘Consumption: Food-Aesthetic’. However, the subsets differ in their dominant thematic categories. In the SDS, the most frequent category is ‘Pineapple Production’, whereas in the EDS, ‘Consumption: Food-Aesthetic’ is predominant. This distinction suggests that English-language texts circulating on the Internet focus more on promoting pineapple consumption, including products such as Pinkglow. Conversely, Spanish-language texts more frequently address topics related to pineapple production.

This difference can be attributed to the fact that pineapples are produced in several Latin American countries (e.g., Costa Rica, Ecuador, Cuba, Nicaragua) and represent an important export product, particularly in Costa Rica. Consequently, Spanish-language texts prioritize

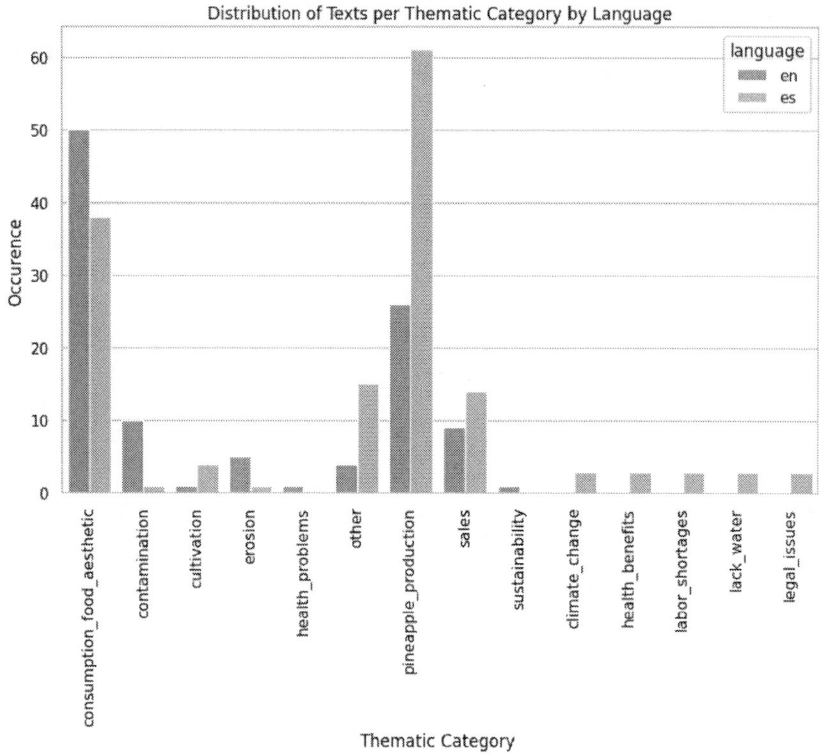


Figure 6: Distribution of Texts per Thematic Category by Language.

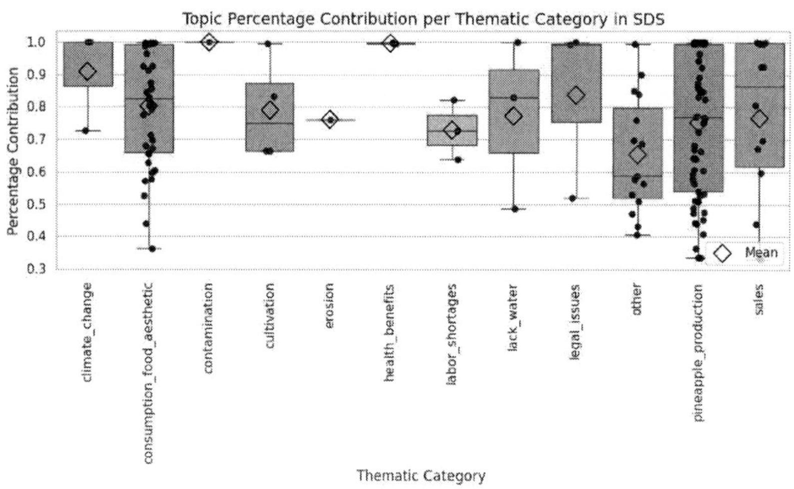


Figure 7: Topic Percentage Contribution per Thematic Category in SDS.

production-related themes over the promotion of consumption. On the other hand, English-language texts have broader international reach, as English is the primary language for global marketing communication. Therefore, it is unsurprising that 'Consumption: Food-Aesthetic' appears more

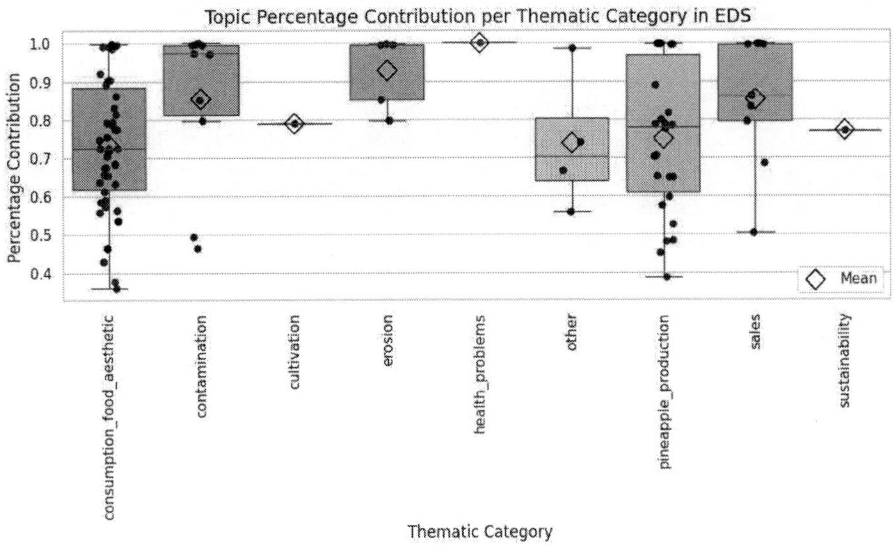


Figure 8: Topic Percentage Contribution per Thematic Category in EDS.

frequently in English-language texts.

In both the SDS and EDS, references to environmental topics are minimal. When combining categories such as ‘Contamination’, ‘Erosion’, ‘Lack of Water’, ‘Climate Change’, and ‘Health Problems’, these topics constitute only 9% in the SDS and 13% in the EDS. This finding indicates that most online texts in Spanish and English fail to address the serious environmental issues caused by pineapple monoculture in Latin American countries, particularly in Costa Rica. Instead, the Internet perpetuates an image of pineapples as an appealing fruit for consumption, obscuring the environmental consequences of their production. Such an image may not only bolster a positive perception of pineapples but also introduce biases for researchers working with Internet-based datasets on this topic.

It is important to note that computational models perform more accurately with English texts than with Spanish texts. This discrepancy may influence the results, which can only be validated through human review. While such a process is slow and labor-intensive, it is essential for improving computational models and the research relying on them.

The thematic categories were developed based on texts addressing pineapple production and marketing in Costa Rica. The classification of dominant topics within each category was derived from the ten most frequent words [2] associated with each topic. However, the analysis did not involve a thorough review of the content of individual texts to confirm the alignment of the dominant topics with the thematic categories. Consequently, there was no human verification to ensure that: (1) the dominant topics were consistent with the main themes or frequent words in the texts, and (2) the primary topics in the texts aligned with the thematic categories used in the research. To address these limitations, future studies should incorporate human verification steps to confirm the relationship between topics, keywords, and the content of the texts.

Future research could also focus on improving the methodology in several ways. First, the corpus should be expanded, as the number of texts collected for this study was relatively small compared to the volume of texts available online. Alternative methods for collecting online texts should be explored. Second, the research scope could be broadened to include other agricultural products from Costa Rica, such as bananas, cocoa, coffee,

[2]These words do not include fillers or stop words.

and palm. This expanded scope would increase the corpus size and help determine whether the low prevalence of environmental topics is consistent across other crops.

Third, new categories could be added for corpus classification, such as main topics, perspectives and source ideologies. Depending on the size of the corpus, a dataset could be created to train computational models to classify texts according to these new categories. This approach would provide greater clarity regarding the relationship between topics, content, perspectives, and sources. Finally, sentiment analysis could be integrated to assess the sentiment associated with different topics and thematic categories. This would allow researchers to identify the probable sentiment of various themes and assign it to the thematic categories more systematically.

Lastly, it should be noted that due to space constraints, this paper does not present the results for the most frequent words or the relationship between textual genres and thematic categories.

## 5 Conclusion

Following this exploratory study, we conclude that combining the application of Hierarchical Dirichlet Processes (HDP) with the human construction of thematic categories could effectively identify the main content patterns in texts across different languages. The findings suggest that significant environmental and labor rights issues associated with pineapple production are rarely disseminated on the Internet. This lack of coverage hinders the visibility of the environmental and health problems caused by pineapple monocultures and pesticide use in Costa Rica and other producing countries. Furthermore, this scarcity of information contributes to a lack of awareness among global consumers, who continue to purchase pineapples and represent a potential market for new laboratory-developed variants created by corporations.

Despite the insights gained, it is important to acknowledge the limitations of this exploratory study when interpreting the results and considering directions for future research. First, the corpus obtained through web scraping was relatively small, limiting the generalization of the findings. Second, we have not yet conducted a human evaluation of the assignment of dominant topics to individual texts, which would provide a more robust verification of topic classification within the thematic categories.

## References


Ahmed Al-Rawi, Oumar Kane, and Aimé-Jules Bizimana. 2021. Topic modelling of public Twitter discourses, part bot, part active human user, on climate change and global warming. *Journal of Environmental Media*, 2(1):31–53.

Marco Baroni and Silvia Bernardini. 2004. BootCaT: Bootstrapping Corpora and Terms from the Web. In *Proceedings of the Fourth International Conference on Language Resources and Evaluation (LREC'04)*, Lisbon, Portugal. European Language Resources Association (ELRA).

David M. Blei, Andrew Y. Ng, and Michael I. Jordan. 2003. Latent Dirichlet Allocation. *Journal of Machine Learning Research*, 3:993–1022.

Eva Carazo and Javiera Aravena. 2016. *Condiciones de producción, impactos humanos y ambientales en el sector piña en Costa Rica*. Asociación Regional Centroamericana para el Agua y el Ambiente, San Jose, Costa Rica.

José M. de Cózar. 2019. *El Antropoceno*. Catarata, Madrid, Spain.

Biraj Dahal, Sathish Alampalayam Kumar, and Zhenlong Li. 2019. Topic Modeling and Sentiment Analysis of Global Climate Change Tweets. *Social Network Analysis and Mining*, 9(1):1–20.

Del Monte. 2020. Pinkglow. pineapple. `https://www.pinkglowpineapple.com/`. Last accessed on 2024-12-12.

Waqas Ejaz, Muhammad Ittefaq, and Sadia Jamil. 2022. Politics Triumphs: A Topic Modeling Approach for Analyzing News Media Coverage of Climate Change in Pakistan. *Journal of Science Communication*, 22:1–18.

FAO. 2024. *Principales Frutas Tropicales. Análisis del mercado. Resultados preliminares 2023*. FAO, Roma, Italy.

Francesca Grasso, Stefano Locci, Giovanni Siragusa, and Luigi Di Caro. 2024. EcoVerse: An annotated Twitter dataset for eco-relevance classification, environmental impact analysis, and stance detection. In *Proceedings of the 2024 Joint International Conference on Computational Linguistics, Language Resources and Evaluation (LREC-COLING 2024)*, pages 5461–5472, Torino, Italia. ELRA and ICCL.

Ye Jiang, Xingyi Song, Jackie Harrison, Shaun Quegan, and Diana Maynard. 2017. Comparing Attitudes to Climate Change in the Media using sentiment analysis based on Latent Dirichlet Allocation. In *Proceedings of the 2017 EMNLP Work-*

*shop: Natural Language Processing meets Journalism*, pages 25–30, Copenhagen, Denmark. Association for Computational Linguistics.

Joohee Kim and Yoomi Kim. 2024. Using Structural Topic Modeling to Explore the Climate Change Discourse about the Paris Agreement on Social Media. *Telematics and Informatics Reports*, 15:1–13.

Taeyong Kim, Hyemin Park, Junyong Heo, and Minjune Yang. 2021. Topic Model Analysis of Research Themes and Trends in the Journal of Economic and Environmental Geology. *Journal of Economic and Environmental Geology*, 54(3):353–364.

Ajay Krishnan and V. S. Anoop. 2023. ClimateNLP: Analyzing Public Sentiment Towards Climate Change Using Natural Language Processing.

Thomas K. Landauer and Susan Dumais. 2008. Latent Semantic Analysis. *Scholarpedia*, 3.

Andrés León and Valeria Montoya. 2021. La función de la frontera en la economía política de las plantaciones piñeras en Costa Rica. *Trace*, 80:116–137.

Yiwei Luo, Dallas Card, and Dan Jurafsky. 2020. Detecting Stance in Media On Global Warming. In *Findings of the Association for Computational Linguistics: EMNLP 2020*, pages 3296–3315, Online. Association for Computational Linguistics.

Tanwi Mallick, John Murphy, Joshua David Bergerson, Duane R. Verner, John K Hutchison, and Leslie-Anne Levy. 2024. Analyzing Regional Impacts of Climate Change using Natural Language Processing Techniques.

Lucy McAllister, Siddharth Vedula, Wenxi Pu, and Maxwell Boykoff. 2024. Vulnerable Voices: Using Topic Modeling to Analyze Newspaper Coverage of Climate Change in 26 Non-Annex I Countries (2010–2020). *Environmental Research Letters*, 19(2):1–14.

Zhewei Mi and Hongwei Zhan. 2023. Text Mining Attitudes towards Climate Change: Emotion and Sentiment Analysis of the Twitter Corpus. *Weather, Climate, and Society*, 15(2):277–287.

Saif Mohammad, Svetlana Kiritchenko, Parinaz Sobhani, Xiaodan Zhu, and Colin Cherry. 2016. SemEval-2016 Task 6: Detecting Stance in Tweets. In *Proceedings of the 10th International Workshop on Semantic Evaluation (SemEval-2016)*, pages 31–41, San Diego, California. Association for Computational Linguistics.

Costanza Navarretta and Dorte H. Hansen. 2023. According to BERTopic, what do Danish Parties Debate on when they Address Energy and Environment? In *Proceedings of the 3rd Workshop on Computational Linguistics for the Political and Social Sciences*, pages 59–68, Ingolstadt, Germany. Association for Computational Lingustics.

Alexa Obando. 2020. Acciones y omisiones del Estado costarricense en la expansión piñera: el caso de la Zona Norte-Norte de Costa Rica. *Anuario del Centro de Investigación y Estudios Políticos,*, 11:22–55.

Florian Rabitz, Audronė Telešienė, and Eimantė Zolubienė. 2021. Topic Modelling the News Media Representation of Climate Change. *Environmental Sociology*, 7(3):214–224.

Riviera. 2024. Pinkglow pineapple – everything you need to know about this new summer sensation. `https://www.rivieraproduce.com/pinkglow-pineapple-everything-you-need-to-know-about-this-new-summer-sensation/`. Last accessed on 2024-12-12.

Michael Röder, Andreas Both, and Alexander Hinneburg. 2015. Exploring the Space of Topic Coherence Measures. In *Proceedings of the Eighth ACM International Conference on Web Search and Data Mining*, WSDM '15, page 399–408, New York, NY, USA. Association for Computing Machinery.

Tania Rodríguez and Delphine Prunier. 2020. Extractivismo agrícola, frontera y fuerza de trabajo migrante: La expansión del monocultivo de piña en Costa Rica. *Frontera norte*, 32.

Moisés Salgado and Marylaura Acuña. 2021. Trabajo asalariado en el monocultivo de piña en la Región Huetar Norte. *Revista Reflexiones. Dossier especialX Jornadas de Investigación*, pages 1–17.

Robin Schaefer and Manfred Stede. 2022. GerCCT: An Annotated Corpus for Mining Arguments in German Tweets on Climate Change. In *Proceedings of the Thirteenth Language Resources and Evaluation Conference*, pages 6121–6130, Marseille, France. European Language Resources Association.

Nabila M. Sham and Azlinah Mohamed. 2022. Climate Change Sentiment Analysis Using Lexicon, Machine Learning and Hybrid Approaches. *Sustainability*, 14(8).

Manfred Stede, Yannic Bracke, Luka Borec, Neele Charlotte Kinkel, and Maria Skeppstedt. 2023. Framing Climate Change in Nature and Science Editorials: Applications of Supervised and Unsupervised Text Categorization. *Journal of Computational Social Science*, 6:485–513.

Manfred Stede and Ronny Patz. 2021. The Climate Change Debate and Natural Language Processing. In *Proceedings of the 1st Workshop on NLP for Positive Impact*, pages 8–18, Online. Association for Computational Linguistics.

Samson E. Uthirapathy and Sandanam Dominic. 2023. Topic Modelling and Opinion Analysis on Climate Change Twitter Data USing LDA and BERT Model. *Procedia Computer Science*, 218:908–917.

Bernal Valverde and Lilliana Chaves. 2020. The Banning of Bromacil in Costa Rica. *Weed Science*, 68(3):240–245.

Francesco S. Varini, Jordan Boyd-Graber, Massimiliano Ciaramita, and Markus Leippold. 2021. Climatext: A Dataset for Climate Change Topic Detection.

Marcelo Werneck and André Gomes. 2023. The Interface between Research Funding and Environmental Policies in an Emergent Economy using Neural Topic Modeling: Proposals for a Research Agenda. *Review of Policy Research*, pages 1–25.

Yee Whye Teh, Michael I. Jordan, Matthew J. Beal, and David M. Blei. 2006. Hierarchical Dirichlet Processes. *Journal of the American Statistical Association*, 101(476):1566–1581.

## A Appendix. Description of Textual Genres.

| **Gender Categories** | **Description** |
|---|---|
| *News article* | Texts produced by the media on various current topics. |
| *Divulgative note* | Texts that present scientific topics to the general public. |
| *Narrative note* | Texts in which the author describes an experience (e.g., visiting a restaurant or place, tasting food or drink, or using an object) without a critical perspective. |
| *Blog post* | Texts published on blogs. |
| *Website description* | Texts that describe or briefly summarize the content of a webpage. |
| *Product description* | Texts that describe or introduce products. |
| *Scientific article* | Texts that present research results and are published in academic journals or books. |
| *Opinion article* | Texts that express individuals' opinions and perspectives on various topics. |
| *Report* | Texts that present the results of a professional analysis or research conducted for companies or organizations. |
| *Manual* | Texts that explain how to use or apply an object, methodology, or theory, or how a person should act. |
| *Wikipedia* | Texts that explain various topics within the Wikipedia platform. |
| *Academic article* | Texts that present scientific topics to an academic audience but are not published on web pages, in academic journals, or in books. |
| *Paper abstract* | Texts that summarize the contents of a scientific article. |

Table 3: Typology of Textual Genres in Dataset (own creation).

# Entity Linking using LLMs for Automated Product Carbon Footprint Estimation

**Steffen Castle** **Julian Moreno Schneider** **Leonhard Hennig** **Georg Rehm**

German Research Center for Artificial Intelligence (DFKI)
first.last@dfki.de

## Abstract

Growing concerns about climate change and sustainability are driving manufacturers to take significant steps toward reducing their carbon footprints. For these manufacturers, a first step towards this goal is to identify the environmental impact of the individual components of their products. We propose a system leveraging large language models (LLMs) to automatically map components from manufacturer Bills of Materials (BOMs) to Life Cycle Assessment (LCA) database entries by using LLMs to expand on available component information. Our approach reduces the need for manual data processing, paving the way for more accessible sustainability practices.

## 1 Introduction

Increasing awareness of climate change and sustainability has put pressure on manufacturers to reduce their carbon footprints. Regulation such as the EU Corporate Sustainability Reporting Directive (CSRD) and the European Green Deal has further emphasized the need for transparent and accurate environmental impact assessments. A fundamental step in this process is determining the environmental impact of a product, particularly the carbon emissions generated during production. LCA databases, such as ecoinvent (Wernet et al., 2016), provide detailed information for this purpose. However, linking the raw components of a product, represented in a BOM, to relevant entries in an LCA database remains a labor-intensive task requiring specialized knowledge of manufacturing materials and processes.

Recent advances in artificial intelligence, particularly large language models (LLMs), present an opportunity to automate this process. Because they are trained on vast amounts of information and are able to efficiently synthesize their knowledge as textual data, they may be capable of providing additional context in order to link components to their production processes in a LCA database.

In this work, we investigate the use of LLMs to streamline the product carbon footprint estimation process by mapping components from BOMs directly to a LCA database. We propose a multi-step approach using a pretrained LLM to identify and summarize component information and mapping this summary to a database using semantic similarity.

## 2 Related Work

Semantic similarity techniques are well-explored in entity linking, where embedding models match textual mentions to corresponding database entries. Hou et al. introduced a method that enhances entity embeddings by incorporating fine-grained semantic information, thereby improving the learning of contextual commonality and achieving state-of-the-art performance in entity linking (Hou et al., 2020). Similarly, Pereira and Ferreira proposed E-BELA, an approach that aligns vector representations of mentions and entities in a shared space using literal embeddings, facilitating effective linking through similarity metrics (Pereira and Ferreira, 2024). These methodologies are particularly effective in domains with straightforward entity disambiguation requirements, where minimal additional context is necessary.

Existing methods for carbon footprint estimation rely heavily on manual mapping of product components to LCA databases. This is a challenging task, requiring both LCA expertise and specialist knowledge of components and materials. Several studies have explored machine learning approaches to partially automate this process.



*Proceedings of the 1st Workshop on Ecology, Environment, and Natural Language Processing (NLP4Ecology2025)*, pages 56–60
March 2, 2025 

Flamingo (Balaji et al., 2023a) uses semantic similarity to match end products to environmental impact factors such as carbon emissions in the ecoinvent database. It does not make use of the fine-grained component details present in a BOM, and additionally it uses a private dataset and supervised approach to train an auxiliary classifier. This classifier is used in conjunction with zero-shot semantic similarity matching to find database matches. Similarly, CaML (Balaji et al., 2023b) maps product text descriptions to industry sector codes, which can be used to make a coarse-grained estimate of carbon production.

## 3 Background

### 3.1 LCA Database

In order to determine the environmental impact of a component, the first step is to map it to its corresponding entry in the LCA database. LCA databases contain lists of manufacturing process names along with technical descriptions and other information. Our approach uses ecoinvent (Wernet et al., 2016) as the primary LCA database. A sample of these two fields for illustrative purposes is shown in Figure 1. For each entry, the database includes additional information describing process inputs and outputs and other life cycle information. The most task-relevant of this data is the environmental impact data including carbon emissions. Once a component has been mapped to a database entry, this information can be used in a relatively straightforward way to estimate the total carbon footprint of a product by summing the emissions for each component. Our method thus focuses on the main challenge to the carbon footprint estimation, which is linking the components from the BOM to the LCA database.

The current manual process for linking items to the LCA database involves two sequential stages. First, a non-specialist conducts a preliminary appraisal to filter straightforward matches. Using the item's material and description, they generate a shortlist of initial candidates (typically around five entries). These potential matches are then reviewed by an LCA expert, who validates their accuracy. In cases of mismatches, the expert manually corrects the mappings in the second stage. While expert oversight remains essential for quality assurance, our objective is to optimize this workflow by automating the preliminary non-specialist tasks. This eliminates manual effort while preserving the critical role of expert verification.

**Steel production, electric arc furnace, EU**

This process models the production of steel using an electric arc furnace (EAF) within the European Union. The process includes the melting of recycled steel scrap and the subsequent refinement to meet industry-grade specifications. Electricity consumption and emissions are based on averages from EU-wide data. Additional inputs include limestone for slag formation and oxygen for decarburization. Outputs include steel billets ready for further processing and slag as a by-product for use in construction applications.
This dataset represents a cradle-to-gate assessment, capturing the production of steel billets up to the point of factory gate, excluding downstream processing (e.g., rolling or shaping). Energy mix and emission profiles align with EU 27 averages for 2023.

Figure 1: An illustrative example of the process name and description from a LCA database.

### 3.2 Bills of Materials

A BOM is an industry-standard document produced by a manufacturer listing the components that make up a product. This document often contains information such as the name of the component, the supplier of the component and the material name, when available and is often required to be produced for regulatory reasons. An example is shown in Figure 2. Although knowledge of the main material of a component is often enough to determine a suitable match to a process in the database, the material name provided by the supplier is often an internal name for the material, a specification code, or other non-straightforward description of the material. Due to the complexity of correctly mapping component materials to the process used to produce them, specialist knowledge is usually required.

### 3.3 Component Datasheets

For some components, a technical datasheet is produced by the manufacturer. Typically, this lists

| Component Name | Material | Supplier |
|---|---|---|
| SPIRALGEHÄUSE | EN-GJL-250/A48 CL 35B | Mechatronik GmbH |
| WELLE | C45+N | Technikbau AG |
| SPALTRING | JL/GUSSEISEN LAMELLENGRAFIT | GussForm Solutions |
| SPANNRING | STAHL+KATAPHORESE | StahlPro Engineering |
| SPALTRING | JL/GUSSEISEN LAMELLENGRAFIT | GussTech Industries |
| STIFTSCHRAUBE | 8.8 | FixFast Components |
| STIFTSCHRAUBE | 8.8 | SchraubenWerk AG |
| STIFTSCHRAUBE | 5.8+A2A | PrecisionParts GmbH |

Figure 2: An excerpt from a BOM. Note that material codes are often ambiguous or obscure, requiring specialized knowledge to correctly identify.

properties of the component or the materials that make up the component. This information can provide useful context that helps to identify the process name for the component. Datasheets are not usually available for all components; they are only supplied by the manufacturer in some instances. We investigate including the information from datasheets in the entity mapping process.

## 4 Methodology

Our key contributions are:

1. Utilize fine-grained information from BOMs to provide a more accurate assessment of carbon emissions

2. Introduce LLMs into the entity mapping process in order to provide additional context, and

3. Integrate additional context from component datasheets in order to further improve context.

We break the process of mapping components to database entries into three connected steps, outlined below. An illustration of the complete pipeline is shown in Figure 3.

### 4.1 Datasheet Selection

Given a pool of datasheets, we must select the document from the pool corresponding to the BOM entry of interest to provide additional context about the component. In order to determine the matching document, we evaluate the textual similarity between the concatenation of the filename and text of the datasheet, and the concatenation of the component name, manufacturer and material from the BOM entry. Similarity is measured by the cosine similarity of the two embeddings generated by a text embedding model. After manual evaluation, we chose a threshold value of 0.5 or higher for the cosine similarity to indicate a match. If a match is found, the text from the datasheet is included in further processing in order to match the BOM entry to the process name.

### 4.2 LLM Querying

We utilize a LLM agent fine-tuned for chat as the LLM in our pipeline. We create a prompt for the model that includes all relevant context and instructs the model to produce a description of the manufacturing process used to create the component. Context includes the BOM entry information (component name, supplier, and material) along with the content of the datasheet, if available. The exact prompt can be found in our publicly available code[1]. The output of the model is then used in further processing. A sample showing typical responses from the LLM is shown in Figure 4.2. We use a local instance of Llama 3.1 with 8 billion parameters (Dubey et al., 2024) as the LLM in our experiments.

### 4.3 Semantic Similarity Matching

As a preprocessing step, we create embeddings for each database entry using the process name and description. We store these embeddings in a FAISS (Douze et al., 2024) vector store. To find a match for a BOM entry, we create an embedding of the LLM response from the previous step and compare this embedding to the vector store. Using the cosine similarity as a distance measure, we are able to obtain a ranking of database entries. For

[1] https://github.com/DFKI-NLP/eco-link

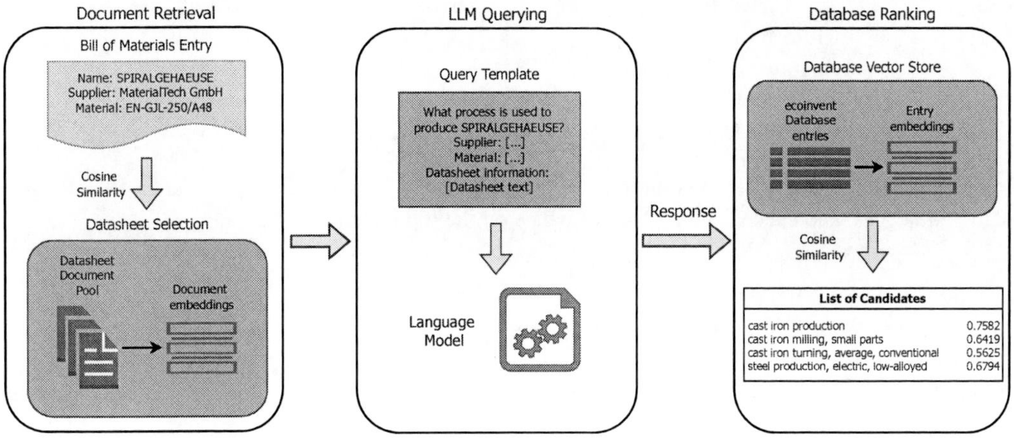


Figure 3: Architecture of the proposed pipeline, made up of three modules: Document retrieval, LLM querying, and database ranking.

**Component:** Ibitech 57 coated Normalausführung 2 mm weiss (Woven polypropylene)

**With Datasheet Context**

Activity name: Polyester film production, coating
Activity information:
Polyethylene terephthalate (PET) film coated with a polyester-based material, assumed to be the product of a process that transforms ethylene glycol and terephthalic acid into PET and then coats it. Transformation process of transforming ethylene glycol and terephthalic acid into polyethylene terephthalate (PET) and applying a coating.

**Without Datasheet Context**

Activity name: Polypropylene production, film or sheet
Activity information:
Synthetic fibres-based non-woven with a polypropylene scrim coating, assumed to consist of 50% synthetic fibers, 35% synthetic resin, and 15% polypropylene textile reinforcement. The transformation process includes the application of a synthetic resin in a water dispersion onto a base material consisting of synthetic fibers and a polypropylene scrim. Transformation process includes non-woven production and coating process with a polypropylene production as precursor for the scrim component.

Figure 4: Sample LLM response for a BOM component. Inclusion of datasheet context appears to considerably improve reliability of responses.

both the datasheet selection and semantic similarity ranking, we use `gte-large-en-v1.5` (Li et al., 2023).

## 5 Results and Discussion

Because of limitations in data availability due to lack of large-scale public datasets, data privacy, and preservation of trade secrecy, we can only evaluate on a small set of BOM entries. Our set of labeled evaluation data consists of only 21 compo-

| Method | Hits@5 | Hits@1 |
|---|---|---|
| Human (non-expert) | **0.48** | 0.19 |
| Semantic similarity only | 0.05 | 0.00 |
| LLM | 0.43 | 0.19 |
| LLM + Datasheet | **0.48** | **0.24** |

Figure 5: Results of evaluation. Our proposed approach is able to match the performance of a human on the top 5 matches, and exceeds human performance on the top match.

nents from 3 different BOMs.

We evaluate by comparing human performance to both the full and ablated pipeline. **Semantic Similarity** uses only the Database Ranking module and semantic similarity between the database entries and the component name, supplier and material. **LLM** uses both the LLM and Database Ranking modules to match the LLM's response , and **LLM + Datasheet** includes the Document Retrieval component. We use $Hits@n$ as the metric, which is defined for a recommender system as the proportion of instances the correct item is present in the top $n$ recommendations. This metric corresponds to our use case, where a shortlist of recommendations is provided by the non-expert recommender. The results are shown in Figure 5.

Our approach was found to be acceptable given the challenging nature of the task — on par or slightly better than non-expert human performance. While not enough to completely automate the entire entity mapping process, these results indicate that our method could take the place of the non-expert human in this process.

## 6 Conclusion and Future Work

This paper presents a novel approach to estimate product carbon footprints using LLMs to map BOM components to LCA database entries. The proposed pipeline streamlines the traditionally manual process, achieving reasonable accuracy and scalability. Future work includes an expanded evaluation with a larger evaluation dataset and integration of additional context from sources such as web search results.

## Acknowledgments

This paper has received funding from the European Union under the grant agreement no. 101058573 (SciLake) and by the German Bundesministerium für Umwelt, Naturschutz, nukleare Sicherheit und Verbraucherschutz (BMUV) under the Green AI Hub Mittelstand initiative.

## References

Bharathan Balaji, Venkata Sai Gargeya Vunnava, Nina Domingo, Shikhar Gupta, Harsh Gupta, Geoffrey Guest, and Aravind Srinivasan. 2023a. Flamingo: Environmental impact factor matching for life cycle assessment with zero-shot machine learning. *ACM Journal on Computing and Sustainable Societies*, 1(2):1–23.

Bharathan Balaji, Venkata Sai Gargeya Vunnava, Geoffrey Guest, and Jared Kramer. 2023b. Caml: Carbon footprinting of household products with zero-shot semantic text similarity. In *Proceedings of the ACM Web Conference 2023*, pages 4004–4014.

Matthijs Douze, Alexandr Guzhva, Chengqi Deng, Jeff Johnson, Gergely Szilvasy, Pierre-Emmanuel Mazaré, Maria Lomeli, Lucas Hosseini, and Hervé Jégou. 2024. https://arxiv.org/abs/2401.08281 The faiss library. *arXiv preprint arXiv:2401.08281*.

Abhimanyu Dubey, Abhinav Jauhri, Abhinav Pandey, Abhishek Kadian, Ahmad Al-Dahle, Aiesha Letman, Akhil Mathur, Alan Schelten, Amy Yang, Angela Fan, et al. 2024. The llama 3 herd of models. *arXiv preprint arXiv:2407.21783*.

Feng Hou, Ruili Wang, Jun He, and Yi Zhou. 2020. https://aclanthology.org/2020.acl-main.612/ Improving entity linking through semantic reinforced entity embeddings. In *Proceedings of the 58th Annual Meeting of the Association for Computational Linguistics*, pages 6843–6848. Association for Computational Linguistics.

Zehan Li, Xin Zhang, Yanzhao Zhang, Dingkun Long, Pengjun Xie, and Meishan Zhang. 2023. Towards general text embeddings with multi-stage contrastive learning. *arXiv preprint arXiv:2308.03281*.

Ítalo M. Pereira and Anderson A. Ferreira. 2024. E-bela: Enhanced embedding-based entity linking approach. *Proceedings of the Brazilian Symposium on Multimedia and the Web (WebMedia)*.

Gregor Wernet, Christian Bauer, Bernhard Steubing, Juergen Reinhard, Emilia Moreno Ruiz, and Bo Weidema. 2016. https://doi.org/10.1007/s11367-016-1087-8 The ecoinvent database version 3 (part i): Overview and methodology. *The International Journal of Life Cycle Assessment*, 21:1–13.

# Quantification of Biodiversity from Historical Survey Text with LLM-based Best-Worst Scaling

**Thomas Haider, Tobias Perschl, Malte Rehbein**
Chair of Computational Humanities
University of Passau
firstname.lastname@uni-passau.de

## Abstract

In this study, we evaluate methods to determine the frequency of species via quantity estimation from historical survey text. To that end, we formulate classification tasks and finally show that this problem can be adequately framed as a regression task using Best-Worst Scaling (BWS) with Large Language Models (LLMs). We test Ministral-8B, DeepSeek-V3, and GPT-4, finding that the latter two have reasonable agreement with humans and each other. We conclude that this approach is more cost-effective and similarly robust compared to a fine-grained multi-class approach, allowing automated quantity estimation across species.

## 1 Introduction

Long-term observation data plays a vital role in shaping policies for preventing biodiversity loss caused by habitat destruction, climate change, pollution, or resource overexploitation (Dornelas et al., 2013; Hoque and Sultana, 2024). However, these efforts depend on the availability of reliable and relevant historical data and robust analytical methods, a significant challenge due to the heterogeneity of records representing such data.

The available biodiversity data varies widely in resolution, ranging from detailed records (e.g., point occurrences, trait measurements) to aggregated compilations (e.g., Floras, taxonomic monographs) (König et al., 2019). Many projects, such as the *Global Biodiversity Information Facility* (GBIF), focus largely on the disaggregated end of the spectrum, particularly with presence/absence data (Dorazio et al., 2011; Iknayan et al., 2014). Furthermore, despite their utility, longitudinal data is largely confined to records from after 1970 (van Goethem and van Zanden, 2021), leaving significant historical gaps.

Natural history collections and records from the archives of societies present valuable opportunities to extend data further back in time (Johnson et al., 2011; Brönnimann et al., 2018). Such sources are rich, but typically unstructured and require sophisticated extraction tools to produce meaningful quantitative information. Recent advances in NLP have shown promising potential for retrieval-based biodiversity detection from (mostly scientific) literature (Kommineni et al., 2024; Langer et al., 2024; Lücking et al., 2022).

This paper focuses on evaluating methods for biodiversity quantification from semi-structured historical survey texts. To achieve this, we test tasks to distill meaningful metrics from textual information found in survey records. A particular focus lies on the feasibility of Best-Worst Scaling (BWS) with a Large Language Model (LLM) as an annotator, which promises greater efficiency and cost-effectiveness compared to manual annotation (Bagdon et al., 2024). In the following, we describe the data, outline the tasks and machine learning methods, and finally present a case study.

## 2 Data

In 1845, the Bavarian Ministry of Finance issued a survey to evaluate biodiversity in the Bavarian Kingdom, a region that encompasses a variety of different ecosystems and landscapes. To that end, 119 forestry offices were contacted to complete a standardized questionnaire. Namely, trained local foresters recorded in free text how frequently 44 selected vertebrate species occurred in the respective administrative territory, and in which habitats and locations they could be found.

Figure 1 shows the facsimile of a digitized survey page. It features a header containing instructions and a number of records describing animal species with their respective responses. These historical survey documents are preserved by the Bavarian State Archives (cf. Rehbein et al., 2024).



*Proceedings of the 1st Workshop on Ecology, Environment, and Natural Language Processing (NLP4Ecology2025)*, pages 61–67

| Animal | Text | Binary | BWS | Multi-Classification | |
|---|---|---|---|---|---|
| Ducks | Bedecken Isar-Strom, wie Amper und Moosach in ganzen Schwärmen.<br>*Cover Isar-stream, likewise Amper and Moosach in whole swarms.* | 1 | 1.00 | 5 | ABUNDANT |
| Roe Deer | Ist hier zu Hause, und beinahe in allen Waldtheilen zu finden.<br>*Is at home here and can be found in almost all parts of the forest.* | 1 | 0.88 | 4 | COMMON |
| European Adder | Kommt wohl aber eben nicht häufig vor.<br>*Does indeed appear but just not that often.* | 1 | 0.44 | 3 | COMMON TO RARE |
| Lynx | Höchst selten wechseln derlei Thiere von Tyrol herüber.<br>*Very rarely do such animals cross over from Tyrol.* | 1 | 0.12 | 2 | RARE |
| Wild Goose | Kommt nur äußerst selten zur Winterszeit vor.<br>*Occurs only very rarely at winter time.* | 1 | 0.06 | 1 | VERY RARE |
| Owl | Horstet dahier nicht und verstreicht sich auch nicht in diese Gegend.<br>*Does not nest here and does not stray into this area.* | 0 | 0.00 | 0 | ABSENT |
| Wolf | Kommt nicht mehr vor.<br>*No longer occurs.* | 0 | 0.00 | -1 | EXTINCT |

Table 1: Data Examples with Annotation (our own translations)

The archival sources were digitized, transcribed from the handwritten original and enriched with metadata, including, among others, taxonomic norm data according to the GBIF-database[1] (Telenius, 2011) and geographical references to forestry offices. This data set is freely available on Zenodo (Rehbein et al., 2024).

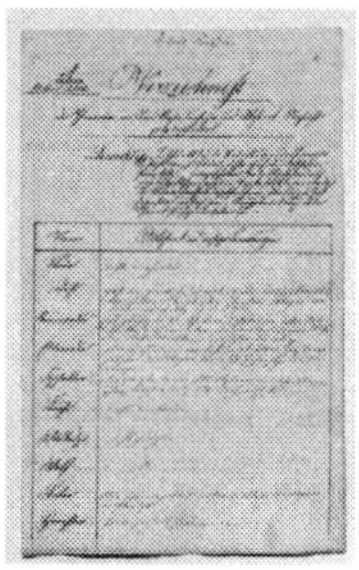

Figure 1: Facsimile of a survey page, Freysing forestry office in the Upper Bavaria district.

In total, the data set contains 5,467 entries[2] among which are also a number of empty (striked out) or 'see above'-type responses. The unique set we used for our experiments contains 2,555 texts. We find that the foresters' replies vary considerably in length where most texts contain 3 to 10 tokens and only a few texts more than 20 tokens. Table 1 provides examples with annotation according to the tasks detailed in the next section.

## 3 Tasks & Experiments

The main task in this paper is to assign a quantity label to a text, indicating the frequency with which an animal species occurs in a specific area. This can be operationalized in various ways, either through a classification task or through regression. In both, it can be as difficult to obtain consistent labels by asking humans to assign a value from a rating scale (Schuman and Presser, 1996; Likert, 1932). Likewise, it is also difficult for researchers to design rating scales, considering design decisions such as scale point descriptions or granularity may bias the annotators.

We evaluate three different task setups,[3] as detailed in Table 1: Binary 'Presence vs. Absence' Classification, a 7-ary Multi-Class setup (Abundant to Extinct), and continuous values scaled to $[0, 1]$. For the first two tasks, we use manual annotation, while continuous values are derived through BWS with LLMs (Bagdon et al., 2024).

### 3.1 Binary Classification

The simplest form of animal occurrence quantification is a binary distinction between the absence (0) or presence (1) of a given species, an annotation scheme as popular as it is problematic in biodiversity estimation.[4] In our annotation, the label PRESENT is given when a species is described in the historical dataset as having been observed in that particular locality at the time of the survey (thus excluding mentions of past occurrences, i.e., extinctions). The annotation workflow consists of iterative steps with discussions. Agreement is nearly perfect. Overall, from the set of 2,555 unique texts, 1,992 (78%) fall into class PRESENT, 563 (22%) into ABSENT.[5]

[1] gbif.org

[2] Including species that were not explicity prompted.

[3] Code: github.org/maelkolb/biodivquant

[4] Since ABSENCE may just stem from non-detection, rather than real absence (Dorazio et al., 2011; Iknayan et al., 2014; Kestemont et al., 2022).

[5] In the complete dataset, absence texts make up more than half of all text descriptions, but often amount to empty or 'strike-out' responses. Thus, the task would be easier on the full dataset, because many instances are trivial to predict.

To test the feasibility of the binary task, we create training curves with different models, namely BERT against Logistic Regression, SVM, and Random Forest on Unigrams. We use 20% of the data for testing, and take another 20% from the training set for hyperparameter search at each cumulative 100 text increment. Despite the 78% majority baseline, we find that the models perform well and training requires only a few hundred texts to reach an F1-macro score in the high 90s.

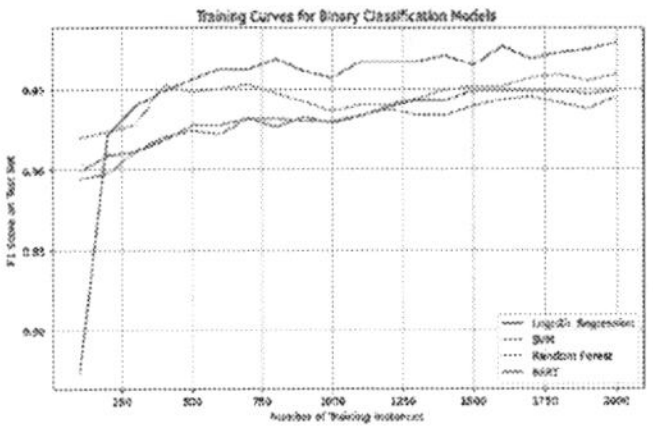


Figure 2: Training Curves of different models on incremental training data (binary classification)

Upon feature weight interpretation of the Logistic Regression and LIME on BERT (Ribeiro et al., 2016), we find that there is some bias in the data: Classification decisions occur on tokens that are not explicit quantifiers and easily substitutable without changing the classification result (e.g., common toponyms such as 'Danube'). This presents a case of spurious correlations—an interesting future research direction, but a matching (Wang and Culotta, 2020) or counterfactual approach (Qian et al., 2021) appears challenging for this heterogeneous data. Yet, we annotate the best features with regard to their 'spuriousness' and find that classifiers are still robust without spurious features. This annotation also gives us a list of quantifiers which we utilize for transfer learning of a regression model (section 3.3).

### 3.2 Multi-Classification

Since the quantification of species frequency in practice exceeds the binary differentiation between presence and absence of animals, a multi-class approach provides more details. We use a 7-class system, categorizing texts based on the schema as shown by the descriptors in Table 1, ranging from ABUNDANT (5) to EXTINCT (-1). We decided to annotate data of four species for our case study (section 4): Roe deer, Eurasian Otter, Eurasian Beaver, Western Capercaille, each within the 119 forestry offices (with one annotator).

A second person annotates a random sample of 100 texts, resulting in a Cohen's $\kappa$ of 0.78, indicating high agreement.

We then train a few models with a 5-fold cross validation, and find that the language agnostic sentence encoder model LaBSE (Feng et al., 2022) performs better than monolingual BERT-models and a Logistic Regression. We also test a zero shot classification with GPT-4 and Deepseek-V3. See appendix for the prompt.

| Model | F1 Micro | F1 Macro |
|---|---|---|
| Logistic Regression | 0.69 | 0.61 |
| gbert-base | 0.63 | 0.51 |
| bert-base-german | 0.73 | 0.63 |
| LaBSE | **0.77** | **0.68** |
| GPT4 Zero Shot | 0.70 | 0.56 |
| DSV3 Zero Shot | 0.66 | 0.66 |

Table 2: Multi-class model performance.

As seen in Table 2, this task is generally quite challenging. We find that the main problem is posed by the underrepresented classes, as shown by the discrepancy between micro and macro scores, indicating that more data would help, which is, however, expensive to obtain. Zero shot classification with GPT-4 in turn is biased towards the RARE classes, such that COMMON categories are harder to predict, while DeepSeek-V3 (DSV3) shows a more balanced response.

### 3.3 Continuous Quantification

Finally, we experiment with operationalizing our task as a regression problem with the aim of generalizing the quantification problem to less arbitrary categories and a possibly imbalanced data set (Berggren et al., 2019). While a naïve labeling of quantifiers showed promising results, it is a challenge to create a comprehensive test set based on heuristic annotation. Thus, we experiment with Best-Worst Scaling, aided by LLMs.

#### 3.3.1 Best-Worst Scaling with LLMs

Best-Worst Scaling (BWS) is a comparative judgment technique that helps in ranking items by identifying the best and worst elements within a set. This approach is easier to accomplish than manual labeling and there are fewer design decisions to make. In a BWS setting, the amount of annotations needed to rank a given number of text instances depends on three variables, namely 1) corpus size (total number of texts used), 2) set size (number of texts in each comparison set), and 3) number of comparison sets each text appears in.

The number of comparisons divided by set size is regarded as the variable $N$, where $N = 2$ generally yields good results in the literature (Kiritchenko and Mohammad, 2017). A reliable set size is 4, since choosing the best and worst text instance from a 4-tuple set essentially provides the same number of comparisons as five out of six possible pairwise comparisons (ibid).

We take a random sample of 1,000 texts (excluding texts with ABSENCE annotation, thus making the task harder, but giving us a more realistic distribution). With a set size of 4 and $N = 2$, every text occurs in exactly 8 different sets and we get 2,000 comparison sets (tuples). These are then individually prompted to three LLMs: the relatively small Ministral-8B,[6] OpenAI's GPT-4 (Achiam et al., 2023), and the DeepSeek-V3 open source model (Liu et al., 2024).

| | Annotator1 | Annotator2 | B | W | B + W |
|---|---|---|---|---|---|
| LLM-LLM | GPT4 | DeepseekV3 | 0.73 | 0.69 | 0.56 |
| | Ministral8B | DeepseekV3 | 0.54 | 0.54 | 0.36 |
| | GPT4 | Ministral8B | 0.57 | 0.50 | 0.38 |
| **Average** | | | 0.61 | 0.57 | 0.43 |
| Human-Human | AR | DS | 0.56 | 0.65 | 0.45 |
| | DS | KB | 0.56 | 0.62 | 0.40 |
| | MR | AR | 0.51 | 0.65 | 0.39 |
| | TP | AO | 0.73 | 0.55 | 0.48 |
| | MP | MR | 0.59 | 0.52 | 0.41 |
| **Average** | | | 0.59 | 0.60 | 0.43 |
| Human-LLM | AO | Ministral8B | 0.43 | 0.31 | 0.23 |
| | AR | Ministral8B | 0.47 | 0.58 | 0.38 |
| | DS | Ministral8B | 0.43 | 0.42 | 0.23 |
| | KB | Ministral8B | 0.53 | 0.61 | 0.46 |
| | MP | Ministral8B | 0.45 | 0.43 | 0.30 |
| | MR | Ministral8B | 0.55 | 0.48 | 0.38 |
| | TP | Ministral8B | 0.49 | 0.31 | 0.24 |
| **Average** | | | 0.48 | 0.45 | 0.32 |
| Human-LLM | AO | GPT4 | 0.68 | 0.55 | 0.45 |
| | AR | GPT4 | 0.49 | 0.57 | 0.34 |
| | DS | GPT4 | 0.44 | 0.71 | 0.43 |
| | KB | GPT4 | 0.47 | 0.68 | 0.41 |
| | MP | GPT4 | 0.57 | 0.62 | 0.41 |
| | MR | GPT4 | 0.49 | 0.63 | 0.41 |
| | TP | GPT4 | 0.63 | 0.57 | 0.43 |
| **Average** | | | 0.54 | 0.62 | 0.41 |
| Human-LLM | AO | DeepseekV3 | 0.61 | 0.59 | 0.45 |
| | AR | DeepseekV3 | 0.55 | 0.68 | 0.41 |
| | DS | DeepseekV3 | 0.62 | 0.63 | 0.46 |
| | KB | DeepseekV3 | 0.57 | 0.62 | 0.41 |
| | MP | DeepseekV3 | 0.69 | 0.53 | 0.41 |
| | MR | DeepseekV3 | 0.59 | 0.68 | 0.46 |
| | TP | DeepseekV3 | 0.58 | 0.58 | 0.41 |
| **Average** | | | 0.60 | 0.62 | 0.43 |

Table 3: Cohen's $\kappa$ Agreement between humans and LLMs in Best-Worst-Annotation (B: Best, W: Worst, B+W: Best + Worst). Two-letter shorthands for humans.

Whereas Ministral-8B is run locally, we use the OpenAI API to access GPT-4 and the fireworks.ai API endpoint for DeepSeek-V3, since the DeepSeek-webservices are limited at the time of the experiment and hardware limitations hamper local deployment. Prompts are in the appendix.

We ask seven native German post-graduates to annotate one of two subsets of 50 tuples each with a custom browser-based annotation interface. Table 3 shows Cohen's $\kappa$ agreement across humans and LLMs. We find that agreement among humans is largely on par with agreement between humans and the two larger LLMs, while the lower agreement between Ministral-8B and humans, as well as the other machine annotators, indicates a limited capability of this model for the task at hand. It appears that it is easier to identify the worst instance than the best, which is likely an artifact of our data. Interestingly, agreement between GPT-4 and DeepSeek-V3 is the highest overall, which could lend itself either to a) the task being easier for the LLMs than for humans, or b) that the models are overall fairly similar. We find no significant difference ($p = .118$) between GPT-4 and DeepSeek-V3 in Human-LLM comparison.

$$s(i) = \frac{\#best(i) - \#worst(i)}{\#overall(i)} \quad (1)$$

By counting how often each text was chosen as the best, worst, or as one of two other texts, we calculate a score $s(i)$ as detailed in equation (1), resulting in an interval scale $[-1, 1]$, which we normalize to a scale $[0, 1]$. This scales (and ranks) the entire dataset, so it can be used for regression. It should be noted that the scores come in increments of $\frac{1}{8}$ (determined by number of comparisons of instance $i$), resulting in 17 discrete values. We find a flat unimodal inverted U-shape in the score distribution without notable outliers.

### 3.3.2 Regression Models

We train a variety of different regression models with 5-fold cross validation to optimize for the values generated by Best-Worst Scaling, as shown in Table 4. We compare a Kernel Ridge Regression (KRR) baseline against BERT-style-models with regression head, and test a transfer learning setup, for which we scale the 114 n-gram quantifiers as extracted from the binary Logistic Regression with another GPT-4 BWS, then match these scores to the texts and tune a LaBSE model on the same train/test split before using it for the final task.

Curiously, KRR with LaBSE embedding features benefits substantially from hyperparameter

[6] https://huggingface.co/mistralai/Ministral-8B-Instruct-2410

| Features/Training Strategy | Model | MAE | | $R^2$ | |
|---|---|---|---|---|---|
| | | GPT4 | DSV3 | GPT4 | DSV3 |
| Unigrams | KRR | 0.159 | 0.158 | 0.514 | 0.515 |
| Frozen LaBSE Embeddings | KRR | 0.118 | 0.117 | 0.678 | 0.686 |
| Regression Head | bert-base-german | 0.149 | 0.158 | 0.516 | 0.490 |
| Regression Head | LaBSE | 0.133 | 0.127 | 0.607 | 0.657 |
| Reg. Head + Transfer | LaBSE | **0.107** | 0.117 | **0.730** | 0.710 |

Table 4: Comparison of different training strategies for regression based on BWS-Scaling. GPT4: GPT-4 BWS annotation, DSV3: Deepseek-V3 BWS annotation

tuning, reaching superior results over LaBSE with regression head. The Transfer Model on GPT4 BWS offers the best performance, with acceptably high explained variance ($R^2 = .73$) and only .11 Mean Absolute Error (MAE), which makes this model useful for downstream prediction as in the case study below. However, more data would likely also help, since training curves show continuous improvement.

## 4 Case Study

For a proof of concept, we map the predictions of the regression model (LaBSE transfer regression model based on GPT-4 BWS) to the multi-class human annotation. Figure 3 shows a strong relationship between multi-class labels and regression scores for the entire dataset (four species), but also that the extinction class is not properly represented in the regression, and furthermore that higher values are challenging to predict.

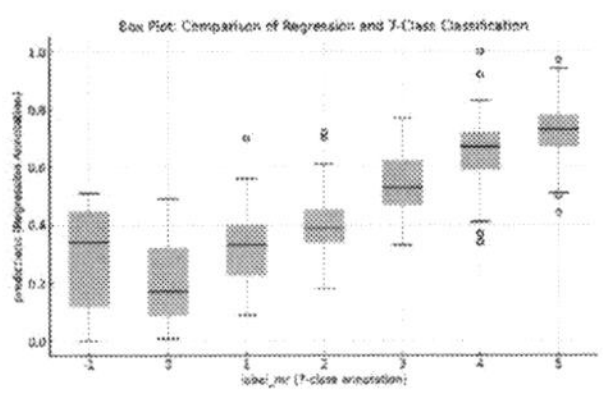

Figure 3: Multi-Class vs. Regression Distribution

Figure 4 shows specie-specific distributions for Roe deer and Eurasian otter across all 119 offices, indicating a fairly good alignment between the regression result (top) and the multi-class annotation (bottom). However, the mapping is not unambiguous due to 1) shortcomings of the regression, such as the inability to model extinction and difficulty in predicting high values, and 2) imperfect alignment with class intervals, which are fuzzy with regard to the continuous values. However, pending further research, we find that our method performs well and produces plausible results.

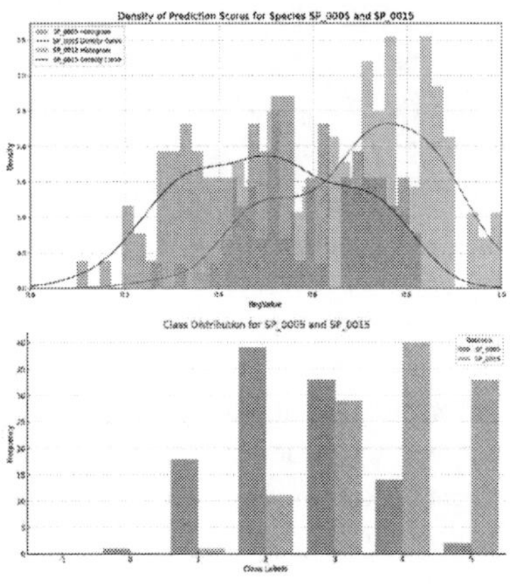

Figure 4: Density histogram of regressor prediction (top) and multi-class (bottom) distribution for Roe deer (SP_0015, red) and Eurasian otter (SP_0005, grey).

## 5 Conclusion & Future Work

This study demonstrates that information of occurrence frequencies from semi-structured historical biodiversity survey texts can be adequately modeled with Best-Worst Scaling through LLMs. While a simple classification approach performs well with minimal training data, a more complex classification struggles with design decisions and imbalanced data. BWS meets this by eliminating rating scale design decisions. In addition, it is cognitively and computationally less expensive, since no manual annotation of training data is necessary, while still offering similarly accurate results with much finer granularity through regression.

The robustness of methods and models should be further tested, not exclusive to biodiversity surveys, lending itself to a number of tasks. Yet, similar data to ours likely exists, e.g., on 19th century Bavarian flora, Württembergische Oberamtsbeschreibungen (1824–1886), or data in biodiversitylibrary.org, making our methods valuable.

## Limitations

The accuracy of the method depends heavily on the capabilities of the specific LLM used. If a model lacks domain-specific knowledge or has biases, it may impact results. Furthermore, without a reliable dataset to benchmark against, it is difficult to assess the absolute accuracy of the BWS-based regression approach, because we also test on BWS values. While we measured agreement on the BWS task with humans, it is impractical to scale the entire dataset with both LLMs and humans, and thus our agreement calculation may suffer from sampling bias.

The effectiveness of the approach on different text sources or structured data remains uncertain. Differences in linguistic styles, terminologies, and data availability across domains may limit generalization. The approach assumes that frequency-related information in historical texts can be accurately mapped to numerical frequency estimates. If the original texts contain qualitative descriptions rather than explicit quantifiers, this may introduce errors. Also, older survey texts may reflect sampling biases, observer subjectivity, or incomplete data. If LLMs learn from these biases, the resulting quantity estimations may reinforce historical inaccuracies rather than correct them.

## Acknowledgements

We thank our annotators from the Journal Club, and the colleagues in the Computational Historical Ecology group at the Chair for Computational Humanities at the University of Passau for their feedback.

## References

Josh Achiam, Steven Adler, Sandhini Agarwal, Lama Ahmad, Ilge Akkaya, Florencia Leoni Aleman, Diogo Almeida, Janko Altenschmidt, Sam Altman, Shyamal Anadkat, et al. 2023. Gpt-4 technical report. *arXiv preprint arXiv:2303.08774*.

Christopher Bagdon, Prathamesh Karmalkar, Harsha Gurulingappa, and Roman Klinger. 2024. "you are an expert annotator": Automatic best–worst-scaling annotations for emotion intensity modeling. In *Proceedings of the 2024 Conference of the North American Chapter of the Association for Computational Linguistics: Human Language Technologies (Volume 1: Long Papers)*, pages 7924–7936, Mexico City, Mexico. Association for Computational Linguistics.

Stig Johan Berggren, Taraka Rama, and Lilja Øvrelid. 2019. Regression or classification? automated essay scoring for Norwegian. In *Proceedings of the Fourteenth Workshop on Innovative Use of NLP for Building Educational Applications*, pages 92–102, Florence, Italy. Association for Computational Linguistics.

Stefan Brönnimann, Christian Pfister, and Sam White. 2018. Archives of nature and archives of societies. In *The Palgrave Handbook of Climate History*, pages 27–36. Palgrave Macmillan UK, London.

Robert M Dorazio, Nicholas J Gotelli, and Aaron M Ellison. 2011. Modern methods of estimating biodiversity from presence-absence surveys. *Biodiversity loss in a changing planet*, pages 277–302.

Maria Dornelas, Anne E. Magurran, Stephen T. Buckland, Anne Chao, Robin L. Chazdon, Robert K. Colwell, Tom Curtis, Kevin J. Gaston, Nicholas J. Gotelli, Matthew A. Kosnik, Brian McGill, Jenny L. McCune, Hélène Morlon, Peter J. Mumby, Lise Øvreås, Angelika Studeny, and Mark Vellend. 2013. Quantifying temporal change in biodiversity: challenges and opportunities. *Proceedings of the Royal Society*, 280.

Fangxiaoyu Feng, Yinfei Yang, Daniel Cer, Naveen Arivazhagan, and Wei Wang. 2022. Language-agnostic bert sentence embedding.

Thomas van Goethem and Jan Luiten van Zanden. 2021. Biodiversity trends in a historical perspective. In *How Was Life? Volume II: New Perspectives on Well-being and Global Inequality since 1820*. Organisation for Economic Co-Operation and Development (OECD).

Sk Rezaul Hoque and Sk Rima Sultana. 2024. Addressing global environmental problems: Challenges, solutions, and opportunities. *The Social Science Review: A Multidisciplinary Journal*, 2(2):124–130.

Kelly J Iknayan, Morgan W Tingley, Brett J Furnas, and Steven R Beissinger. 2014. Detecting diversity: emerging methods to estimate species diversity. *Trends in ecology & evolution*, 29(2):97–106.

Kenneth G Johnson, Stephen J Brooks, Phillip B Fenberg, Adrian G Glover, Karen E James, Adrian M Lister, Ellinor Michel, Mark Spencer, Jonathan A Todd, Eugenia Valsami-Jones, Jeremy R Young, and John R Stewart. 2011. Climate change and biosphere response: Unlocking the collections vault. *Bioscience*, 61(2):147–153.

Mike Kestemont, Folgert Karsdorp, Elisabeth de Bruijn, Matthew Driscoll, Katarzyna A Kapitan, Pádraig Ó Macháin, Daniel Sawyer, Remco Sleiderink, and Anne Chao. 2022. Forgotten books: The application of unseen species models to the survival of culture. *Science*, 375(6582):765–769.

Svetlana Kiritchenko and Saif Mohammad. 2017. Best-worst scaling more reliable than rating scales: A case study on sentiment intensity annotation. In *Proceedings of the 55th Annual Meeting of the Association for Computational Linguistics (Volume 2: Short Papers)*, pages 465–470, Vancouver, Canada. Association for Computational Linguistics.

Vamsi Krishna Kommineni, Waqas Ahmed, Birgitta Koenig-Ries, and Sheeba Samuel. 2024. Automating information retrieval from biodiversity literature using large language models: A case study. *Biodivers. Inf. Sci. Stand.*, 8.

Christian König, Patrick Weigelt, Julian Schrader, Amanda Taylor, Jens Kattge, and Holger Kreft. 2019. Biodiversity data integration—the significance of data resolution and domain. *PLoS biology*, 17(3):e3000183.

Lars Langer, Manuel Burghardt, Roland Borgards, Ronny Richter, and Christian Wirth. 2024. The relation between biodiversity in literature and social and spatial situation of authors: Reflections on the nature–culture entanglement. *People and Nature*, 6(1):54–74.

Rensis Likert. 1932. A technique for the measurement of attitudes. *Archives of Psychology*.

Aixin Liu, Bei Feng, Bing Xue, Bingxuan Wang, Bochao Wu, Chengda Lu, Chenggang Zhao, Chengqi Deng, Chenyu Zhang, Chong Ruan, et al. 2024. Deepseek-v3 technical report. *arXiv preprint arXiv:2412.19437*.

Andy Lücking, Christine Driller, Manuel Stoeckel, Giuseppe Abrami, Adrian Pachzelt, and Alexander Mehler. 2022. Multiple annotation for biodiversity: developing an annotation framework among biology, linguistics and text technology. *Language resources and evaluation*, 56(3):807–855.

Chen Qian, Fuli Feng, Lijie Wen, Chunping Ma, and Pengjun Xie. 2021. Counterfactual inference for text classification debiasing. In *Proceedings of the 59th Annual Meeting of the Association for Computational Linguistics and the 11th International Joint Conference on Natural Language Processing (Volume 1: Long Papers)*, pages 5434–5445, Online. Association for Computational Linguistics.

Malte Rehbein, Andrea Belen Escobari Vargas, Sarah Fischer, Anton Güntsch, Bettina Haas, Giada Matheisen, Tobias Perschl, Alois Wieshuber, and Thore Engel. 2024. Historical animal observation records by bavarian forestry offices (1845): Description of the data sets. Version 1.3 as of 2024-10-29, `https://doi.org/10.5281/zenodo.14008158`.

Marco Tulio Ribeiro, Sameer Singh, and Carlos Guestrin. 2016. " why should i trust you?" explaining the predictions of any classifier. In *Proceedings of the 22nd ACM SIGKDD international conference on knowledge discovery and data mining*, pages 1135–1144.

Howard Schuman and Stanley Presser. 1996. *Questions and answers in attitude surveys: Experiments on question form, wording, and context*. Sage.

Anders Telenius. 2011. Biodiversity information goes public: Gbif at your service. *Nordic Journal of Botany*, 29(3):378–381.

Zhao Wang and Aron Culotta. 2020. Identifying spurious correlations for robust text classification. In *Findings of the Association for Computational Linguistics: EMNLP 2020*, pages 3431–3440, Online. Association for Computational Linguistics.

Württembergische Oberamtsbeschreibungen. 1824–1886. Wikisource. Accessed: 30 Jan. 2025.

## APPENDIX: PROMPTS

### Multi-Classification Prompt

**System-prompt:** You are a German native expert in text classification. Use the provided classification scheme to classify German texts based on species frequency descriptions.

**User-prompt:** You are a classification model. Classify the given German text into one of the following categories:
- Abundant (5): Species is very frequently observed or present.
- Common (4): Species is commonly found in the area.
- Common to Rare (3): Species is observed, but not very frequently.
- Rare (2): Species is rarely seen in the area.
- Very Rare (1): Species is seen only in exceptional circumstances.
- Absent (0): Species is not observed in the area.
- Extinct (-1): Species no longer exists in the area.

Read the provided text and classify it according to this scheme. Here is the text to classify:
Text

### Best-Worst Scaling Prompt

**System-prompt:** You are an expert annotator specializing in Best-Worst Scaling of German texts based on quantity information about animal occurrences.

**User-prompt:** (Texts 1 to 4 were substituted with the actual texts of a tuple): Task: From the following German texts about animal occurrence, identify:

Best: The text conveying the highest quantity (e.g., presence, frequency, population size)

Worst: The text conveying the lowest quantity.

1. Text 1
2. Text 2
3. Text 3
4. Text 4

JSON format for your answer:

{ "Best": [Text Number],
"Worst": [Text Number]}

# Analyzing the Online Communication of Environmental Movement Organizations: NLP Approaches to Topics, Sentiment, and Emotions

**Christina S. Barz**
Darmstadt University
of Applied Sciences
Haardtring 100
64295 Darmstadt
Germany
christina.barz@h-da.de

**Melanie Siegel**
Darmstadt University
of Applied Sciences
Schöfferstraße 3
64295 Darmstadt
Germany
melanie.siegel@h-da.de

**Daniel Hanss**
Darmstadt University
of Applied Sciences
Haardtring 100
64295 Darmstadt
Germany
daniel.hanss@h-da.de

**Abstract**

This project employs state-of-the-art Natural Language Processing (NLP) techniques to analyze the online communication of international Environmental Movement Organizations (EMOs). First, we introduce our overall EMO dataset and describe it through topic modeling. Second, we evaluate current sentiment and emotion classification models for our specific dataset. Third, as we are currently in our annotation process, we evaluate our current progress and issues to determine the most effective approach for creating a high-quality annotated dataset that captures the nuances of EMO communication. Finally, we emphasize the need for domain-specific datasets and tailored NLP tools and suggest refinements for our annotation process moving forward.

## 1 Introduction

In order to address the escalating environmental crises of our time, it is imperative that individuals and groups worldwide act in a collective manner. Investigating current environmental movements is crucial as they play a significant role in motivating collective environmental action, shaping public opinion, and influencing policy decisions. The online communication of Environmental Movement Organizations (EMOs) provides valuable insights into their strategic approaches, thematic content and emotional appeals (Gulliver et al., 2021; Ackland and O'Neil, 2011). Concurrently, the success of these organizations can be ascertained through the examination of various reactions of other users, such as likes and comments. Therefore, the objective of our project is to analyze four years of X (former Twitter) data, which we refer to as tweets, from a range of international EMOs, including *Greenpeace*, *Friends of the Earth*, *Fridays for Future*, *Extinction Rebellion*, and *Climate Action Network (CAN)* in order to gain a deeper understanding of their communication. We intend to assess the sentiment and emotions conveyed in the EMOs' language, utilizing and evaluating state-of-the-art Natural Language Processing (NLP) models. As part of this research, our ultimate goal is to create a comprehensive and annotated dataset tailored to climate- and environment-specific content, in the future. In this paper, we present an interim stage of our project, focusing on a critical assessment of our current annotation process to refine and enhance its robustness, with the goal of creating a high-quality annotated dataset. The paper is structured as follows: First, we review related work and outline our research questions. Next, we describe our methodology, including the annotation process and the evaluation of existing sentiment and emotion models. We then present our results, highlighting key findings and insights gained from this evaluation. Finally, we conclude by discussing the limitations of our approach and proposing avenues for future research, including further dataset development and model fine-tuning for climate- and environment-related communication.

### 1.1 Related Work & Research Questions

Sentiment and emotion analysis is rarely applied to climate and environmental contexts. Instead, most research in this field focuses on more general applications, such as product analysis or the determination of stock market trends (Wankhade et al., 2022). Moreover, there is a paucity of datasets and models that have been specifically designed for the purpose of understanding climate-related text in social media. Available datasets include the *ClimaConvo* dataset, which comprises 15,309 tweets from the year 2022 labeled as *relevance*, *stance*, *hate speech*, *direction of hate*, and *humor* (Shiwakoti et al., 2024) and the *Twitter Climate Change Sentiment Dataset* (Qian, 2021) with a to-



*Proceedings of the 1st Workshop on Ecology, Environment, and Natural Language Processing (NLP4Ecology2025)*, pages 68–76
March 2, 2025 

tal of 43,943 tweets spanning from 2015 to 2018. Here each tweet was classified into one of four categories: *news*, *pro*, *neutral*, or *anti*.

A significant challenge in the research field is posed by the ambiguity of sentiment and emotions, particularly in social media, where context and tone vary greatly (Pozzi et al., 2016). In contrast to studies that analyze individual users' posts (Dahal et al., 2019; El Barachi et al., 2021), our research exclusively examines content created by groups. It seems probable that the content of posts from EMOs reflects strategic communication approaches pursued by an organization rather than an expression of individual members' sentiments or emotional states. This raises the question of whether state-of-the-art NLP models are capable of adequately capturing the nuances of environmental and climate communication from EMOs. Our study addresses these gaps in the literature by investigating the following research questions: (1) *How effectively do state-of-the-art NLP models perform in analyzing online communication of EMOs?* and (2) *How effective and reliable is our current annotation process in capturing sentiment and emotion in climate- and environment-related tweets and what refinements are necessary to ensure the creation of a high-quality, domain-specific annotated dataset?*

To this end, we first employ topic modeling to describe our dataset and then test the performance of the ClimateBERT sentiment model for sentiment analysis (Webersinke et al., 2021) and the emotion model *bhadresh-savani/bert-base-uncased-emotion* for emotion classification (Savani, 2020). Our analyses regarding the second research question should provide insights for addressing challenges that may arise during our annotation process, such as inter-annotator agreement (IAA), and enhance the reliability of future annotations.

| EMO | Number of Documents |
|---|---|
| Greenpeace | 14420 |
| Extinction Rebellion | 12004 |
| CAN | 5152 |
| Fridays for Future | 2353 |
| Friends of the Earth | 2230 |

Table 1: Document Distribution in Dataset

## 2 Methodology

### 2.1 Data

The dataset extracted in September 2024 comprises 36,159 tweets from five prominent international EMOs, namely *Greenpeace*, *Extinction Rebellion*, *Friends of the Earth*, *Fridays for Future*, and *CAN*, see Table 1. The tweets were published between 2019 and 2024. The dataset comprises the following information for each document: group name, time, retweet count, reply count, like count and tweet text. All analyses were performed in Python (version 3.11.11) using the *bertopic*, *pandas*, and *Scikit-learn* packages (pandas development team, 2020; Pedregosa et al., 2011; Grootendorst, 2020).

### 2.2 Annotation Process

A first sub-dataset of 1399 tweets was independently annotated by three annotators. To facilitate this process, an annotation guideline was developed, which provided clear definitions for all constructs and illustrative examples, see osf.io for our guidelines. Annotators were instructed to label sentiment and expressions of the emotions joy, anger, fear, and sadness. The annotation process commenced with a preliminary phase, during which the annotators labelled an initial set of 10 tweets. This was followed by a feedback session, during which ambiguities were addressed and alignment on the labeling criteria was ensured. Subsequently, feedback sessions were conducted at regular intervals, with each session focusing on a specific subset of 500 tweets. As discrepancies are typical in annotation tasks of this nature (Uma et al., 2021), we established a gold standard dataset through majority voting. In instances where all three annotators reached a differing conclusion (this could only occur with sentiment annotations), these cases were subjected to further analysis and resolution through group discussions in order to achieve a consensus. This approach ensured a balance between individual judgments and collaborative decision-making, thereby enhancing the reliability of the annotations.

### 2.3 Topic Modeling

To describe and analyze the themes present within the whole dataset (36,159), we employed BERTopic, a recently developed topic modeling approach that utilizes embedding-based techniques in contrast to the traditional bag-of-words methods, such as LDA (Jelodar et al., 2019; Grootendorst, 2022). BERTopic uses semantic embeddings to cluster documents and utilizes parameters such as *n_neighbors* and *min_cluster_size* to refine the granularity of topics. In contrast to LDA, BERTopic does not necessitate the pre-definition of the number of topics. Unlike other approaches, the model is designed to determine the number of clusters based on the data itself. A more detailed representation of themes was given priority, which informed our selection of parameters. The complete parameter settings are available for consultation at osf.io.

### 2.4 Sentiment Classification

In order to conduct a sentiment analysis, we utilized the ClimateBERT sentiment model, which has been specifically trained on texts pertaining to climate-related issues (Webersinke et al., 2021). In their model, the researchers conceptualized sentiment as a framing, categorizing climate-related text as either positive (opportunity), neutral, or negative (risk). It is noteworthy that ClimateBERT was trained on longer documents, such as news articles or financial reports, and its performance on shorter social media texts remains untested. The present study assesses the applicability of this approach to short-form content, such as tweets.

### 2.5 Emotion Classification

Emotion analysis was conducted using the emotion model *bhadresh-savani/bert-base-uncased-emotion* that had been trained on general tweets (Savani, 2020). The model identifies a number of emotions, from which we selected four for our analysis that overlap with our annotations, i.e. *joy*, *anger*, *sadness*, and *fear*. Despite having been trained on a generic social media dataset, such models typically necessitate fine-tuning for specific domains. Nonetheless, prior to the fine-tuning of a model, a preliminary evaluation is conducted to assess the functionality of existing models. Therefore, in this analysis, the model's capacity to categorize emotions within the context of climate change and environmental issues is assessed without additional fine-tuning.

## 3 Results

### 3.1 IAA & Class Distributions

In order to assess the quality of our gold standard, we have calculated the Fleiss' Kappa coefficient, see Table 2, for our sub-data set (1,399 tweets) and examined the class distributions (Fleiss, 1971). We had slight to moderate Kappa depending on sentiment or the specific emotion. Despite the provision of guidelines and feedback sessions, there was a notable discrepancy in the interpretation of sentiment and emotions by the annotators. The feedback conversations revealed that the annotations contained a bias toward personal emotional reactions to the text. This means that annotators tended to label tweets with emotions if the tweets evoked certain emotions in them. For example, neutral texts reporting on extreme weather events were often rated with sadness, fear or anger, even though the texts were written without emotional tone. We found the least agreement for the emotions anger (0.2472) and fear (0.0379).

| **Construct** | **Fleiss' Kappa** |
|---|---|
| Sentiment | 0.4574 |
| Joy | 0.4708 |
| Anger | 0.2472 |
| Fear | 0.0379 |
| Sadness | 0.1825 |

Table 2: Inter-Annotator Agreement (IAA) measured by Fleiss' Kappa

| **Class** | **Label** | **Count** |
|---|---|---|
| | **Sentiment** | |
| Neutral | 0 | 1054 |
| Risk | -1 | 325 |
| Opportunity | 1 | 20 |
| | **Joy** | |
| No Joy | 0 | 1378 |
| Joy | 1 | 21 |
| | **Anger** | |
| No Anger | 0 | 1298 |
| Anger | 1 | 101 |
| | **Fear** | |
| No Fear | 0 | 1389 |
| Fear | 1 | 10 |
| | **Sadness** | |
| No Sadness | 0 | 1391 |
| Sadness | 1 | 8 |

Table 3: Class Distribution for Sentiment and Emotion Labels

Nevertheless, we have created a majority voting gold standard to evaluate the current models. In 14 cases, a lack of consensus was observed among the three annotators, necessitating a collective dis-

| Topic | Topic Name | Number of Documents |
|---|---|---|
| 0 | Climate Change, Fossil Fuels & Finance | 22711 |
| 1 | Indigenous People & Biodiversity | 1387 |
| 2 | Ocean | 1231 |
| 3 | Plastic | 1049 |
| 4 | Noise | 1039 |
| 5 | Indigenous People, Brazil & Amazon | 751 |
| 6 | Noise: Posts in other Languages | 600 |
| 7 | Women & Gender | 623 |
| 8 | Forest & Deforestation | 620 |
| 9 | Support XR Groups & Activists | 460 |
| 10 | Food & Agriculture | 607 |
| 11 | Australia & Wildfires | 530 |
| 12 | Stop Shell | 480 |
| 13 | Air Pollution | 385 |
| 14 | Meat & Dairy | 329 |
| 15 | Deep Sea Mining | 295 |
| 16 | Ban Private Jets | 272 |
| 17 | Nuclear Energy & War | 255 |
| 18 | Transport & Mobility | 318 |
| 19 | Indonesia & Palm Oil | 430 |
| 20 | Policing Bill | 321 |
| 21 | Palestine | 269 |
| 22 | Noise: Apply for Climate Jobs | 186 |
| 23 | Fossil of the Day Award | 200 |
| 24 | Vaccine & Covid19 | 142 |
| 25 | Black Friday & Buying | 168 |
| 26 | Cars & Vehicles | 152 |
| 27 | Countries | 232 |
| 28 | Human Rights Act | 117 |

Table 4: Identified Topics, Labels, and Frequencies from Initial Topic Modeling

cussion to resolve the discrepancy. The class distribution in our gold standard is very unbalanced, see Table 3. For example, in our annotations we have more labels for climate change as risk (23.23 %; 325 posts) compared to opportunity (1.43 %; 20 posts), which suggests that EMOs view climate change as a high risk. In terms of emotions, we only had 1.50 % joy (21 posts), 0.71 % fear (10 posts) and 0.57 % sadness (8 posts), compared to a higher incidence of anger with 7.22% (101 posts). The distribution of emotional language used by EMOs indicates a lack of emotional expression, with anger being the most prevalent emotion.

### 3.2 Topic Modeling

Our initial topic analysis yielded 29 topics, which were then subjected to a manual review by one researcher. Three topics consisting solely of documents labeled as *Noise* due to their lack of meaningful content or content not in English (e.g., 'Clearly.', 'Hmm.' or 'Starting in about 1 hour! Make sure to tune in!'), were excluded from further analysis. For each remaining topic, an in-depth analysis of the representative documents and word representations was conducted, which resulted in the ten most frequently discussed topics: *'Climate Change, Fossil Fuels & Finance'*, *'Indigenous People & Biodiversity'*, *'Ocean'*, *'Plastic'*, *'Indigenous People, Brazil & Amazon'*, *'Women & Gender'*, *'Forest & Deforestation'*, *'Support XR Groups & Activists'*, *'Food & Agriculture'* and *Australia & Wildfires*. For a comprehensive list of all 29 topics and their corresponding labels, please refer to Table 4.

A thorough examination of the most frequently occurring topics across EMOs reveals distinct pat-

| Author | Topic | Description | Frequency |
|---|---|---|---|
| CAN | 0 | Climate Change, Fossil Fuels & Finance | 4376 |
| CAN | 23 | Fossil of the Day Award | 142 |
| CAN | 1 | Indigenous People & Biodiversity | 114 |
| CAN | 21 | Palestine | 64 |
| CAN | 7 | Women & Gender | 50 |
| Extinction Rebellion | 0 | Climate Change, Fossil Fuels & Finance | 8323 |
| Extinction Rebellion | 9 | Support XR Groups & Activists | 450 |
| Extinction Rebellion | 1 | Indigenous People & Biodiversity | 293 |
| Extinction Rebellion | 11 | Australia & Wildfires | 272 |
| Extinction Rebellion | 20 | Policing Bill | 222 |
| Friends of the Earth | 0 | Climate Change, Fossil Fuels & Finance | 977 |
| Friends of the Earth | 1 | Indigenous People & Biodiversity | 352 |
| Friends of the Earth | 10 | Food & Agriculture | 179 |
| Friends of the Earth | 7 | Women & Gender | 126 |
| Friends of the Earth | 21 | Palestine | 98 |
| Fridays for Future | 0 | Climate Change, Fossil Fuels & Finance | 1693 |
| Fridays for Future | 27 | Activism in diverse Countries | 107 |
| Fridays for Future | 1 | Indigenous People & Biodiversity | 102 |
| Fridays for Future | 21 | Palestine | 59 |
| Fridays for Future | 20 | Policing Bill | 42 |
| Greenpeace | 0 | Climate Change, Fossil Fuels & Finance | 7342 |
| Greenpeace | 2 | Ocean | 1067 |
| Greenpeace | 3 | Plastic | 829 |
| Greenpeace | 5 | Indigenous People, Brazil & Amazon | 532 |
| Greenpeace | 1 | Indigenous People & Biodiversity | 526 |

Table 5: Distribution of Topics by Author After Initial Topic Modeling Analysis

terns that reflect the issues these groups prioritize and the strategies they employ. For instance, both Extinction Rebellion and Fridays for Future have most frequent topics which are activism related, such as *'Support XR Groups & Activists'* for Extinction Rebellion and *'Activism in diverse Countries'* for Fridays for Future. In addition, both groups have the topic of *'Policing Bill'* in their most common themes, which includes restrictions on unacceptable protest behavior. These subjects, which have been derived from the topic modeling, reflect the identity and strategies of the groups, as Extinction Rebellion and Fridays For Future are more akin to a protest movement in comparison to larger EMOs such as Greenpeace and Friends of the Earth. Furthermore, Greenpeace appears to prioritize subjects such as *'Ocean'* and *'Plastic'*, in contrast to other groups. It should also be noted that the topic of *'Women & Gender'* only appeared frequently at the CAN and Friends of the Earth. For all topic frequencies and representative documents refer to Table 5.

Since the most frequent topic *'Climate Change, Fossil Fuels & Finance'* encompassed the majority of the documents, we conducted another round of topic modeling using only the documents from this topic (22,711) to explore its content in more detail. This analysis revealed several specific subtopics, as shown in Table 6. Further breakdown of these topics by organization provided valuable insights, see Table 7. For example, CAN primarily posts about COP (Conference of the Parties) and financial issues, while Greenpeace frequently communicates about fossil fuels. Extinction Rebellion focuses heavily on peaceful protest and rights, emphasizing advocacy and activism in its messaging. Fridays for Future, on the other hand, focuses almost exclusively on activism-related issues. Their communication strategy is particularly inviting and action-oriented, as reflected in common themes such as *'Join Fridays for Future Strike'* and *'Friendly Reminder to Act Now'*. These findings underscore the different thematic focuses and strategic communication approaches of each organization, shedding

| Topic | Topic Name | Number of Documents |
|---|---|---|
| 0 | COP, Loss and Damage & Finance | 3009 |
| 1 | Fossil Fuels | 2631 |
| 2 | Noise: Article, Link, Source, Join & Share | 1420 |
| 3 | Climate Emergency & Denial | 1029 |
| 4 | Peaceful Protest & Protest Rights | 953 |
| 5 | Carbon Emissions & Net Zero | 840 |
| 6 | Fight for Freedom, Peaceful & Just World | 812 |
| 7 | Flood | 760 |
| 8 | Nature & Sustainable Future | 760 |
| 9 | Join Fridays for Future Strike | 663 |
| 10 | Climate Justice & Court | 622 |
| 11 | Climate Crisis Solutions | 613 |
| 12 | Heat | 561 |
| 13 | Covid19 | 539 |
| 14 | Friendly Reminder to Act Now | 495 |
| 15 | Environmental Crisis | 494 |
| 16 | Economic Growth | 479 |
| 17 | Climate, Gender & Racial Justice | 472 |
| 18 | Global Warming, Climate Breakdown & Extreme Weather | 443 |
| 19 | Activism Works | 433 |
| 20 | ISDS | 403 |
| 21 | Greenpeace | 379 |
| 22 | Africa & Energy | 371 |
| 23 | Renewable Energy | 369 |
| 24 | (Youth) Climate Activists | 342 |
| 25 | Coal Mine | 324 |
| 26 | Hope & Love | 303 |
| 27 | Extreme Weather Events | 277 |
| 28 | Rebellion & Resistance | 257 |
| 29 | 2021 Session of the UNFCCC Subsidiary Bodies | 221 |
| 30 | IPCC | 200 |
| 31 | Ice & Glacier Melting | 194 |
| 32 | Anxiety, Grief & Hope | 193 |
| 33 | Extinction Rebellion | 191 |
| 34 | Philippines & Typhoons | 180 |
| 35 | Vanuatu & Pacific Islands | 166 |
| 36 | Norway, Denmark, Oil & Coal | 160 |
| 37 | Citizens Assemblies | 153 |

Table 6: Identified Topics, Labels, and Frequencies from Second Topic Modeling

light on their priorities and methods of engagement.

### 3.3 Sentiment Classification

We tested the application of the model on our gold standard. Using the ClimateBERT sentiment model, we achieved an F1 score of 0.4333 (Precision = 0.6504, Recall = 0.3283). This result can be explained by the training data set of the ClimateBERT sentiment model, which consists of longer documents such as financial reports (Webersinke et al., 2021). We conclude that the application to social media posts is not possible without limitations. According to the results, the model should be fine tuned with social media data before it is applied.

| Author | Topic | Description | Frequency |
|---|---|---|---|
| CAN | 0 | COP, Loss and Damage & Finance | 2034 |
| CAN | 1 | Fossil Fuels | 437 |
| CAN | 29 | 2021 Session of the UNFCCC Subsidiary Bodies | 158 |
| CAN | 10 | Climate Justice & Court | 149 |
| CAN | 5 | Carbon Emissions & Net Zero | 148 |
| Extinction Rebellion | 1 | Fossil Fuels | 883 |
| Extinction Rebellion | 4 | Peaceful Protest & Protest Rights | 707 |
| Extinction Rebellion | 6 | Fight for Freedom, Peaceful & Just World | 447 |
| Extinction Rebellion | 7 | Flood | 417 |
| Extinction Rebellion | 0 | COP, Loss and Damage & Finance | 394 |
| Friends of the Earth | 0 | COP, Loss and Damage & Finance | 199 |
| Friends of the Earth | 5 | Carbon Emissions & Net Zero | 119 |
| Friends of the Earth | 1 | Fossil Fuels | 79 |
| Friends of the Earth | 10 | Climate Justice & Court | 64 |
| Friends of the Earth | 22 | Africa & Energy | 53 |
| Fridays for Future | 9 | Join Fridays for Future Strike | 471 |
| Fridays for Future | 1 | Fossil Fuels | 100 |
| Fridays for Future | 24 | (Youth) Climate Activists | 80 |
| Fridays for Future | 14 | Friendly Reminder to Act Now | 74 |
| Fridays for Future | 4 | Peaceful Protest & Protest Rights | 65 |
| Greenpeace | 1 | Fossil Fuels | 1132 |
| Greenpeace | 3 | Climate Emergency & Denial | 477 |
| Greenpeace | 8 | Nature & Sustainable Future | 320 |
| Greenpeace | 0 | COP, Loss and Damage & Finance | 318 |
| Greenpeace | 21 | Greenpeace | 308 |

Table 7: Distribution of Topics by Author After Second Topic Modeling Analysis

### 3.4 Emotion Classification

We tested the application of the emotion model *bhadresh-savani/bert-base-uncased-emotion* on our gold standard. Based on the model's prediction, continuous emotion outputs were generated for each document, such as 0.45959. In two separate analyses, we applied thresholds of 0.2 and 0.5 to these outputs to compare them to our gold standard. Since we categorized emotions as either present (1) or absent (0), regardless of their intensity, values between 0.2 and 1, or 0.5 and 1, were considered indicative of the presence of an emotion. These two thresholds were used to examine whether the choice of threshold influenced the model's performance. The performance metrics for both thresholds are presented in the corresponding Tables 8 and 9. The choice of cutoff only had a minimal effect on performance, with the 0.5 cutoff showing a slight improvement. F1 scores ranged from 0.0270 to 0.1847 for the 0.2 cutoff and from 0.0496 to 0.2302 for the 0.5 cutoff. However, we conclude that the overall performance remained inadequate and unsuitable for practical use in analyzing environmental and climate-related texts. Given the obtained F1 scores, fine-tuning the model for climate and environmental contexts may prove challenging. Therefore, the use of alternative or more advanced models, such as Large Language Models, may be necessary to improve performance.

| Emotion | Precision | Recall | F1 Score |
|---|---|---|---|
| Joy | 0.0278 | 0.9048 | 0.0540 |
| Anger | 0.1081 | 0.6337 | 0.1847 |
| Fear | 0.0142 | 0.3000 | 0.0270 |
| Sadness | 0.0174 | 0.6250 | 0.0339 |

Table 8: Model Performance with 0.2 Cutoff

## 4 Limitations

This study has several limitations that should be considered when interpreting the results. First, only 1,399 tweets were used as the gold standard for model evaluation, which may limit the generaliz-

| Emotion | Precision | Recall | F1 Score |
|---|---|---|---|
| Joy | 0.0335 | 0.9048 | 0.0645 |
| Anger | 0.1422 | 0.6040 | 0.2302 |
| Fear | 0.0270 | 0.3000 | 0.0496 |
| Sadness | 0.0296 | 0.6250 | 0.0565 |

Table 9: Model Performance with 0.5 Cutoff

ability of our findings. These tweets were annotated by three annotators, with the final dataset created using majority voting. While this approach is standard, the IAA was only slight to moderate (ranging from 0.1825 to 0.4708), which complicates the evaluation of the models. Disagreements among annotators, especially for emotions like anger (IAA = 0.2472) and fear (IAA = 0.0379), are not unusual but highlight the subjective nature of the task. Annotators may interpret climate- and environment-related texts in different ways, given their complexity and the challenge of reading such texts neutrally. We question whether an unbiased annotation of such texts is possible, since the various climate and environmental issues addressed in the documents are difficult to read neutrally. We attribute some of the disagreement in sentiment to the possibility of multiple sentiment framings within a single post. For example, a tweet may present both a risk and an opportunity framing, requiring annotators to choose a single sentiment, which can lead to varied interpretations. This additional room for interpretation may explain some of the discrepancies in sentiment. We would like to emphasize that our previous annotations have primarily shown that texts related to climate and environmental issues seem to be difficult to interpret and evaluate, which crystallizes them as a very challenging area in NLP where there still seems to be a need for research, annotation, and training.

Second, the highly imbalanced class distributions in the dataset pose a significant challenge for evaluating model performance. The presence of floor effects further complicates the accuracy of contemporary sentiment and emotion models, making it difficult to assess their full potential.

Third, our analysis was limited to tweets, which may not fully capture the broader communication patterns of EMOs across different social media platforms. Additionally, this study did not account for the impact of Elon Musk's acquisition of Twitter in October 2022, which led to significant changes to the platform's structure and policies. These changes could have influenced the communication strategies of EMOs in ways that our dataset does not reflect, thus limiting the scope of our findings. Lastly, the use of topic modeling tools, such as BERTopic, also has limitations. While helpful in organizing large datasets, such tools are not infallible. They may fail to identify certain topics or assign topics inaccurately, which could impact the interpretation of the results.

## 5 Conclusion and Future Work

Despite these limitations, our findings provide valuable insights into the strategic communication of EMOs and the challenges associated with annotating data as well as applying current NLP models to climate- and environment-related group discourse. Our study underscores the need for handling disagreement in data annotation, domain-specific datasets, and models to address the unique challenges posed by analyzing climate- and environment-related content. Our preliminary evaluation of the annotation process serves as a crucial step towards refining and enhancing its robustness. It is imperative that future efforts dedicate greater attention to the resolution of disagreement in climate- and environment-related text annotations. Overall, future research should prioritize the development of robust domain-specific datasets and the fine-tuning of models to improve accuracy and interpretability. Additionally, exploring other psychological constructs, such as efficacy beliefs, alongside traditional sentiment and emotion analysis, should provide a more comprehensive understanding of online climate and environment communication. Expanding beyond the current focus on sentiment, emotion, and hate speech to include such constructs can yield a richer and more nuanced perspective on EMO strategies and their impact on public discourse.

## References


Robert Ackland and Mathieu O'Neil. 2011. Online collective identity: The case of the environmental movement. *Social Networks*, 33(3):177–190.

Biraj Dahal, Sathish AP Kumar, and Zhenlong Li. 2019. Topic modeling and sentiment analysis of global climate change tweets. *Social network analysis and mining*, 9:1–20.

May El Barachi, Manar AlKhatib, Sujith Mathew, and Farhad Oroumchian. 2021. A novel sentiment analysis framework for monitoring the evolving public opinion in real-time: Case study on climate change. *Journal of Cleaner Production*, 312:127820.

Joseph L Fleiss. 1971. Measuring nominal scale agreement among many raters. *Psychological bulletin*, 76(5):378.

Maarten Grootendorst. 2020. Bertopic: A topic modeling technique using bert embeddings. Accessed: 2024-12-30.

Maarten Grootendorst. 2022. Bertopic: Neural topic modeling with a class-based tf-idf procedure. *arXiv preprint arXiv:2203.05794*.

Robyn Gulliver, Kelly S Fielding, and Winnifred R Louis. 2021. Assessing the mobilization potential of environmental advocacy communication. *Journal of Environmental Psychology*, 74:101563.

Hamed Jelodar, Yongli Wang, Chi Yuan, Xia Feng, Xiahui Jiang, Yanchao Li, and Liang Zhao. 2019. Latent dirichlet allocation (lda) and topic modeling: models, applications, a survey. *Multimedia tools and applications*, 78:15169–15211.

Fabian Pedregosa, Gaël Varoquaux, Alexandre Gramfort, Vincent Michel, Bertrand Thirion, Olivier Grisel, Mathieu Blondel, Peter Prettenhofer, Ron Weiss, Vincent Dubourg, et al. 2011. Scikit-learn: Machine learning in python. *the Journal of machine Learning research*, 12:2825–2830.

Federico Alberto Pozzi, Elisabetta Fersini, Enza Messina, and Bing Liu. 2016. *Sentiment analysis in social networks*. Morgan Kaufmann.

Ed Qian. 2021. Twitter climate change sentiment dataset. Accessed: 2024-12-30.

Bhadresh Savani. 2020. Bert-base-uncased emotion. Accessed: 2024-12-30.

Shuvam Shiwakoti, Surendrabikram Thapa, Kritesh Rauniyar, Akshyat Shah, Aashish Bhandari, and Usman Naseem. 2024. Analyzing the dynamics of climate change discourse on twitter: A new annotated corpus and multi-aspect classification. In *Proceedings of the 2024 Joint International Conference on Computational Linguistics, Language Resources and Evaluation (LREC-COLING 2024)*, pages 984–994.

The pandas development team. 2020. pandas-dev/pandas: Pandas. *Zenodo*.

Alexandra N Uma, Tommaso Fornaciari, Dirk Hovy, Silviu Paun, Barbara Plank, and Massimo Poesio. 2021. Learning from disagreement: A survey. *Journal of Artificial Intelligence Research*, 72:1385–1470.

Mayur Wankhade, Annavarapu Chandra Sekhara Rao, and Chaitanya Kulkarni. 2022. A survey on sentiment analysis methods, applications, and challenges. *Artificial Intelligence Review*, 55(7):5731–5780.

Nicolas Webersinke, Mathias Kraus, Julia Anna Bingler, and Markus Leippold. 2021. Climatebert: A pretrained language model for climate-related text. *arXiv preprint arXiv:2110.12010*.

# No AI on a Dead Planet: Sentiment and Emotion Analysis Across Reddit Communities on AI and the Environment

**Arianna Longo***
Università di Torino / Turin, Italy
arianna.longo401@edu.unito.it

**Alessandro Y. Longo***
CNRS / Paris, France
REINCANTAMENTO[†]
alessandrolongo1@protonmail.com

## Abstract

This paper investigates how different online communities perceive and discuss the environmental impact of AI through sentiment analysis and emotion detection. We analyze Reddit discussion from r/artificial and r/climatechange, using pre-trained models fine-tuned on social media data. Our analysis reveals distinct patterns in how these communities engage with AI's environmental implications: the AI community demonstrates a shift from predominantly neutral and positive sentiment in posts to more balanced perspectives in comments, while the climate community maintains a more critical stance throughout discussions. The findings contribute to our understanding of how different communities conceptualize and respond to the environmental challenges of AI development.

## 1 Introduction

The debate on the impact of Artificial Intelligence (AI) is multifaceted, encompassing different areas of society and, more broadly, environmental sustainability (Crawford, 2021). One of the most pressing issues is the ecological footprint of AI systems, primarily due to their intensive computational requirements and consequent energy consumption of increasingly larger models (OECD, 2022; Wang et al., 2024). The extensive training of these models leads to substantial $CO_2$ emissions and water consumption, with projections suggesting Large Language Models (LLMs) could potentially reach over 30% of the world's total energy consumption by 2030 (Bolón-Canedo et al., 2024). The environmental cost extends beyond training to daily usage. The public release of ChatGPT, powered by GPT-3, sparked widespread adoption of AI assistants, leading to a dramatic increase in their collective energy usage. For instance, each ChatGPT query during inference consumes energy equivalent to running a 5-watt LED bulb for 1 hour and 20 minutes. Furthermore, the carbon footprint of these systems is intertwined with broader issues of extractivism, both material and immaterial. This includes the resource mining, energy consumption, and product obsolescence cycles required to manufacture the hardware and infrastructure supporting AI (Brevini, 2023). These are all issues that must be addressed within the NLP scholar community, as our research work relies more heavily on LLMs.

Several efforts have been devoted to understanding and reducing the environmental impact of AI techniques (Verdecchia et al., 2023). For example, researchers have developed a carbon emission tracking tool for models training process (Budennyy et al., 2022), a lighter version of existing models (Lan et al., 2019) and they created optimized techniques for a better efficiency-consumption trade off like the Gaussian Process-based Bayesian Optimization (Candelieri et al., 2021).

Despite growing evidence of AI's environmental impact, studies have shown that these technologies are often perceived as more sustainable, or less environmentally harmful than they actually are (Yeh et al., 2021).

Building on previous research (Bosco et al., 2023), this paper investigates the online discourse surrounding AI's environmental impact through sentiment analysis (SA) and emotion detection. In particular, we focus on two interest-based communities on Reddit, the forum social network: the subreddits r/artificial and r/climatechange. By examining and comparing these two distinct threads of online conversation, this paper aims to shed

*The authors contributed equally to this work.
[†]https://reincantamentox.substack.com



*Proceedings of the 1st Workshop on Ecology, Environment, and Natural Language Processing (NLP4Ecology2025)*, pages 77–83
March 2, 2025 

light on the emotional gradient of online conversations on the matter.

The paper is structured as follows. Section 2 reviews existing studies on SA in climate change-related discourse; Section 3 presents our methodology and collected data, describes the models that were used to perform the analysis; Section 4 discusses the results of the analysis; and Section 5 outlines conclusions and future research directions.

## 2 Related Work

In recent years, the application of Natural Language Processing (NLP) and Sentiment Analysis (SA) to analyze the discourse on climate change (CC) and related environmental matters increased.

NLP methodologies were adopted for stance classification (Mohammad et al., 2016; Luo et al., 2020), entity recognition in environmental texts (Abdelmageed et al., 2022), bias detection in corporate communication (Moodaley and Telukdarie, 2023) and sustainability reports (Ning et al., 2021). Moreover, a growing body of research has examined bias in environmental discourse. Scholars like Leach et al. (Leach et al., 2021) and Takeshita et al.(Takeshita et al., 2022) have explored anthropocentric and speciesist biases in language, and developed methods to address these issues. The framing of environmental topics in media and political arenas has also been studied, investigating how these frames shape public perceptions and influence policymaking (Dehler-Holland et al., 2021).

Sentiment analysis in particular was adopted to analyze tweets corpora to capture the broad public feeling on climate change (Dahal et al., 2019; Mi and Zhan, 2023). Similarly, existing work focuses on public opinion or emotional responses towards particular ecological events or phenomena (Duong et al., 2023; Roberts et al., 2018).

Despite the growing environmental implications of AI systems, the field of Natural Language Processing has insufficiently explored how different communities perceive and discuss these ecological impacts. This study addresses this research gap through a comparative analysis of sentiment and emotional patterns in discussions across AI-focused and climate-focused online communities, offering insights into how distinct epistemic communities conceptualize the environmental implications of AI technologies.

## 3 Methodology

### 3.1 Data Collection and Preprocessing

We collected textual data from two Reddit subreddits: r/artificial and r/climatechange. These subreddits were chosen for their high levels of activity and engagement, with r/artificial hosting over 900k members and frequent discussions. The inclusion of r/climatechange was further supported by the alignment with prior research that identifies this subreddit as one of the five most significant climate communities on Reddit (Parsa et al., 2022). For each subreddit, we retrieved posts by searching for three predefined keywords: 'emissions', 'energy consumption', and 'climate change' for r/artificial; and 'artificial intelligence', 'AI', and 'machine learning' for r/climatechange. The selection of keywords was grounded in our preliminary analysis of the most frequently occurring technical terms in each subreddit when discussing the intersection of AI and environmental issues. Using the Reddit API via PRAW, the search was performed with top sorting method. Posts without any text content were then filtered out. For each remaining post, comments were recursively collected, including nested replies, ensuring a comprehensive dataset. The extracted data included post IDs, titles, bodies, and all associated comments with their metadata. The preprocessing phase involved concatenating post titles and bodies into a 'full_post' column. While links and URLs were removed, we preserved punctuation, emojis, and other textual features to maintain the original sentiment and tone. The resulting corpora are:

**AI Corpus**. 783 entries derived from discussion threads focused on environmental concerns in AI development, containing 47k tokens. Posts address directly environmental concerns in AI development, such as computational costs and energy consumption, averaging 338 words with 1,943 unique tokens. Comments primarily emerge from technical discussions, often focusing on potential solutions and technological optimizations. They average 50 words and contain 5,361 unique tokens.

**Climate Corpus**. 870 entries with a total of 66k tokens. Posts average 187 words with 1,130 unique tokens, while comments average 71 words with 6,439 unique tokens. Discussions center on technological interventions in climate change, where AI emerges mostly as a subtopic.

### 3.2 Sentiment and Emotion Analysis

For the sentiment and emotion analysis of the Reddit data, we selected two pre-trained models based on their relevance to the domain and the social media context. For sentiment classification, we used cardiffnlp/twitter-roberta-base-sentiment-latest (Barbieri et al., 2020), a RoBERTa variant fine-tuned on Twitter data. Despite being trained on Twitter, the model is suitable for Reddit analysis due to similar social media linguistic patterns. For emotion detection, we used monologg/bert-base-cased-goemotions-original (Park, 2020), which was fine-tuned on the GoEmotions dataset: a dataset of 58,000 Reddit comments. This model distinguishes between 28 distinct emotions, providing granular emotional analysis specifically calibrated for Reddit's conversational style. This expanded range of emotions allows for a more detailed understanding of emotional nuances in the discussions, which is crucial for our specific analysis.

## 4 Results and Discussion

The sentiment and emotion analysis reveals distinctive discourse patterns across two specialized communities under analysis. The analysis shows robust reliability with average confidence scores of 71% for sentiment classification and 85% for emotion classification across both datasets, with particularly high confidence in detecting the most frequent emotions.

The findings are presented first through an individual corpus analysis and then through a comparative analysis supported by representative examples that highlights divergences in framing, response patterns, and community engagement dynamics. Table 1 summarizes the sentiment distribution for posts and comments in both corpora.

### 4.1 Results on the AI corpus

Posts in r/artificial demonstrate a predominantly neutral outlook (50%) when discussing AI's environmental impact, with positive sentiments following (35%) and negative sentiment representing a minority (15%).

The community frames AI as a potential solution to environmental challenges, rather than emphasizing its role as a contributor to climate change, reflecting a characteristic techno-optimistic perspective within the AI community and the broader tech industry. In short, the dominating opinion seems to be that automatic technology like AI is a key to tackle and solve CC (Danaher, 2022).

In the comments neutral responses predominate (51.7%), followed by negative (29%) and positive (19.3%) sentiments.

Emotionally (Table 2), posts exhibit high neutrality (50%), followed by confusion (15%) and optimism (15%), realization (10%) and a small presence of approval (5%) and admiration (5%). The emotional landscape in comments shows a more diverse spectrum with a strong presence of neutral expressions (45.7%), followed by a mix of positive emotions including approval (9.1%), curiosity (7.0%), and admiration (5.1%). Notably, even when criticism appears in comments, it manifests as measured skepticism rather than hostility, with annoyance (3.3%) and disapproval (2.9%) being the most frequent negative responses. This distribution suggests that while the community engages critically with AI's environmental impact, it maintains a predominantly analytical rather than emotional discourse.

### 4.2 Results on the Climate corpus

Posts in the Climate corpus demonstrate a markedly cautious perspective, with neutral sentiments strongly predominating (81.3%), followed by negative sentiments (12.5%), while positive sentiments represent a smaller fraction (6.3%). This distribution suggests how the climate change community approaches AI developments with reservation and skepticism. The sentiment distribution in the comments section shows an even more critical stance, where negative responses become the majority (45.5%), closely followed by neutral perspectives (43%), while positive sentiments remain minimal (11.5%). The community discussions tend to emphasize concerns about AI's role in environmental issues, potentially focusing on its energy consumption and environmental costs rather than its solutions-oriented potential.

The emotion detection analysis (Table 3) of posts reveals an interesting contrast: while posts express curiosity (31.3%), they also show confusion (12.6%) and present a small percentage of fear (6.3%), an emotion that did not appear at all in the first corpus. This emotional spectrum suggests that while there's recognition of AI's potential capabilities in doing good in the fight against CC, there's also uncertainty and apprehension about its

| Sentiment | AI Posts | AI Comments | Climate Posts | Climate Comments |
|---|---|---|---|---|
| Positive | 35% | 19.3% | 6.3% | 11.5% |
| Neutral | 50% | 51.7% | 81.3% | 43% |
| Negative | 15% | 29% | 12.5% | 45.5% |

Table 1: Sentiment distribution in the AI and Climate corpora (posts and comments)

| Emotion | Posts | Comments |
|---|---|---|
| Neutral | 50% | 45.7% |
| Confusion | 15% | 4.5% |
| Optimism | 15% | 3.8% |
| Realization | 10% | 3.1% |
| Approval | 5% | 9.1% |
| Admiration | 5% | 5.1% |
| Curiosity | - | 7.0% |
| Amusement | - | 4.1% |
| Annoyance | - | 3.3% |

Table 2: Most frequent emotions in AI corpus (>3%)

| Emotion | Posts | Comments |
|---|---|---|
| Neutral | 37.5% | 44.3% |
| Curiosity | 31.3% | 7.9% |
| Confusion | 12.6% | 3.6% |
| Admiration | 6.3% | 5.5% |
| Fear | 6.3% | - |
| Gratitude | 6.3% | - |
| Approval | - | 8.0% |
| Optimism | - | 5.1% |
| Disapproval | - | 4.9% |
| Realization | - | 3.9% |
| Annoyance | - | 3.8% |

Table 3: Most frequent emotions in Climate corpus (>3%)

environmental implications.

Comments maintain this complexity, with similar prevalence of neutral expressions (44.3%), but a different emotional spectrum. While approval (8.0%) and curiosity (7.9%) remain high, there's a stronger presence of critical emotions, with disapproval (4.9%) and annoyance (3.8%) appearing more frequently than in the AI corpus. This emotional pattern, combined with higher levels of realization (3.9%) and confusion (3.6%), suggests a more questioning approach to AI's role in environmental issues.

### 4.3 Qualitative Insights and Comparative Analysis

To complement the quantitative findings presented earlier, we draw on an extensive qualitative content analysis conducted on our dataset, examining hundreds comments from both communities to identify recurring patterns and themes. While the examples discussed below illustrate key dynamics, our broader observations are derived from a systematic review of full posts and associated comment threads. Through this analysis, we identified distinct patterns in how each community frames and react to environmental concerns.

The selected examples illustrate these broader patterns:

**Example 1**. The post "*AI already uses as much energy as a small country. It's only the beginning*" presents the International Energy Agency's prediction about data centers' future energy usage, which could become equivalent to Japan's consumption by 2026. Despite the worrying prediction suggested by the title, the body of the post adopts a report-like, fact-based narrative that aligns the AI community's tendency toward neutral, technical discourse. This consistency in style likely explains why the model classified it as neutral. The comments section displays a characteristic tendency toward constructive and solution-oriented approach. For instance, one user asks how the energy cost of AI compares to that of gaming, expressing curiosity. Subsequent comments frequently pivot toward potential solutions, discussing fusion energy and improved GPU efficiency, reflecting the community's tendency to view environmental challenges as technical problems awaiting solutions rather than insurmountable obstacles.

**Example 2**. An illustrative example of the Climate community dynamics can be found in this post: "*AI for Ocean Cleanup: A Better Use of Robotics? Found this good question on another platform. 'Can we get some AI to pick plastic out of the ocean or do all robots need to be screenwriters?' instead of replacing all other human* *job titles. Why not use AI for the environment and betterment, aside from using it for profit?"*. It was classified with neutral sentiment and confusion emotion, probably because it poses a series of consecutive questions. However, the comments reveal a more complex spectrum of emotions. Some responses show cautious optimism, classified by the model as desire ('I would really like to see AI be used like this'), while others, negative and classified as showing disapproval and disappointment, express technical skepticism ('Ai is a significant contributing factor to carbon production. It's not environmentally friendly at all.') or point to broader systemic issues ('There's not enough clean energy. It's a problem. Data centers also use a large amount of fresh water. I'm so sick of hypothetical answers from technocrats').

**Example 3**. Another post, titled "*Big Tech's thirst for AI dominance may bring literal thirst for everyone else*" highlights critical concerns about data centers' water consumption. The post was classified as neutral and realization, but it triggers diverse emotional responses in the comments: from existential concerns classified as negative with sadness ('Bruh we are all going to die slow and painful deaths'), to the curiosity that emerges in questions about cooling systems' efficiency.

**Example 4**. The post titled "*AI and Climate Change - Our best hope*" promotes a podcast featuring a scientist discussing machine learning's potential for climate change mitigation. The post, classified with positive sentiment and optimism emotion, exemplifies the techno-optimistic framing often found in the AI community. The comments section reveals overwhelmingly positive reactions, with multiple expressions of gratitude and admiration ('Awesome stuff - really banking on AI being what leads us away from our worlds current political and climate situation'). However, this optimism is occasionally tempered by critical perspectives, as seen in comments like 'Yeah, that's humans mentality - keep on messing up', classified with negative sentiment.

These examples showcase the different approaches detected for the two different communities. Within the AI subreddit, environmental predictions are often addressed through constructive and techno-optimistic perspectives, demonstrating a tendency to overlook the environmental risks of unrestricted AI system growth. On the other hand, the climate community is predominantly wary of the framing that sees AI as a valid tool in the fight against CC.

## 5 Conclusion and Future Work

This study presents an analysis of sentiment and emotion patterns in discussions about AI's environmental impact across two Reddit communities. The AI community shows a neutral-positive sentiment, while the climate community is more neutral in posts but varies between negative and neutral in comments. Emotionally, AI discussions feature approval, curiosity and admiration; the climate corpus reveals a slightly broader emotional spectrum, with higher frequencies of critical emotions like disapproval and annoyance. Qualitative analysis reveals different problem-framing approaches. The AI community tends to approach environmental concerns as technical challenges amenable to optimization, often transforming warnings about energy consumption into discussions of efficiency improvements. The climate community's responses indicate attention to systemic environmental impacts, with a marked skepticism toward technological solutions.

Future work will address current limitations of this study through the development of a high-quality, manually annotated dataset focused on the topic of our interest. The creation of a gold standard dataset will enable proper evaluation of different models' performances on our specific domain. To this end, we will develop annotation guidelines, conduct inter-annotator agreement studies, and create a corpus capturing the language patterns that are present in discussions about AI's environmental impact. Such a resource would not only allow for more reliable model evaluation but could also serve as training data for fine-tuning models specifically for this domain. Expanding the analysis to include more diverse online communities could also enrich the findings and reveal additional patterns.

Finally, the differences between AI and climate subreddits highlight the need to foster connections and encourage collaboration between commmunities. Future research could create a more productive dialogue, perhaps through development of shared tools or frameworks that combine both approaches to assess and tackle AI's environmental impact.

## References


N. Abdelmageed, F. Löffler, L. Feddoul, A. Algergawy, S. Samuel, J. Gaikwad, A. Kazem, and B. König-Ries. 2022. Biodivnere: Gold standard corpora for named entity recognition and relation extraction in the biodiversity domain. *Biodiversity Data Journal*, 10:e89481.

Francesco Barbieri, Jose Camacho-Collados, Luis Espinosa Anke, and Leonardo Neves. 2020. TweetEval: Unified benchmark and comparative evaluation for tweet classification. In *Findings of the Association for Computational Linguistics: EMNLP 2020*, pages 1644–1650, Online. Association for Computational Linguistics.

Verónica Bolón-Canedo, Laura Morán-Fernández, Brais Cancela, and Amparo Alonso-Betanzos. 2024. A review of green artificial intelligence: Towards a more sustainable future. *Neurocomputing*, 599:128096.

Cristina Bosco, Muhammad Okky Ibrohim, Valerio Basile, and Indra Budi. 2023. How green is sentiment analysis? environmental topics in corpora at the university of turin. In *Proceedings of the 9th Italian Conference on Computational Linguistics (CLiC-it 2023)*, volume 3596, pages 1–7, Ca' Foscari University, Italy. CEUR-WS.

Benedetta Brevini. 2023. *Artificial intelligence, artificial solutions: placing the climate emergency at the center of AI developments*, pages 23–34. Routledge, New York, NY.

S. A. Budennyy, V. D. Lazarev, N. N. Zakharenko, A. N. Korovin, O. Plosskaya, D. V. Dimitrov, V. Akhripkin, I. Pavlov, I. V. Oseledets, and I. S. Barsola. 2022. Eco2ai: Carbon emissions tracking of machine learning models as the first step towards sustainable ai. *Doklady Mathematics*, 106:S118–S128.

A. Candelieri, R. Perego, and F. Archetti. 2021. Green machine learning via augmented gaussian processes and multi-information source optimization. *Soft Computing*, 25:12591–12603.

Kate Crawford. 2021. *Atlas of AI*. Yale University Press.

Biraj Dahal, Sathish Alampalayam Kumar, and Zhenlong Li. 2019. Topic modeling and sentiment analysis of global climate change tweets. *Social Network Analysis and Mining*, 9. N. pag.

J. Danaher. 2022. Techno-optimism: an analysis, an evaluation and a modest defence. *Philosophy & Technology*, 35:54.

Joris Dehler-Holland, Kira Schumacher, and Wolf Fichtner. 2021. Topic modeling uncovers shifts in media framing of the german renewable energy act. *Patterns*, 2(1).

Cuc Duong, Vethavikashini Chithrra, Amos Chungwon Lee Raghuram, Rui Mao, Gianmarco Mengaldo, and E. Cambria. 2023. Neurosymbolic ai for mining public opinions about wildfires. *Cogn. Comput.*, 16:1531–1553.

Z. Lan, M. Chen, S. Goodman, K. Gimpel, P. Sharma, and R. Soricut. 2019. Albert: A lite bert for self-supervised learning of language representations. *arXiv preprint*, arXiv:1909.11942.

L.L. Leach, N.J. Hanovice, S.M. George, A.E. Gabriel, and J.M. Gross. 2021. The immune response is a critical regulator of zebrafish retinal pigment epithelium regeneration. *Proceedings of the National Academy of Sciences of the United States of America*, 118(21).

Yiwei Luo, Dallas Card, and Dan Jurafsky. 2020. Desmog: Detecting stance in media on global warming. *Findings*.

Zhewei Mi and Hongwei Zhan. 2023. Text mining attitudes towards climate change: Emotion and sentiment analysis of the twitter corpus. *Weather, Climate, and Society*. N. pag.

Saif M. Mohammad, Svetlana Kiritchenko, Parinaz Sobhani, Xiao-Dan Zhu, and Colin Cherry. 2016. Semeval-2016 task 6: Detecting stance in tweets. In *International Workshop on Semantic Evaluation*.

Wayne Moodaley and Arnesh Telukdarie. 2023. Greenwashing, sustainability reporting, and artificial intelligence: A systematic literature review. *Sustainability*, 15(2):1481.

X. Ning, D. Yim, and J. Khuntia. 2021. Online sustainability reporting and firm performance: Lessons learned from text mining. *Sustainability*, 13:1069.

OECD. 2022. Measuring the environmental impacts of artificial intelligence compute and applications: The ai footprint. *OECD Digital Economy Papers*.

Jangwon Park. 2020. bert-base-cased-goemotions-original. `https://huggingface.co/monologg/bert-base-cased-goemotions-original`. Accessed: 2024-12.

Mohammad Parsa, Haoqi Shi, Yihao Xu, Aaron Yim, Yaolun Yin, and Lukasz Golab. 2022. Analyzing climate change discussions on reddit. In *The 2022 International Conference on Computational Science and Computational Intelligence*.

Helen Roberts, Bernd Resch, Jonathan Sadler, Lee Chapman, Andreas Petutschnig, and Stefan Zimmer. 2018. Investigating the emotional responses of individuals to urban green space using twitter data: A critical comparison of three different methods of sentiment analysis. *Urban Planning*, 3:21.

Masashi Takeshita, Rafal Rzepka, and Kenji Araki. 2022. Speciesist language and nonhuman animal bias in english masked language models. *Information Processing &; Management*, 59(5):103050.

Roberto Verdecchia, June Sallou, and Luis Cruz. 2023. A systematic review of green ai.

Qiang Wang, Yuanfan Li, and Rongrong Li. 2024. Ecological footprints, carbon emissions, and energy transitions: the impact of artificial intelligence (ai). *Humanities and Social Sciences Communications*, 11:1043.

Shin-Cheng Yeh, Ai-Wei Wu, Hui-Ching Yu, Homer C. Wu, Yi-Ping Kuo, and Pei-Xuan Chen. 2021. Public perception of artificial intelligence and its connections to the sustainable development goals. *Sustainability*, 13(16):9165.

# Towards Addressing Anthropocentric Bias in Large Language Models

**Francesca Grasso, Stefano Locci, Luigi Di Caro**
Department of Computer Science, University of Turin
Corso Svizzera 185, 10149 - Turin, Italy
{fr.grasso, stefano.locci, luigi.dicaro}@unito.it

## Abstract

The widespread use of Large Language Models (LLMs), particularly among non-expert users, has raised ethical concerns about the propagation of harmful biases. While much research has addressed social biases, few works, if any, have examined *anthropocentric bias* in Natural Language Processing (NLP) technology. Anthropocentric language prioritizes human value, framing non-human animals, living entities, and natural elements solely by their utility to humans; a perspective that contributes to the ecological crisis. In this paper, we evaluate anthropocentric bias in OpenAI's GPT-4o across various target entities, including sentient beings, non-sentient entities, and natural elements. Using prompts eliciting neutral, anthropocentric, and ecocentric perspectives, we analyze the model's outputs and introduce a manually curated glossary of 424 anthropocentric terms as a resource for future ecocritical research. Our findings reveal a strong anthropocentric bias in the model's responses, underscoring the need to address human-centered language use in AI-generated text to promote ecological well-being.

## 1 Introduction

The rapid propagation of Large Language Models (LLMs) among both expert and non-expert users has raised pressing questions and concerns regarding their safety and ethical implications (Liang et al., 2021). Alongside the growing hype surrounding these systems, an increasing body of work has begun to address the biases they can generate and/or propagate through language use (Blodgett et al., 2020; Cheng et al., 2023). The state-of-the-art shows several studies aimed at identifying, assessing, and ultimately limiting the propagation of social biases—such as gender, political, and racial biases—in LLMs. However, while much of this attention has focused on phenomena harmful to humans, very few efforts have examined an equally pressing issue: *anthropocentric bias*. Anthropocentrism is a worldview that places humans at the center of all value considerations, and has been shown to be one of the main drivers behind our current ecological crisis (Lewis and Maslin, 2020). This view is encoded in language use, as seen in expressions like "ecosystem *services*" or "*fattening pig*", which underscore a human-centered framing of reality (Heuberger, 2017). By normalizing and reproducing language that frames non-human entities solely by their utility to humans, LLMs risk reinforcing harmful perspectives that undermine efforts to address urgent environmental challenges. Although the ever-growing popularity of LLMs has naturally led the NLP and AI communities to address ethical issues concerning harmful content in language generation, their role in reproducing such biases remains underexplored.

In this paper, we present a preliminary study and evaluation of anthropocentric bias in OpenAI's GPT-4o[1], one of the most widely used LLMs. We analyze the model's responses across four main topics: (effects of) climate change, non-human animals, living entities, and non-living entities. For each designed prompt, we created three versions: one explicitly aimed at eliciting an anthropocentric response, one aimed at eliciting an ecocentric[2] output, and one intended to be neutral. The ecocentric and anthropocentric

[1] https://openai.com/index/hello-gpt-4o/

[2] As an antonymic term of anthropocentrism, **ecocentrism** is a perspective that prioritizes ecological systems and the intrinsic value of all living and non-living entities.



*Proceedings of the 1st Workshop on Ecology, Environment, and Natural Language Processing (NLP4Ecology2025)*, pages 84–93
March 2, 2025 

prompts served as controls, allowing us to contextualize the anthropocentric bias in the neutral prompts by comparing it systematically against outputs explicitly directed to adopt specific perspectives. To ensure diversity and comprehensiveness, we formulated prompts in various formats, resulting in a total of 48 different prompts. To facilitate both qualitative and quantitative analysis, we extracted lists of lexical elements—noun phrases (NPs) and verbs—from the model's outputs. Based on these extractions, we manually curated a glossary of 424 terms associated with anthropocentric language, marking our second contribution, which can serve as a resource for future ecocritical studies. Using this glossary, we quantitatively assessed the prevalence of anthropocentric terms across the three output sets: neutral, anthropocentric, and ecocentric. Subsequently, we analyzed the frequency distribution of verbs, followed by a qualitative analysis of both NPs and verbs. Our results reveal a strong anthropocentric bias in GPT-4o's responses, such as defining animals primarily in terms of food production and framing non-living entities in terms of human leisure and exploitation. This analysis underscores the importance of addressing anthropocentric language use in AI-generated text to mitigate its potential ecological and ethical implications.

## 2 Anthropocentrism in Language Use

*Anthropocentrism* can be defined as "a form of human-centredness that subordinates everything in nature to human concerns" (Stibbe, 2012). This worldview, stemming from the ancient philosophical perspective typical of many Western cultures, sharply divides "nature" from "culture" (Latour, 2016; Descola, 2005). It implies that non-human entities, such as animals and other living and non-living entities, lack intrinsic value unless they serve human needs (Kopnina et al., 2018). A prominent manifestation of this perspective is *utilitarian anthropocentrism*, which is the most common form of human-centeredness in language (Jung, 2001). It manifests in many aspects of the relationship between humans and nature and seems so natural that it is rarely called into question (Fill, 2015). Utilitarian anthropocentrism, and its linguistic manifestations, equates nature (understood as the complexity of every non-human entity) with a resource for human use. For example, utilitarian linguistic practices name and categorize animals and their behaviors according to human requirements and standards. Based on domestication, animals are differentiated as *pets*, *livestock* or *farm animals*, and *wildlife* or *wild animals* (Trampe, 2017). 'Domestic animals' can be further subdivided into categories such as *laying hens*, *milk cows*, and *porkers*. Similarly, plants are categorized as *pot plants*, *bedding plants*, or *houseplants*. Even places are often named from a utilitarian-anthropocentric perspective, with examples including *skiing area* or *no-man's land* (Heuberger, 2017). This form of human-centered language use is reflected in many linguistic expressions, ranging from syntactic strategies (e.g., the use of passive constructions like "the pigs have been slaughtered" which obscures the agent of the action) to the lexicon, including both nouns and verbs. For example, fishes are often referred to as *"marine resources"* to *exploit*; chickens are *bred* specifically for *"egg production"*; and living ecosystems are reduced to *crops* to be *harvested*. Why is this problematic? Language that reduces non-human entities to mere means for human use and fails to recognize their intrinsic value entails numerous issues. Not only is such a notion debatable from an ethical point of view, but its environmental consequences are also pervasive. As many historians, philosophers, and anthropologists agree, the anthropocentric view of nature as a resource to exploit has led to the ecological crises we are currently facing, culminating in the Anthropocene—a proposed epoch in which human activity dominates Earth's environment and climate (Lewis and Maslin, 2020; White Jr, 1967). Beyond endangering the well-being of non-human animals and ecosystems, this form of bias ultimately threatens human welfare as well, given the interconnectedness of all living (and non-living) systems (Adami, 2013; Stibbe, 2015). As language encodes and shapes reality, the way we speak about and frame nature strongly influences our thinking and behavior. For this reason, critiquing language forms that contribute to ecological destruction and aiding the search for new forms of language that inspire people to protect the natural world is central (Stibbe, 2015).

## 3 Related Work

The investigation of ecologically disruptive language has primarily been conducted within the humanities, particularly in the field of ecolinguistics (Kuha, 2017; Alexander and Stibbe, 2014). Within the broader study of anthropocentrism in language use, Heuberger (2003) analyze monolingual English dictionaries to explore the lexicographic treatment of faunal terminology, while Heuberger (2007) provide an overview of anthropocentric and speciesist[3] usage in English at both lexical and discourse levels. Furthermore, Cook and Sealey (2017) examine the discursive representation of animals, highlighting how language frames them in human-centered ways.

In NLP research, much attention has been devoted to societal biases present in the training data of language models (Liang et al., 2021; Blodgett et al., 2020). For instance, significant efforts have focused on detecting and mitigating gender biases in both large language models and transformer-based architectures (Kotek et al., 2023; Cai et al., 2024; Vig et al., 2020). Similarly, other studies have addressed racial and religious biases (An et al., 2024; Nadeem et al., 2020; Torres et al., 2024), demonstrating how language models propagate stereotypes through professions and associations (Cheng et al., 2023). While these works provide valuable insights into societal biases, they are limited to human-centric concerns.

Speciesism in NLP has received some attention in recent years. For example, Leach et al. (2023) analyze word embedding models, showing that words denoting concern and value are more closely associated with humans than with other animals. Hagendorff et al. (2023) investigate speciesist content in AI applications, including both word embeddings and large language models in their analysis. Takeshita et al. (2022) focus on speciesist language and non-human animal bias in English masked language models. Most recently, Takeshita and Rzepka (2024) provide a systematic investigation of speciesism in NLP research, highlighting how models amplify anthropocentric perspectives on non-human animals. However, these studies are restricted to species-related biases and do not explore broader anthropocentric language involving both living and non-living entities.

[3]*Speciesism* is "the unjustified comparatively worse consideration or treatment of those who do not belong to a certain species" (Horta and Albersmeier, 2020).

## 4 Methodolology

### 4.1 Study Design and Scope

**Model selection** The aim of our study is to assess and evaluate the presence of anthropocentric language bias in the output of a large language model (LLM). We selected OpenAI's GPT-4o, as it is one of the most widely used models, particularly among non-expert users. Its widespread use increases the risk of perpetuating biases, making it a representative and relevant subject for this investigation.

**Study Scope and Target Entities** Unlike previous studies that primarily focused on speciesist biases, that is, particularly harmful language frames about animals, our study extends the analysis to include both living and non-living entities. To achieve this, we identified representative target entities that cover a broad spectrum of categories:

- *Non-human animals*: We included the generic target "animal" as well as representative examples from three subcategories: domestic (dogs, pigs, and horses), farm (chickens and cows), and wild animals (wolves and fishes).
- *Living entities*: Trees were selected as a representative example for this category.
- *Non-living entities*: Soil, mountains, rivers, and the sea were included to represent various natural inanimate entities.

We developed three perspective-based prompts to systematically compare outputs aligned with distinct viewpoints: (i) Neutral prompt: designed to elicit a general, unbiased response; (ii) Anthropocentric prompt: designed to encourage a human-centered perspective; (iii) Ecocentric prompt: designed to elicit a nature-centered perspective.

### 4.2 Exploratory Study

Before conducting the main study, we first assessed GPT-4o's reliability in adopting different perspectives (anthropocentric and ecocentric) based on specific prompting instructions, alongside a baseline condition with no specified viewpoint (neutral). This exploratory phase was also essential for refining the prompt format and model setup, given that small adjustments in prompt phrasing can significantly impact results (Deldjoo, 2023). We evaluated the model's output using three main criteria:

1. **Adherence to instructions**: Did the model follow the directive to present an anthropocentric or ecocentric standpoint?

2. **Internal consistency**: Were the arguments and statements consistently aligned with the chosen perspective throughout the response?

3. **Differentiation between viewpoints**: Did the model clearly contrast anthropocentric and ecocentric worldviews (e.g., a human-centered vs. ecosystem-centered rationale)?

This evaluation was divided into two tasks:
**Task 1: Testing conceptual awareness**: To verify the model's understanding of anthropocentric and ecocentric worldviews, we prompted it to provide definitions for each term. Examining the generated definitions allowed us to confirm whether the model demonstrated basic conceptual awareness of how these perspectives differ.
**Task 2: Testing viewpoint adherence**: We assessed whether GPT-4o could reliably adopt each perspective when explicitly prompted. This phase allowed us to monitor variations in the outputs and refine the prompts to ensure clarity and consistency.

By the end of this phase, we confirmed that GPT-4o could reliably assume the specified viewpoints and remain coherent in its responses. Based on these findings, we finalized the prompts and proceeded with the main study.

### 4.3 Main Study: Prompt Design and Experimental Setup

**Prompt Design and Formats** To ensure diversity and comprehensiveness, we formulated prompts in various formats, inspired by the current literature on speciesist bias analysis (e.g. Hagendorff et al. (2023)). Specifically, we included:
**Open-ended questions**: These allowed us to explore the model's general framing of entities, e.g., *"What are animals for?"*;
**Descriptive requests**: These prompts targeted more explicit and detailed responses, e.g., *"Provide a description of chickens"*;
**Sentence completions**: Designed to elicit structured, context-specific language, e.g., *"Complete this sentence: pigs are... "*.

The choice to use multiple formats was motivated by the need to capture different styles of language use, such as how the model frames entities in general terms, through detailed descriptions, or within specific contexts. While not all target entities were covered by every prompt format, this approach allowed us to balance breadth in the range of entities with variability in prompt design, ensuring a comprehensive exploration of anthropocentric bias without redundancy.

As anticipated, for each prompt, we designed three versions to systematically elicit different perspectives:

1. **Neutral baseline**: A version with no specific instructions regarding viewpoint, to elicit possibly problematic responses. e.g., *"What are animals for?"*.

2. **Anthropocentric viewpoint**: A version explicitly instructing the model to adopt a human-centered perspective, e.g., *"Adopt an anthropocentric viewpoint and answer the question while staying in strict accordance with the nature of this viewpoint. Answer the question: ...."*.

3. **Ecocentric viewpoint**: A version instructing the model to adopt a nature-centered perspective, e.g., *"Adopt an ecocentric viewpoint and answer the question while staying in strict accordance with the nature of this viewpoint. Answer the question: ...."*.

A complete overview of the prompts used is provided in Table 1.

**Experimental setup** The experiments were conducted on the Google Colab platform using the free CPU-based standard configuration, "Backend Google Compute Engine Python 3". To prompt the `gpt-4o` model, we utilized the OpenAI APIs[4]. During the generation process, we adopted a temperature scaling approach, varying temperature values between 0.0 and 0.9, and generating 10 responses per prompt. For each target entity, we aggregated these responses into a single JSON data file containing the 10 neutral, 10 anthropocentric, and 10 ecocentric responses. This approach allowed the model to explore both high-probability, deterministic predictions and low-probability, diverse responses. This

[4]`https://openai.com/index/openai-api/`

| Category | Prompts |
|---|---|
| **Open-ended Questions** | • *What are animals for?*<br>- Neutral: *What are animals for?*<br>-Anthropocentric: *Adopt an anthropocentric viewpoint and answer the questions while staying in strict accordance with the nature of this viewpoint. Answer the question: What are animals for?*<br>- Ecocentric: *Adopt an ecocentric viewpoint and answer the questions while staying in strict accordance with the nature of this viewpoint. Answer the question: What are animals for?*<br><br>•*What is the soil for?*<br>• *What are mountains for?* |
| **Questions on Climate Change** | - Neutral: *What are the negative effects of climate change?*<br>- Anthropocentric: *What are the negative effects of climate change on humans?*<br>- Ecocentric: *What are the negative effects of climate change on non-human entities?* |
| **Descriptive Requests**<br>For each descriptive request, the model was prompted from three perspectives as shown in the first example. | • *Provide a description of chickens*<br>• *Provide a description of cows*<br>•*Provide a description of wolves*<br>•*Provide a description of fishes*<br>•*Provide a description of trees*<br>•*Provide a description of soil*<br>•*Provide a description of mountains.* |
| **Sentence Completion**<br>For each sentence completion task, the model was prompted from three perspectives as shown in the first example. | • *Complete this sentence providing at least three sentences: pigs are...*<br>• *Complete this sentence providing at least three sentences: dogs are...*<br>•*Complete this sentence providing at least three sentences: horses are...*<br>• *Complete this sentence providing at least three sentences: rivers are...*<br>• *Complete this sentence providing at least three sentences: the sea is....* |

Table 1: Overview of the prompts used in the study. The example of "What are animals for?" illustrates how neutral, anthropocentric, and ecocentric prompts were applied. All other prompts followed this three-perspective structure.

variability facilitated the generation of complementary answers, enabling a richer analysis of linguistic patterns and biases while extending coverage across the selected entities.
All the generated outputs, the Python code and all the derived data representation are available in a GitHub repository[5].

## 5 Results and Discussion

To empirically evaluate the presence of anthropocentric bias in the model's output, we focused primarily on the "neutral" outputs. Ideally, if the model were unbiased, neutral outputs would not predominantly reflect a human-centered perspective. However, by comparing neutral outputs with anthropocentric and ecocentric responses, we gained insights into the underlying biases in the model. Since lexical items better reveal such biases, we concentrated our analysis on words, particularly noun phrases and verbs. Both quantitative and qualitative analyses were conducted to assess these findings.

### 5.1 Data preparation

To facilitate the analysis, we applied a series of preprocessing steps to the aggregated outputs using the SpaCy library[6]. We first removed stopwords and performed lemmatization: these steps reduced noise and ensured uniformity in the data,

[5]https://github.com/stefanolocci/Anthropocentric_Bias_LLMs

[6]https://spacy.io/

making it easier to compare lexical items across outputs. Moreover, a dependency parsing was conducted: this enabled us to identify specific subject-verb relationships, allowing for deeper syntactic analysis and the extraction of meaningful noun phrases (NPs) and verbs relevant to anthropocentric bias analysis. These steps prepared the data for subsequent analyses, including frequency comparisons, overlap evaluations, and syntactic pattern analyses.

### 5.2 Anthropocentric Glossary Construction

From the processed outputs, we extracted all noun phrases (NPs) and sorted them by frequency. Through manual inspection, we identified and categorized terms indicative of anthropocentric language, referencing prior work in ecolinguistics to inform our selection process (Fill, 2015; Stibbe, 2015, 2021). The glossary include, for example, terms like "dairy products", "fur", and "meat", frequently associated with animals and that highlight the utilitarian view of them. Moreover, words like "skiing", "leisure", and "recreational fishing" emerged from descriptions of mountains and rivers, highlighting the human-centered view of these entities. The glossary was lemmatized to ensure consistency and facilitate further analysis, leading to a total of 424 unique entries. The complete glossary is provided in the GitHub repository presented in footnote 5 and we release it for future eco-critical research.

### 5.3 Analysis of NPs

Leveraging the manually curated glossary, we quantitatively measured the presence of anthropocentric terms across the neutral, anthropocentric, and ecocentric outputs. This analysis focused on the frequency of glossary terms and their overlap across the three output categories. To do so, we assessed the presence of glossary terms in each set of responses, and counted their frequency to determine their prevalence. The results indicate a significant overlap of neutral outputs with the anthropocentric glossary (37.14%), suggesting that even the neutral prompts tend to reflect a human-centered perspective. This overlap is highest in the anthropocentric responses (45.22%), as expected, and lowest in the ecocentric outputs (29.70%); however, although low, this indicates that even if prompted to provide an ecocentric perspective, the model still shows anthropocentric language use. Table 2 summarizes the total and unique lemmas in each category, as well as their overlaps with the anthropocentric glossary.

Figure 1 provides a visual summary of the shared unique vocabulary within each set, illustrating the intersection of lemmas from the neutral, anthropocentric, and ecocentric outputs. The Venn diagrams highlight how much of the vocabulary is shared with the anthropocentric glossary and between categories, supporting numerical findings.

### 5.4 Analysis of Verbs

Leveraging the dependency parsing results, we conducted an investigation of the verbs associated with the targeted entities. Verbs are crucial in framing relationships between humans, nonhuman animals, and ecosystems, offering insights into anthropocentric or ecocentric perspectives. To identify relevant verbs, we extracted verbal heads directly linked to the entities under study (e.g., animals, soil, mountains). However, this approach proved insufficient, as not all verbs semantically related to the entities constituted their syntactic "head", due to the model's tendency to generate periphrastic constructions[7]. To address this limitation, we expanded our analysis by extracting all verbs using part-of-speech (POS) tagging and then manually verifying whether the verbs semantically referred to the target entities. This combined approach allowed us to compile a comprehensive list of relevant verbs, which were subsequently sorted by frequency for quantitative and qualitative analysis.

| Cat | L | L (U) | O | O (U) | % |
|---|---|---|---|---|---|
| E | 16221 | 1283 | 4819 | 194 | 29,70 |
| A | 12950 | 1305 | 5856 | 367 | 45,22 |
| N | 12784 | 1257 | 4749 | 263 | 37,14 |

Table 2: Lemma statistics across categories. **Cat**: Category (**E**: Ecocentric, **A**: Anthropocentric, **N**: Neutral). **L**: Total lemmas (with repetition), **L (U)**: Unique lemmas (no repetition), **O**: Overlap with the Anthropocentric Glossary (with repetition), **O (U)**: Overlap with the Anthropocentric Glossary (no repetition), **%**: Percentage overlap (with repetition).

Figure 2 illustrates the frequency distribution of selected verbs across neutral, anthropocentric, and ecocentric prompts, and they can be categorized

[7]For example, a frequent output pattern was "[entity] plays a crucial role in [verb]", where the direct syntactic relation is with "plays", rather than the semantically relevant verb. Copulas were often present too.

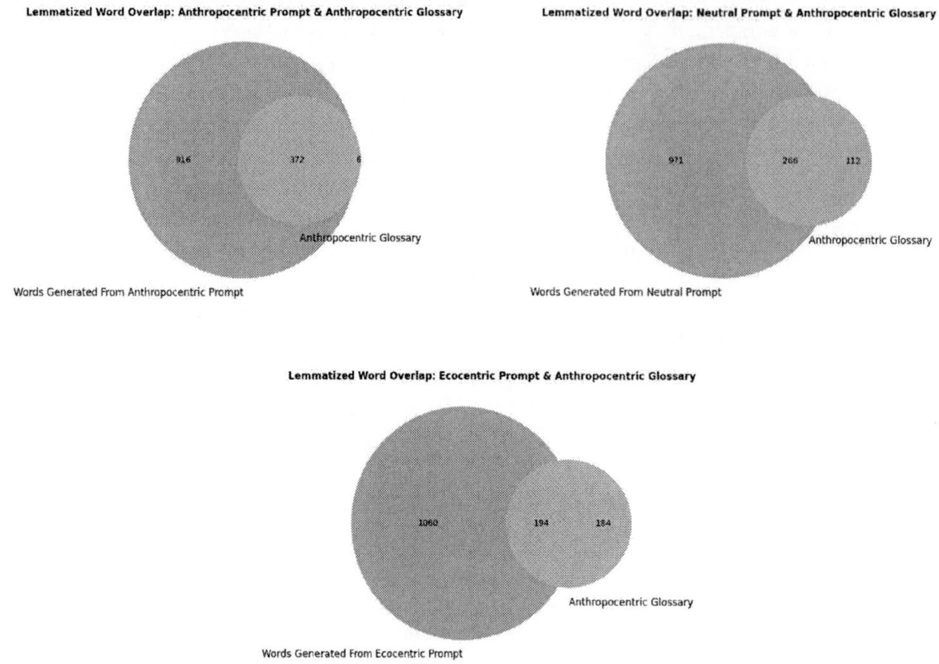


Figure 1: Venn diagrams showing the intersection of Anthropocentric terms within the three output categories. The red set represent of words generated from the three prompt categories (Anthropocentric, Neutral, and Ecocentric), the green set the Anthropocentric glossary words, and the yellow set contains the overlapping words between the two.

as ecologically positive or negative. Ecologically "positive" verbs, such as *protect*, *sustain*, *respect*, and *thrive*, dominate ecocentric outputs, aligning with nature-centered perspectives. In contrast, anthropocentric outputs emphasize "negative" verbs, such as *breed*, *domesticate*, and *serve*, reflecting human-centered control or exploitation of non-human entities. Neutral prompts display a mixed distribution of positive and negative verbs. While verbs like *protect* and *sustain* appear, their lower frequency compared to ecocentric outputs suggests weaker ecological framing. Meanwhile, the frequent occurrence of *domesticate* and *serve* reveals an implicit anthropocentric bias, indicating that the model's neutral responses often default to human-centered language patterns.

**Qualitative insights** To better understand the model's output and highlight differences between ecocentric and anthropocentric perspectives, we present qualitative insights from the neutral prompt answers, focusing on the semantics of verbs and noun phrases (NPs). We also considered the sequential order and distribution of information in the text to evaluate the degree of anthropocentrism. For instance, among the first listed "key functions" of **animals** is that they "*serve*" humans by being "*raised* for *food*, *providing* nutrients and *proteins* for humans." They are "*livestock*": cows, pigs, and chickens are described as "commonly *consumed* for *meat*, *milk*, and *eggs*," while they also "*provide companionship* and *emotional support* to humans" and are used "in scientific research." In the case of **soil**, it is described as "supporting human activities, such as *agriculture* and *construction*," and being "important for *forestry* and *landscaping*." While **trees** are acknowledged for ecocentric roles such as "providing oxygen, filtering air pollutants, and offering habitats for various animals," they are also framed anthropocentrically as "a vital *resource* for humans, *providing wood* for *construction*, *fuel*, and various other products." Similarly, the **sea** is described as "*providing vital resources* such as *food*, *minerals*, and *transportation routes* for human

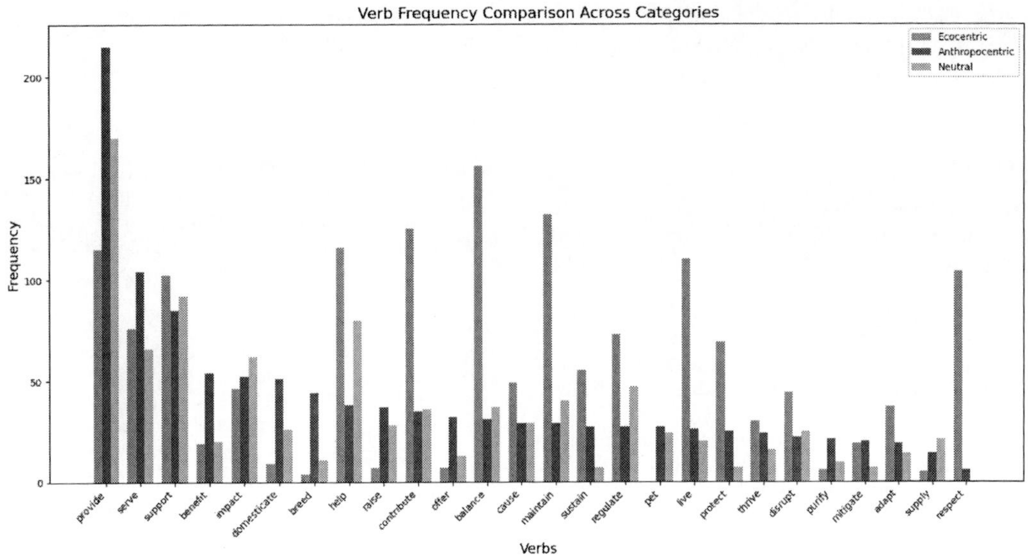


Figure 2: Verb Frequency Comparison Across Neutral, Anthropocentric, and Ecocentric Outputs.

trading." However, these anthropocentric views appear later in the answer, with more descriptive and ecocentric views prioritized earlier. **Mountains** follow a similar pattern, with references to "*recreational opportunities*" and "*resource extraction*" appearing shortly after their ecological characteristics. For **rivers**, the initial focus is on their importance to human civilization, described as a "source of *water* for *drinking*, *agriculture*, and *transportation*." Additionally, their "economic importance, serving as centers of human settlement and supporting various *industries* such as *fishing* and *tourism*" is emphasized.

## 6 Limitations

In this work, we take a first step toward addressing anthropocentrism in NLP, presenting a preliminary analysis. However, this also means that our study has several limitations, which we are aware of and plan to address in future research. One key limitation is that our analysis focuses exclusively on a single LLM—OpenAI's GPT-4o. Exploring other widely used LLMs, such as Meta's LLaMA, Claude, or other versions of GPT, could provide additional insights and offer a broader understanding of anthropocentric biases in NLP systems. Another limitation lies in our focus on aggregated outputs. We did not, for example, compare the degree of anthropocentrism between outputs concerning wild animals and farm animals, or between non-sentient living entities and non-living ones. Additionally, our analysis includes only a sample of representative entities; for instance, we selected trees as the sole representative of non-sentient living entities. Despite these limitations, we believe this work represents an important first step in raising awareness of anthropocentric biases in NLP, and we are actively working to address these issues in future studies.

## 7 Conclusion and Future Work

This study presents, to the best of our knowledge, the first investigation of anthropocentric bias in NLP technology, focusing specifically on GPT-4o, a widely used large language model. We examined how the model frames both living and non-living entities across neutral, anthropocentric, and ecocentric prompts. We manually curated and presented a glossary of 424 anthropocentric terms, used in our analysis. Our findings revealed significant anthropocentric tendencies in GPT-4o, even in neutral prompts, where non-human entities were frequently framed as resources for human use. These findings raise important concerns about the implicit biases encoded in language models, which risk perpetuating harmful narratives that contribute to ecological degradation. In future research, we plan to expand this preliminary study by exploring additional models, including a wider range of target entities, conducting comparative analyses, and deepening the linguistic analysis.

## References


Valentina Adami. 2013. Culture, language and environmental rights: The anthropocentrism of english. *Pólemos*, 7(2):335–355.

Richard J. Alexander and Arran Stibbe. 2014. https://api.semanticscholar.org/CorpusID:143894235 From the analysis of ecological discourse to the ecological analysis of discourse. *Language Sciences*, 41:104–110.

Jiafu An, Difang Huang, Chen Lin, and Mingzhu Tai. 2024. Measuring gender and racial biases in large language models. *arXiv preprint arXiv:2403.15281*.

Su Lin Blodgett, Solon Barocas, Hal Daumé III, and Hanna Wallach. 2020. https://doi.org/10.18653/v1/2020.acl-main.485 Language (technology) is power: A critical survey of "bias" in NLP. In *Proceedings of the 58th Annual Meeting of the Association for Computational Linguistics*, pages 5454–5476, Online. Association for Computational Linguistics.

Yuchen Cai, Ding Cao, Rongxi Guo, Yaqin Wen, Guiquan Liu, and Enhong Chen. 2024. Locating and mitigating gender bias in large language models. In *International Conference on Intelligent Computing*, pages 471–482. Springer.

Myra Cheng, Esin Durmus, and Dan Jurafsky. 2023. https://api.semanticscholar.org/CorpusID:258960243 Marked personas: Using natural language prompts to measure stereotypes in language models. *ArXiv*, abs/2305.18189.

Guy Cook and Alison Sealey. 2017. The discursive representation of animals. In *The Routledge handbook of ecolinguistics*, pages 311–324. Routledge.

Yashar Deldjoo. 2023. Fairness of chatgpt and the role of explainable-guided prompts. *ArXiv*, abs/2307.11761.

Philippe Descola. 2005. *Par-delà nature et culture*. Gallimard, Paris.

Alwin Frank Fill. 2015. https://api.semanticscholar.org/CorpusID:148176052 Language creates relations between humans and animals animal stereotypes, linguistic anthropocentrism and anthropomorphism.

Thilo Hagendorff, Leonie N Bossert, Yip Fai Tse, and Peter Singer. 2023. Speciesist bias in ai: how ai applications perpetuate discrimination and unfair outcomes against animals. *AI and Ethics*, 3(3):717–734.

Reinhard Heuberger. 2003. Anthropocentrism in monolingual english dictionaries: An ecolinguistic approach to the lexicographic treatment of faunal terminology. *AAA: Arbeiten aus Anglistik und Amerikanistik*, pages 93–105.

Reinhard Heuberger. 2007. Language and ideology: A brief survey of anthropocentrism and speciesism in english. *Sustaining language: Essays in Applied Ecolinguistics. Edited by Alwin Fill and Hermine Penz. Berlin: Lit Verlag*, pages 107–24.

Reinhard Heuberger. 2017. Overcoming anthropocentrism with anthropomorphic and physiocentric uses of language? In *The Routledge handbook of ecolinguistics*, pages 342–354. Routledge.

Oscar Horta and Frauke Albersmeier. 2020. https://api.semanticscholar.org/CorpusID:243648679 Defining speciesism. *Philosophy Compass*.

Matthias Jung. 2001. Ecological criticism of language. In Alwin Fill and Peter Mühlhäusler, editors, *The Ecolinguistics Reader: Language, Ecology and Environment*, pages 270–285. Continuum, London.

Helen Kopnina, Haydn Washington, Bron Taylor, and John J Piccolo. 2018. Anthropocentrism: More than just a misunderstood problem. *Journal of Agricultural and Environmental Ethics*, 31(1):109–127.

Hadas Kotek, Rikker Dockum, and David Sun. 2023. Gender bias and stereotypes in large language models. In *Proceedings of the ACM collective intelligence conference*, pages 12–24.

Mai Kuha. 2017. The treatment of environmental topics in the language of politics. In *The Routledge handbook of ecolinguistics*, pages 249–260. Routledge.

Bruno Latour. 2016. *Politiques de la nature: comment faire entrer les sciences en démocratie*. La découverte.

Stefan Leach, Andrew P Kitchin, Robbie M Sutton, and Kristof Dhont. 2023. Speciesism in everyday language. *British Journal of Social Psychology*, 62(1):486–502.

Simon L Lewis and Mark A Maslin. 2020. The human planet: How we created the anthropocene. *Global Environment*, 13(3):674–680.

Paul Pu Liang, Chiyu Wu, Louis-Philippe Morency, and Ruslan Salakhutdinov. 2021. Towards understanding and mitigating social biases in language models. In *International Conference on Machine Learning*, pages 6565–6576. PMLR.

Moin Nadeem, Anna Bethke, and Siva Reddy. 2020. Stereoset: Measuring stereotypical bias in pretrained language models. *arXiv preprint arXiv:2004.09456*.

Arran Stibbe. 2012. https://api.semanticscholar.org/CorpusID:132186804 Animals erased: Discourse, ecology, and reconnection with the natural world.

Arran Stibbe. 2015. *Ecolinguistics: Language, ecology and the stories we live by*. Routledge.

Arran Stibbe. 2015, 2021. *Ecolinguistics: Language, ecology and the stories we live by*. Routledge.

Masashi Takeshita and Rafal Rzepka. 2024. Speciesism in natural language processing research. *AI and Ethics*, pages 1–16.

Masashi Takeshita, Rafal Rzepka, and Kenji Araki. 2022. Speciesist language and nonhuman animal bias in english masked language models. *Information Processing & Management*, 59(5):103050.

Nicolás Torres, Catalina Ulloa, Ignacio Araya, Matías Ayala, and Sebastián Jara. 2024. A comprehensive analysis of gender, racial, and prompt-induced biases in large language models. *International Journal of Data Science and Analytics*, pages 1–38.

Wilhelm Trampe. 2017. Euphemisms for killing animals and for other forms of their use. In *The Routledge handbook of ecolinguistics*, pages 325–341. Routledge.

Jesse Vig, Sebastian Gehrmann, Yonatan Belinkov, Sharon Qian, Daniel Nevo, Yaron Singer, and Stuart Shieber. 2020. Investigating gender bias in language models using causal mediation analysis. *Advances in neural information processing systems*, 33:12388–12401.

Lynn White Jr. 1967. The historical roots of our ecologic crisis. *Science*, 155(3767):1203–1207.

# Efficient Scientific Full Text Classification: The Case of EICAT Impact Assessments

**Marc Brinner** and **Sina Zarrieß**
Computational Linguistics, Department of Linguistics
Bielefeld University, Germany
{marc.brinner,sina.zarriess}@uni-bielefeld.de

## Abstract

This study explores strategies for efficiently classifying scientific full texts using both small, BERT-based models and local large language models like Llama-3.1 8B. We focus on developing methods for selecting subsets of input sentences to reduce input size while simultaneously enhancing classification performance. To this end, we compile a novel dataset consisting of full-text scientific papers from the field of invasion biology, specifically addressing the impacts of invasive species. These papers are aligned with publicly available impact assessments created by researchers for the International Union for Conservation of Nature (IUCN). Through extensive experimentation, we demonstrate that various sources like human evidence annotations, LLM-generated annotations or explainability scores can be used to train sentence selection models that improve the performance of both encoder- and decoder-based language models while optimizing efficiency through the reduction in input length, leading to improved results even if compared to models like ModernBERT that are able to handle the complete text as input. Additionally, we find that repeated sampling of shorter inputs proves to be a very effective strategy that, at a slightly increased cost, can further improve classification performance.

## 1 Introduction

The exponential growth of research publications across various domains (Bornmann et al., 2021) has created an increasing need for automated methods to process scientific texts efficiently. To address this, numerous approaches have been developed to optimize general research workflows, such as literature search (Singh et al., 2023) and summarization (Singha Roy and Mercer, 2024). For more specialized tasks, such as extracting specific information from full texts, proprietary large language models (LLMs) offer potential solutions (Dagdelen et al., 2024). However, these models are not locally deployable, making them expensive to use when processing large datasets.

Recently, open-source large language models have emerged as strong competitors to proprietary systems, offering comparable performance (DeepSeek-AI et al., 2024). Nevertheless, a wider adoption from researchers outside the machine learning research community is unlikely within the next years, primarily due to their significant hardware requirements. Furthermore, both proprietary and open-source LLMs of this scale are highly energy-intensive, raising concerns about their sustainability. This highlights the importance of exploring smaller, more efficient models that can deliver similar performance while minimizing resource consumption, or of exploring other strategies to reduce the computational cost of using these models to solve specific tasks.

To address these challenges, we investigate the potential of more efficient BERT-based models alongside slightly more resource-intensive local large language models (LLMs) for classification of scientific full texts. As part of this effort, we introduce the EICAT dataset, which consists of scientific full-text papers focused on specific invasive species and their impact on the native ecosystem, as well as labels specifying the impact category of that species with corresponding evidence sentences that were extracted from the papers.

In our series of experiments, we first evaluate the performance of a standard BERT-based classifier on the EICAT dataset, where full-text inputs must be split into multiple segments due to the



*Proceedings of the 1st Workshop on Ecology, Environment, and Natural Language Processing (NLP4Ecology2025)*, pages 94–103
March 2, 2025 ©2025 University of Tartu Library

limited context length. We then compare its performance to ModernBERT (Warner et al., 2024), a recent BERT variant capable of handling longer contexts, as well as to Llama-3.1 8B (Grattafiori et al., 2024), a state-of-the-art local LLM.

All models face significant challenges due to the large input size, leading us to performing further experiments with training selector models to identify and prioritize the most relevant input sentences for training and evaluation. To ensure the general applicability of this approach, we test various sentence selection strategies, including leveraging human-provided evidence annotations, using LLM-generated selections, and using importance scores extracted from the classifiers.

Our findings indicate that many selection strategies improve classifier performance while simultaneously enhancing the efficiency of the decoder model. For scenarios where efficiency is less critical, we also observe that repeated randomization can improve the classification performance and even make a random selection of input sentences a viable strategy, thus leading to a simple-to-use way of boosting classification results.

Ultimately, this work presents a generalizable pipeline for accelerating inference and improving performance of scientific full-text classification.

The remainder of the paper is organized as follows: Section 2 reviews recent natural language processing approaches for the automated processing of scientific texts. Section 3 introduces the EICAT dataset, while Sections 4 and 5 describe our experiments and present the results. Section 6 provides a discussion of the findings, and Section 7 concludes with final remarks.

## 2 Related Work

### 2.1 Language Models for Scientific Literature

The introduction of the transformer architecture (Vaswani et al., 2017) revolutionized natural language processing, marking a new era in the field, with pretrained language models like BERT (Devlin et al., 2019) significantly advancing performance across a wide range of tasks. This progress quickly extended to the scientific domain, leading to the development of domain-specific models such as SciBERT (Beltagy et al., 2019), which set new benchmarks on various scientific NLP tasks. SciBERT and similar models demonstrate clear advantages over general-purpose models (Lee et al., 2019; Song et al., 2023; Rostam and Kertész, 2024), and have therefore been applied to a variety of tasks within the scientific domain, including literature search and similarity assessment (Singh et al., 2023), classification (Rostam and Kertész, 2024), and summarization (Sefid and Giles, 2022), with similar pretrained models having been trained for the general biomedical domain (Lee et al., 2019; Gu et al., 2021) as well as for the biodiversity domain (Abdelmageed et al., 2023).

More recently, the improved performance of autoregressive language models (Radford et al., 2019) has driven a shift toward leveraging these models for a wide range of tasks. Openly available models, such as Llama-2 (Touvron et al., 2023), alongside proprietary systems like ChatGPT, have established new state-of-the-art results in various scientific document processing tasks, including structured information extraction (Rettenberger et al., 2024; Dagdelen et al., 2024), term extraction (Huang et al., 2024), text classification, named entity recognition and and question answering (Choi and Lee, 2024).

A range of benchmarks has been developed specifically for information extraction from scientific full texts, often accompanied by proposed models. These benchmarks target various tasks, including dataset mention detection (Pan et al., 2023), entity and relation extraction (Zhang et al., 2024), general information extraction (Jain et al., 2020), and summarization (DeYoung et al., 2021).

### 2.2 Language Models for Biodiversity Science

In the specific domain of biodiversity science, transformer encoder architectures have been employed to tackle tasks such as hypothesis classification (Brinner et al., 2022), biodiversity analysis (Arias et al., 2023), named entity recognition and relation extraction (Abdelmageed et al., 2023), as well as hypothesis evidence localization (Brinner et al., 2024; Brinner and Zarrieß, 2024). Additionally, autoregressive models have been applied to tasks such as literature review, question answering (Jiqi Gu, 2024), and structured information extraction (Castro et al., 2024; Kommineni et al., 2024), with further potential applications continuing to emerge (Osawa et al., 2023).

## 3 The EICAT Dataset

We present a new dataset for training and evaluating models on the task of assessing the impact of invasive species on ecosystems based on scientific full texts. This dataset is grounded in the "Environmental Impact Classification for Alien Taxa" (EICAT, IUCN (2020)) standard, a classification standard developed by the International Union for Conservation of Nature (IUCN), which is used by researchers to compile standardized summaries of scientific literature addressing invasive species, along with assessments of the species' impacts as reported in these publications. The impacts are categorized into one of six possible classes: *Minimal Concern*, *Minor*, *Moderate*, *Major Risk*, *Massive*, and *Data Deficient*. Furthermore, researchers extract and include sentences from the full texts as evidence supporting their selected category. These impact assessments for various species are publicly available as Excel files at https://www.iucngisd.org/gisd/.

To construct our dataset, we acquired impact assessment files for as many species as possible. From these files, we extracted publication names and corresponding impact assessments for each species, covering around 800 publications. Using Llama-3 8B, we determined whether each citation represented a scientific paper (as opposed to books, PhD theses, government reports, etc.), since this study focuses exclusively on shorter scientific articles. We then used Crossref (crossref.org) as well as manual scraping to obtain as many full texts as possible.

Since the retrieved documents were in PDF format, we used Grobid (GRO, 2008–2024) to extract the raw text from the publications. We excluded any documents for which text extraction was unsuccessful, resulting in a final dataset with 436 full texts addressing 120 species.

As a final processing step, we matched the evidence sentences from the impact assessments to sentences in the extracted text files. Discrepancies between the version of the paper we obtained and the one used for the assessments, as well as artifacts introduced during the PDF-to-text conversion, made exact matching infeasible in many cases. To address this, we implemented a fuzzy matching strategy, matching two sentences if they contain most of the same words in the same order. For matches slightly below the set similarity threshold, we used Llama-3 to determine whether the sentences were still a valid match. In total, we identified 2,247 evidence sentences, compared to 2,226 sentences in the original annotations. The higher count likely results from imperfect matching, as well as from PDF-to-text conversion artifacts, which sometimes split evidence sentences in the full text into two parts.

We created training, validation, and test splits comprising 82%, 8%, and 10% of the species, respectively. To prevent inflated performance scores caused by the model learning the typical impact category assigned to a specific species across publications, all texts addressing the same species were assigned to the same split.

We publish the dataset containing publication names, impact labels and evidence sentences together with our code on github.com/inas-argumentation/efficient_full_text_classification.

## 4 Baseline Classification Experiments

### 4.1 Experimental Setup

Our initial experiment focuses on establishing baseline performance for both BERT-based models and local instruction-tuned LLMs on our datasets. Specifically, we evaluate 1) PubMedBERT (Gu et al., 2021), which demonstrated strong performance in previous studies on invasion biology (Brinner et al., 2022) 2) ModernBERT (Warner et al., 2024), a recently introduced BERT variant that claims improved performance and efficiency while allowing for input lengths of up to 8192 tokens, and 3) Llama-3.1 8B, a state-of-the-art local LLM capable of handling up to 128K tokens, allowing for full-text processing.

Given that BERT-based models are limited to processing 512 tokens at a time, we split each full text into chunks of up to 512 tokens (with neighboring chunks overlapping for 50 tokens) and average the output logits across all chunks to produce a single score for the entire paper, serving as input to the cross-entropy loss. For ModernBERT, we instead used the whole full-text as input to the model, with tokens exceeding the 8192 token context window being truncated. We perform seven runs per model to obtain average results that mitigate variance in our reported scores.

For the LLM, we design a prompt that includes the full text along with a textual description of the impact categories, extracted from the IUCN EICAT guidelines (IUCN, 2020). The model is prompted to first generate a sentence summarizing

This is a scientific paper about an invasive species: [SCIENTIFIC FULL TEXT]

This is the end of the scientific text. Your task is to classify the impact that the invasive species [SPECIES NAME] has. Note that the text might contain information on other species. Possible classes are the following:
1. Minimal
A taxon is considered to have impacts of Minimal Concern when it causes negligible levels of have impacts on the recipient environment at some level, for example by altering species diversity or community similarity (e.g., biotic homogenisation), and for this reason there is no category equating to "no impact". Only taxa for which changes in the individual performance of natives have been studied but not detected are assigned an MC category. Taxa that have been evaluated under the EICAT process but for which impacts have not been assessed in any study should not be classified in this category, but rather should be classified as Data Deficient.
2. Minor
A taxon is considered to have Minor impacts when it causes reductions in the performance of individuals in the native biota, but no declines in native population sizes, and has no impacts that would cause it to be classified in a higher impact category.
3. Moderate
A taxon is considered to have Moderate impacts when it causes declines in the population size of at least one native taxon, but has not been observed to lead to the local extinction of a native taxon.
4. Major
A taxon is considered to have Major impacts when it causes community changes through the local or sub-population extinction (or presumed extinction) of at least one native taxon, that would be naturally reversible if the alien taxon was no longer present. Its impacts do not lead to naturally irreversible local population, sub-population or global taxon extinctions.
5. Massive
A taxon is considered to have Massive impacts when it causes naturally irreversible community changes through local, sub-population or global extinction (or presumed extinction) of at least one native taxon.
6. Data Deficient
A taxon is categorised as Data Deficient when the best available evidence indicates that it has (or had) individuals existing in a wild state in a region beyond the boundary of its native geographic range, but either there is inadequate information to classify the taxon with respect to its impact, or insufficient time has elapsed since introduction for impacts to have become apparent. It is expected that all introduced taxa will have an impact at some level, because by definition an alien taxon in a new environment has a nonzero impact. However, listing a taxon as Data Deficient recognises that current information is insufficient to assess that level of impact.

Return just the classification and end your answer, and provide one of the following labels as answer: "Minimal", "Minor", "Moderate", "Major", "Massive", "Data Deficient". Provide your answer by just using the following response format, and do not answer anything else in addition to that:
Summary: [One sentence summarizing the key information that you consider for the assessment]
Answer: [Your answer, that is one of the six labels]
END.

Figure 1: The Llama-3.1 8B prompt to classify scientific full texts.

the impact (a step that significantly improves classification results) and then output a single impact category in a structured way (see Figure 1). We used greedy decoding to deterministically generate the most likely answer.

### 4.2 Results

The results of the classification experiment are presented in Table 1 (Deterministic Selection, Sentence Selector: *Complete Input*), where we report both macro F1 and micro F1 scores. Given the dataset's highly uneven label distribution, macro F1 can be strongly influenced by the misclassification of only a few samples, making micro F1 an important complementary metric. The results show that the trained BERT model achieves a macro F1 score of 0.425, thus significantly outperforming the LLM with a rather unsatisfactory macro F1 result of 0.272. We hypothesize that this could be cause by two key factors:

1. Limited context in model prompt: While researchers use the same EICAT impact class descriptions as provided in the prompt for their assessments, they also rely on their domain knowledge and familiarity with existing literature to perform impact assessments as intended. A trained model learns this implicit consensus through exposure to a large, annotated dataset, whereas the LLM lacks this resource and depends solely on the textual descriptions of the classes, which are less informative.

2. Challenges with input length: Full texts contain extensive information, not all of which will be relevant for the classification, thus making it hard to detect the relevant pieces of information to perform the classification.

While the first issue could be addressed by training the LLM on the dataset, this is beyond the scope of this initial analysis. The second issue is supported by the fact that ModernBERT

| Model | Sentence Selector | Deterministic Selection Macro F1 | Deterministic Selection Micro F1 | Randomized Selection Macro F1 | Randomized Selection Micro F1 |
|---|---|---|---|---|---|
| ModernBERT | Complete Input | 0.433 | 0.446 | 0.439 | 0.465 |
| PubMedBERT | Complete Input | 0.425 | 0.446 | - | - |
| PubMedBERT | Evidence | **0.523** | **0.538** | 0.503 | 0.508 |
| PubMedBERT | LLM | 0.457 | 0.460 | 0.494 | <u>0.508</u> |
| PubMedBERT | Entropy | 0.453 | 0.460 | 0.475 | 0.494 |
| PubMedBERT | Importance | 0.442 | 0.460 | 0.479 | 0.479 |
| PubMedBERT | Random | 0.441 | 0.450 | <u>0.496</u> | 0.499 |
| Llama 3.1 8B | Complete Input | 0.272 | 0.373 | - | - |
| Llama 3.1 8B | Evidence | 0.234 | 0.237 | 0.257 | 0.271 |
| Llama 3.1 8B | LLM | 0.228 | 0.271 | 0.230 | 0.305 |
| Llama 3.1 8B | Entropy | 0.322 | 0.373 | 0.358 | 0.441 |
| Llama 3.1 8B | Importance | 0.403 | 0.441 | 0.399 | 0.441 |
| Llama 3.1 8B | Random | 0.265 | 0.339 | 0.356 | 0.407 |

Table 1: Results on the EICAT dataset using PubMedBERT, ModernBERT and Llama-3.1 8B with either the full text input or one of the sentence selectors. Best scores are bold, second-best (from a different model) are underlined.

outperformed the standard BERT variant only marginally, even though it is able to reason about much more information at once, thus again indicating that the abundance of information in a full-text can pose significant challenges. To investigate this issue further, we conducted additional experiments that focus on selecting a subset of relevant sentences during preprocessing and using only those as input for the BERT or Llama models.

## 5 Evidence Sentence Selection

### 5.1 Experimental Setup

We propose a two-step procedure to improve the performance of the models tested in the previous experiments. Our hypothesis is that both models face challenges due to the length of the full-text inputs. For the LLM, identifying the few critical pieces of information within a large block of text can be difficult. For PubMedBERT, the input is often split into more than 15 chunks, many of which might contain little to no relevant information, potentially disrupting the training process.

The proposed procedure involves training a sentence selector model (also based on PubMedBERT) on all sentences from the training set to distinguish important sentences from less relevant ones. Once trained, we use the selector to identify the 15 most relevant sentences for each document. Both models are then trained and evaluated using only these selected sentences, thus significantly reducing the input size while focusing on the most crucial information. For the Llama model, we used the same prompt as before, with the addition of mentioning at the beginning that sentences extracted from a paper are presented, and indicating left-out sentences in the input with "[...]", which lead to improved results.

We evaluate several strategies for training the sentence selector model:

1. *Evidence*: A model trained to recognize the human evidence annotations from the dataset.
2. *LLM*: We provide the EICAT guidelines as background and prompt Llama-3.1 8B to assess each individual sentence from a paper, classifying it as *Not Useful*, *Slightly Useful*, or *Highly Useful*, resulting in a three-class classification task.
3. *Entropy*: We used three of the seven BERT classifiers trained in Section 4 to classify each sentence individually. A low entropy in the predicted distribution is a sign that the sentence is indicative of a specific class.
4. *Importance*: For each sentence in the dataset, we used three of the seven BERT classifiers trained in the earlier experiments to classify the corresponding full text, once with the sentence included and once with it being removed. We then evaluated the absolute change in output logits to assess the importance of the given sentence for the output.

The evidence and LLM-based annotations naturally give rise to two- and three-class classification tasks for training the BERT sentence selection model. The entropy and importance scores, on the other hand, are continuous by nature, but since the absolute values of these scores are less relevant compared to the ranking among sentences within a text, we decided to discretize them into three categories: sentences falling within the bottom 50% of scores within a text, those in the top 20%, and the remaining 30% in between, thus again constituting a three-class classification problem.

The sentence selectors all receive the species name and the three sentences before and after the sentence that they shall assess as context, with the relevant sentence being enclosed by *[SEP]*-tokens. The resulting models can be used for ranking sentences within a document by predicting class probabilities for each sentence individually, and then using the expected value as continuous score.

### 5.2 Results

#### 5.2.1 Sentence Selector Agreement

We begin by comparing the similarities between the predictions of the different sentence selector models (displayed in Table 2) to see if they focus on similar kinds of information. To quantify this, we use the normalized discounted cumulative gain (NDCG), which produces a score between 0 and 1, with higher values indicating greater agreement between the rankings of two models (i.e., highly ranked sentences by one model are also ranked highly by the other model or ground truth).

The rankings generated by the different trained sentence selector models are compared to the test-set ground truth rankings (i.e., the evidence annotations created by human annotators, or the assessments that were directly predicted by the LLM). Notably, the model trained on human evidence annotations achieved only a mediocre NDCG score with regards to alignment with the ground truth evidence annotations. This could be caused by inconsistencies in how evidence sentences were selected across different EICAT assessments, which might be caused by the involvement of many different researchers in their creation. Notably, it proved to be important to provide the surrounding sentences as well as the species name as context, since otherwise the NDCG score drops to just 0.487. The reason for this is, that annotated evidence sentences usually report on actual evidence

| Train Data | Evidence NDCG | LLM NDCG |
|---|---|---|
| Evidence | 0.541 | 0.753 |
| LLM | 0.394 | 0.911 |
| Entropy | 0.362 | 0.691 |
| Importance | 0.344 | 0.674 |
| Random | 0.299 | 0.618 |

Table 2: NDCG scores denoting the match between the different sentence selection strategies and the ground truth sentences from the human evidence annotations or the LLM selections.

collected within a study, so that the model needs to learn to exclude sentences that appear, for example, in a literature review section, which can be hard if that sentence is viewed in isolation. Further, a text might address several species, thus making the species for which the sentence shall be assessed a crucial piece of information.

In contrast to the evidence selector, the LLM demonstrated a high degree of internal consistency, achieving an impressive NDCG score of 0.911 between its own test set predictions and those from the corresponding BERT classifier.

Interestingly, while human and LLM rankings show some correlation, the two BERT-based methods for generating sentence rankings align only marginally better with the human or LLM annotations than a random selector. This raises concerns about the validity of these methods. However, their actual utility for the classification will be further evaluated in the following section.

#### 5.2.2 BERT Classification Results

We evaluate the classification performance of BERT classifiers trained on the 15 most important sentences from each full text, as determined by the various sentence selectors. In most cases, only up to five sentences were chosen as evidence by the human annotators, but we chose the larger number of 15 to increase the likelihood of many relevant sentences being selected even if the selectors perform suboptimal, while still reducing the input size significantly. The results are presented in Table 1 (Deterministic Selection).

For BERT classifiers, the evidence-based selector proves to be the most effective, significantly improving classification performance. A possible explanation is that it removes unnecessary and distracting information, most importantly because it can filter out sentences describing impacts caused by other species, thereby eliminating misleading information and implicitly creating a focus on the target species. In contrast, the BERT and ModernBERT models trained on the full input did not receive the species name, which was necessary to ensure they relied on textual evidence rather than simply associating species names with specific classifications, but leading to potentially incorrect predictions in the case of multiple species being addressed in a text. Since the BERT classifier was used as basis for training the importance and entropy selectors, these models likely did not learn to filter out sentences about other species as well. However, the LLM-based selector may have developed this ability, as the species name was included when generating the LLM assessments used for training. Nevertheless, it only marginally outperforms the entropy and importance selectors.

Overall, all sentence selection strategies improve classification performance, even when compared to ModernBERT, which should have access to the same (and even more) information. This holds even true for a random selection strategy, which selects 15 sentences before a training run starts and does not change this predetermined selection to mirror the deterministic selection by the other models. We see this as evidence that an overflow of information decreases classification performance, thus making our sentence selection strategy highly effective.

### 5.2.3 Llama Classification Results

The results for Llama reveal a different pattern compared to BERT. Despite their potentially beneficial property of filtering our non-relevant impacts, the evidence and LLM selectors do not improve classification performance. In this case, these properties will not be as significant, though, since the LLM does receive the name of the species it shall assess, so that it can filter out unnecessary information on its own.

To explain the decreased performance, we analyzed the distribution of class predictions and found that, for the evidence selector, the model's predictions significantly under-represent the lower-impact classes (*Data Deficient*, *Minimal Concern* and *Minor*). We attribute this to the model receiving condensed information on the impact of the specific invasive species, thus pushing it to a higher impact category that it did not see as justified when assessing the full text.

For the LLM selector, we see a similar distribution, with a few more samples being classified as *Minor*, but even less being classified as *Data Deficient*, which could be caused by the LLM not managing to exclude sentences from, for example, the literature review section, thus making every paper contain some information on potential impacts.

The BERT model, in contrast, is not susceptible to these factors hindering the LLM, since it is additionally trained on these specific inputs and thus learns to draw the right conclusion from them.

Interestingly, sentences identified as important by BERT (i.e., *Entropy* and *Importance*) lead to substantially better results than the other strategies. We see this as a sign that the models indeed learned to identify the sentences that should actually contribute to the classification (as learned by the original BERT model), thus mitigating especially the issues pointed out for the LLM-selector.

### 5.2.4 Randomization

In both experiments, random sentence selection yielded reasonable results, even outperforming using the complete input or other selection methods. This is especially notable for the BERT models, as we fixed the 15 randomly selected sentences for each sample within a training run, thus significantly restricting access to useful information. A similar limitation applies to the other selection strategies, which also reduce the total number of sentences encountered during training.

To explore this further, we conducted additional experiments where a new random input is created each time a text is accessed during training. For the targeted selectors, this random sampling is restricted to the top 30 sentences (with higher-ranking sentences being sampled more often), ensuring that most sentences deemed unimportant were excluded. During evaluation, we generated 10 different input samples per text and determined the final prediction through majority voting.

The results for the randomized classifiers are shown in Table 1 (Randomized Selection). With the exception of the evidence selector, we observe consistent performance improvements across all BERT models. This suggests that, unless the selection is guided by a well-informed approach based on human annotations, exposing the model to a greater variety of sentences during training and making predictions based on diverse inputs is beneficial. Notably, this even makes the random selector a viable competitor to the evidence selector, demonstrating that for large-text classification tasks, this simple strategy can be an effective choice. We hypothesize that targeted selectors focus on specific types of information (such as empirical observations for the evidence selector), which leads to only very narrow relationships being learned during training. In contrast, the random selector's lack of bias increases the variance of inputs and forces the model to generalize more effectively through being trained on a more difficult task, thus enabling it to learn the broader relationships required for accurate classification.

For the Llama model, randomization improves results across most selection strategies, with the random selector again becoming a viable alternative to targeted selection. We hypothesize that specific sentences might throw off the LLM's prediction for a specific input, and sampling many different inputs could instead lead to a classification that is based on the general information provided by a vast number of sentences in the text.

#### 5.2.5 Efficiency Analysis

In the introduction, we emphasized the importance of efficiency for broader adoption of local models outside the machine learning community. Alongside performance improvements, we observed substantial speed gains for the Llama model due to reduced input lengths. For instance, a full test set evaluation with full-text input on an RTX 3090 takes 116 seconds, but this drops to 65 seconds with importance-based sentence selection - including the time for sentence relevance prediction. Notably, this strategy also improves classification performance, breaking the typical tradeoff between efficiency and accuracy. Further increased performance using sampling then leads to vastly increased times that are more than three times longer than using the full-text input.

Smaller models like BERT remain far more efficient, requiring just 6.6 seconds for a test set evaluation with evidence sentence selection. The sampling strategy increases this to 9.8 seconds, thus offering performance gains for most selection strategies in trade for higher computational cost.

## 6 Discussion

In our evaluation, we identified significant challenges when using instruction-tuned LLMs for scientific text processing. On the one hand, extracting a different set of sentences, even if they should contain the necessary information for performing the classification, can easily change classification results and even push the model towards incorrect conclusions. Additionally, a detailed natural language description of our task was insufficient for the Llama model to achieve results comparable to a 70 times smaller BERT classifier, and the explicit selection of highly relevant sentences through the evidence selector did not yield improvements. We interpret this as a sign that sample-level labels, as used by BERT, provide substantially more information than both evidence annotations and natural language descriptions.

The superior informational content of sample-level labels compared to evidence annotations is plausible considering that a single evidence annotation only conveys information about a single sentence, while a sample-level label provides information about every sentence in the whole text. On the other hand, the superior performance of sample-level labels over natural language descriptions is especially significant given the recent trend toward prompting-based approaches rather than extensive labeling efforts. In-context learning (Dong et al., 2024) offers a potential bridge between these approaches, enabling the delivery of rich sample-level information to LLMs without training, typically complementing natural language descriptions within the prompting framework. This combination can thus potentially overcome the challenge of precisely specifying a given task by returning to the classical way of demonstrating desired behavior. However, while this approach has shown success, it becomes impractical for tasks involving lengthy inputs, such as scientific full-text classification. For such cases, finetuning local large language models could present a viable solution, which can be explored in future work.

## 7 Conclusion

We introduced a novel dataset for scientific full-text classification and conducted extensive experiments using smaller encoder and larger decoder architectures. Our results demonstrated that various strategies for reducing input size can simultaneously enhance efficiency and performance, offering a generalizable pipeline adaptable to other tasks. However, as classification scores remain suboptimal, future research could investigate the potential of fine-tuning local LLMs, leveraging recently emerging LLMs with advanced reasoning capabilities (DeepSeek-AI et al., 2025), or testing the performance of larger proprietary models.

## References


2008–2024. Grobid. `https://github.com/kermitt2/grobid`.

Nora Abdelmageed, Felicitas Löffler, and Birgitta König-Ries. 2023. Biodivbert: a pre-trained language model for the biodiversity domain. In *SWAT4HCLS*, pages 62–71.

Pablo Millan Arias, Niousha Sadjadi, Monireh Safari, ZeMing Gong, Austin T. Wang, Scott C. Lowe, Joakim Bruslund Haurum, Iuliia Zarubiieva, Dirk Steinke, Lila Kari, Angel X. Chang, and Graham W. Taylor. 2023. Barcodebert: Transformers for biodiversity analysis.

Iz Beltagy, Kyle Lo, and Arman Cohan. 2019. SciBERT: A pretrained language model for scientific text. In *Proceedings of the 2019 Conference on Empirical Methods in Natural Language Processing and the 9th International Joint Conference on Natural Language Processing (EMNLP-IJCNLP)*, pages 3615–3620, Hong Kong, China. Association for Computational Linguistics.

Lutz Bornmann, Robin Haunschild, and Rüdiger Mutz. 2021. Growth rates of modern science: a latent piecewise growth curve approach to model publication numbers from established and new literature databases. 8(1):1–15. Publisher: Palgrave.

Marc Brinner, Tina Heger, and Sina Zarriess. 2022. Linking a hypothesis network from the domain of invasion biology to a corpus of scientific abstracts: The INAS dataset. In *Proceedings of the first Workshop on Information Extraction from Scientific Publications*, pages 32–42, Online. Association for Computational Linguistics.

Marc Brinner, Sina Zarrieß, and Tina Heger. 2024. Weakly supervised claim localization in scientific abstracts. In *Robust Argumentation Machines*, pages 20–38, Cham. Springer Nature Switzerland.

Marc Felix Brinner and Sina Zarrieß. 2024. Rationalizing transformer predictions via end-to-end differentiable self-training. In *Proceedings of the 2024 Conference on Empirical Methods in Natural Language Processing*, pages 11894–11907, Miami, Florida, USA. Association for Computational Linguistics.

Andry Castro, João Pinto, Luís Reino, Pavel Pipek, and César Capinha. 2024. Large language models overcome the challenges of unstructured text data in ecology. *Ecological Informatics*, 82:102742.

Jaewoong Choi and Byungju Lee. 2024. Accelerating materials language processing with large language models. *Communications Materials*, 5(1):13.

John Dagdelen, Alexander Dunn, Sanghoon Lee, Nicholas Walker, Andrew S Rosen, Gerbrand Ceder, Kristin A Persson, and Anubhav Jain. 2024. Structured information extraction from scientific text with large language models. *Nature Communications*, 15(1):1418.

DeepSeek-AI et al. 2024. Deepseek-v3 technical report.

DeepSeek-AI et al. 2025. Deepseek-r1: Incentivizing reasoning capability in llms via reinforcement learning.

Jacob Devlin, Ming-Wei Chang, Kenton Lee, and Kristina Toutanova. 2019. BERT: Pre-training of deep bidirectional transformers for language understanding. In *Proceedings of the 2019 Conference of the North American Chapter of the Association for Computational Linguistics: Human Language Technologies, Volume 1 (Long and Short Papers)*, pages 4171–4186, Minneapolis, Minnesota. Association for Computational Linguistics.

Jay DeYoung, Iz Beltagy, Madeleine van Zuylen, Bailey Kuehl, and Lucy Lu Wang. 2021. MS^2: Multi-document summarization of medical studies. In *Proceedings of the 2021 Conference on Empirical Methods in Natural Language Processing*, pages 7494–7513, Online and Punta Cana, Dominican Republic. Association for Computational Linguistics.

Qingxiu Dong, Lei Li, Damai Dai, Ce Zheng, Jingyuan Ma, Rui Li, Heming Xia, Jingjing Xu, Zhiyong Wu, Tianyu Liu, Baobao Chang, Xu Sun, Lei Li, and Zhifang Sui. 2024. A survey on in-context learning.

Aaron Grattafiori et al. 2024. The llama 3 herd of models.

Yu Gu, Robert Tinn, Hao Cheng, Michael Lucas, Naoto Usuyama, Xiaodong Liu, Tristan Naumann, Jianfeng Gao, and Hoifung Poon. 2021. Domain-specific language model pretraining for biomedical natural language processing. *ACM Trans. Comput. Healthcare*, 3(1).

Jingwei Huang, Donghan M Yang, Ruichen Rong, Kuroush Nezafati, Colin Treager, Zhikai Chi, Shidan Wang, Xian Cheng, Yujia Guo, Laura J Klesse, et al. 2024. A critical assessment of using chatgpt for extracting structured data from clinical notes. *npj Digital Medicine*, 7(1):106.

IUCN. 2020. Guidelines for using the iucn environmental impact classification for alien taxa (eicat) categories and criteria. version 1.1.

Sarthak Jain, Madeleine van Zuylen, Hannaneh Hajishirzi, and Iz Beltagy. 2020. SciREX: A challenge dataset for document-level information extraction. In *Proceedings of the 58th Annual Meeting of the Association for Computational Linguistics*, pages 7506–7516, Online. Association for Computational Linguistics.

Jiangshan Lai Jiqi Gu, Jianping Chen. 2024. Application of large language models in biodiversity research. *Biodiversity Science*, 32(9):24258.

Vamsi Krishna Kommineni, Waqas Ahmed, Birgitta Koenig-Ries, and Sheeba Samuel. 2024. Automating information retrieval from biodiversity literature using large language models: A case study.

*Biodiversity Information Science and Standards*, 8:e136735.

Jinhyuk Lee, Wonjin Yoon, Sungdong Kim, Donghyeon Kim, Sunkyu Kim, Chan Ho So, and Jaewoo Kang. 2019. Biobert: a pre-trained biomedical language representation model for biomedical text mining. *Bioinformatics*, 36(4):1234–1240.

T Osawa, N Tsutsumida, et al. 2023. The role of large language models in ecology and biodiversity conservation: Opportunities and challenges.

Huitong Pan, Qi Zhang, Eduard Dragut, Cornelia Caragea, and Longin Jan Latecki. 2023. Dmdd: A large-scale dataset for dataset mentions detection. *Transactions of the Association for Computational Linguistics*, 11:1132–1146.

Alec Radford, Jeffrey Wu, Rewon Child, David Luan, Dario Amodei, Ilya Sutskever, et al. 2019. Language models are unsupervised multitask learners. *OpenAI blog*, 1(8):9.

Luca Rettenberger, Marc F. Münker, Mark Schutera, Christof M. Niemeyer, Kersten S. Rabe, and Markus Reischl. 2024. Using large language models for extracting structured information from scientific texts. *Current Directions in Biomedical Engineering*, 10(4):526–529.

Zhyar Rzgar K Rostam and Gábor Kertész. 2024. Finetuning large language models for scientific text classification: A comparative study.

Athar Sefid and C. Lee Giles. 2022. Scibertsum: Extractive summarization for scientific documents. In *Document Analysis Systems*, pages 688–701, Cham. Springer International Publishing.

Amanpreet Singh, Mike D'Arcy, Arman Cohan, Doug Downey, and Sergey Feldman. 2023. SciRepEval: A multi-format benchmark for scientific document representations. In *Proceedings of the 2023 Conference on Empirical Methods in Natural Language Processing*, pages 5548–5566, Singapore. Association for Computational Linguistics.

Sudipta Singha Roy and Robert E. Mercer. 2024. Enhancing scientific document summarization with research community perspective and background knowledge. In *Proceedings of the 2024 Joint International Conference on Computational Linguistics, Language Resources and Evaluation (LREC-COLING 2024)*, pages 6048–6058, Torino, Italia. ELRA and ICCL.

Yu Song, Santiago Miret, and Bang Liu. 2023. MatSci-NLP: Evaluating scientific language models on materials science language tasks using text-to-schema modeling. In *Proceedings of the 61st Annual Meeting of the Association for Computational Linguistics (Volume 1: Long Papers)*, pages 3621–3639, Toronto, Canada. Association for Computational Linguistics.

Hugo Touvron et al. 2023. Llama 2: Open foundation and fine-tuned chat models.

Ashish Vaswani, Noam Shazeer, Niki Parmar, Jakob Uszkoreit, Llion Jones, Aidan N Gomez, Ł ukasz Kaiser, and Illia Polosukhin. 2017. Attention is all you need. In *Advances in Neural Information Processing Systems*, volume 30. Curran Associates, Inc.

Benjamin Warner, Antoine Chaffin, Benjamin Clavié, Orion Weller, Oskar Hallström, Said Taghadouini, Alexis Gallagher, Raja Biswas, Faisal Ladhak, Tom Aarsen, Nathan Cooper, Griffin Adams, Jeremy Howard, and Iacopo Poli. 2024. Smarter, better, faster, longer: A modern bidirectional encoder for fast, memory efficient, and long context finetuning and inference.

Qi Zhang, Zhijia Chen, Huitong Pan, Cornelia Caragea, Longin Jan Latecki, and Eduard Dragut. 2024. SciER: An entity and relation extraction dataset for datasets, methods, and tasks in scientific documents. In *Proceedings of the 2024 Conference on Empirical Methods in Natural Language Processing*, pages 13083–13100, Miami, Florida, USA. Association for Computational Linguistics.

# The Accuracy, Robustness, and Readability of LLM-Generated Sustainability-Related Word Definitions

**Alice Heiman**
Stanford University
aheiman@stanford.edu

## Abstract

A common language with standardized definitions is crucial for effective climate discussions. However, concerns exist about LLMs misrepresenting climate terms. We compared 300 official IPCC glossary definitions with those generated by GPT-4o-mini, Llama3.1 8B, and Mistral 7B, analyzing adherence, robustness, and readability using SBERT sentence embeddings. The LLMs scored an average adherence of $0.57 - 0.59 \pm 0.15$, and their definitions proved harder to read than the originals. Model-generated definitions vary mainly among words with multiple or ambiguous definitions, showing the potential to highlight terms that need standardization. The results show how LLMs could support environmental discourse while emphasizing the need to align model outputs with established terminology for clarity and consistency.

## 1 Introduction

Large language models (LLMs) have proven effective in a range of tasks, such as analyzing climate-related texts (Callaghan et al., 2021) and explaining sustainability reports (Ni et al., 2023). However, as citizens and politicians turn to LLMs for information and inspiration, there is concern that these probabilistic models fail to consistently convey the specificity and accuracy required to discuss climate change. For example, agreeing to a standard set of definitions is essential to achieve common ground in the climate debate (Peter Glavič, 2007). However, streamlining language around climate is already challenging. For instance, Julian Kirchherr (2017) showed that among 114 different definitions for "circular economy," most failed to convey all nuances of the concept. Thus, this can lead to inconsistencies in research and policy-making.

To address this issue, the Interdisciplinary Panel on Climate Change (IPCC) and the United Nations (UN) maintain the online glossaries IPCC Glossary (IPCC, 2019a,b, 2018), and UNTERM (UN, 2024a). Although LLMs have access to these repositories during training, they are not constrained to them during inference. Therefore, LLMs could further diversify and confuse these terms. As more people rely on LLMs, it is of special interest to study how LLM-generated explanations adhere to the official definitions, how robust the completions are, and what lessons we should keep in mind when using these models at ever higher levels of climate discourse. Motivated by this, we analyze the adherence, robustness, and readability of word definitions generated by one closed-source and two open-source models compared to official IPCC definitions.

## 2 Related Work

Pham et al. (2024) showed that word definitions of English words given by OpenAI LLMs agree well with three popular English dictionaries. However, current LLM performance is mainly dependent on prompt engineering. Atil et al. (2024) examined LLM stability and showed that even the same input and parameters can result in variation, which is task-dependent and not normally distributed.

Studies show that sustainability literature can be complex to read (Smeuninx et al., 2020; Barkemeyer et al., 2016). This complexity challenges the accessibility and transparency of sustainability debates and reporting. Studies spanning the sustainability to medical domains use LLMs to simplify these texts and make them interactive (Ni et al., 2023; Yao et al., 2024).



*Proceedings of the 1st Workshop on Ecology, Environment, and Natural Language Processing (NLP4Ecology2025)*, pages 104–109
March 2, 2025 

## 3 Methodology

We present a framework for assessing the adherence and robustness of LLM sustainability word definitions. Specifically, given a term, we let an LLM generate five definitions for each of the five prompt templates (25 completions per term). Then, we use SBERT sentence embeddings to compute the sentence similarity between the official and generated definitions (adherence), as well as the similarity between the generated definitions for a given term and prompt template (robustness). Thus, we define adherence and robustness for each term as follows:

$$\text{adherence} = \frac{1}{n}\sum_{k=1}^{n} \text{sim}(D, M_k)$$

$$\text{robustness} = \frac{1}{\text{cmb(n)}}\sum_{p=1}^{n}\sum_{q=k+1}^{n} \text{sim}(M_p, M_q)$$

where $D$ is the IPCC glossary definition, $M_k$ is the k'th model definition completion across all prompts, cmb(n) the number of unique pairwise combinations using $n$ terms, and sim(A, B) the cosine distance between the SBERT sentence embeddings of the texts A and B. Intuitively, adherence measures how similar model completions are to glossary definitions, while robustness measures the consistency of model completions.

**Dataset collection:** We use Selenium WebBrowser to scrape all terms and definitions from the IPCC glossary website as of December 2024. In total, the glossary contained 911 terms. We limit the terms to those with an overlap in the IPCC 2022 Special Report on Climate Change and Land Annex I Glossary (IPCC, 2022), and get a subset of 300 terms. Finally, we use only the first sentence of each definition and replace all cross-references (such as "See Pathways") with the cited term.

**Models:** We use three different models in the experiments. We use GPT-4o-mini as our closed source model, and Meta-Llama-3.1-8B-Instruct (Meta, 2024) and Mistral-7B-Instruct-v0.2 (Jiang et al., 2023) as our open source models. We use the default parameter settings for all models.

**Prompts:** We prompt ChatGPT with "Write 4 versions of asking 'Define "[TERM]" in one sentence."' resulting in the following list of 5 prompt templates:

- Define "[TERM]" in one sentence.
- How would you define "[TERM]" in a single sentence?
- Can you describe "[TERM]" in just one sentence?
- What is your one-sentence definition of "[TERM]"?
- In one sentence, what does "[TERM]" mean to you?

**Readability analysis:** We use the Python library Readability (Py-Readbility-Metrics, 2019) to compute the two readability metrics Flesch-Kincaid (Kincaid et al., 1975) and Gunning-Fog (Gunning, 1952) for the official definitions and model completions, respectively. Higher Flesh-Kincaid and Gunning-Fog scores indicate more complex material. The metrics require at least 100 words and are not directly applicable to single sentences. Therefore, we use bootstrapping with 1,000 iterations to create longer text samples by sampling 50 random definitions with replacement and assessing the readability of these excerpts.

## 4 Experimental Results

### 4.1 Adherence

The average SBERT similarity scores between all terms and their corresponding official IPCC definitions are shown in Figure 1. The terms vary greatly, ranging from an adherence score of 0.06 to 0.94. Table 1 shows that all three models received similar results, with average adherence scores of $0.57 - 0.59 \pm 0.15$. The terms with the highest and lowest adherence scores are shown in Table 2. Notably, there is a significant overlap between models, with the term "East Asian monsoon (EAsiaM)" scoring highest and "Demand- and supply-side measures" scoring lowest.

### 4.2 Robustness

Table 1 includes the robustness scores across all term completions. The average robustness falls between $0.96 - 1.00 \pm 0.02$ (min 0.89, max 1.00), with no statistical difference between the prompt templates. Some terms produce notable variations, however, in definitions across prompt templates, as listed in Table 3. For instance, GPT-4o-mini's

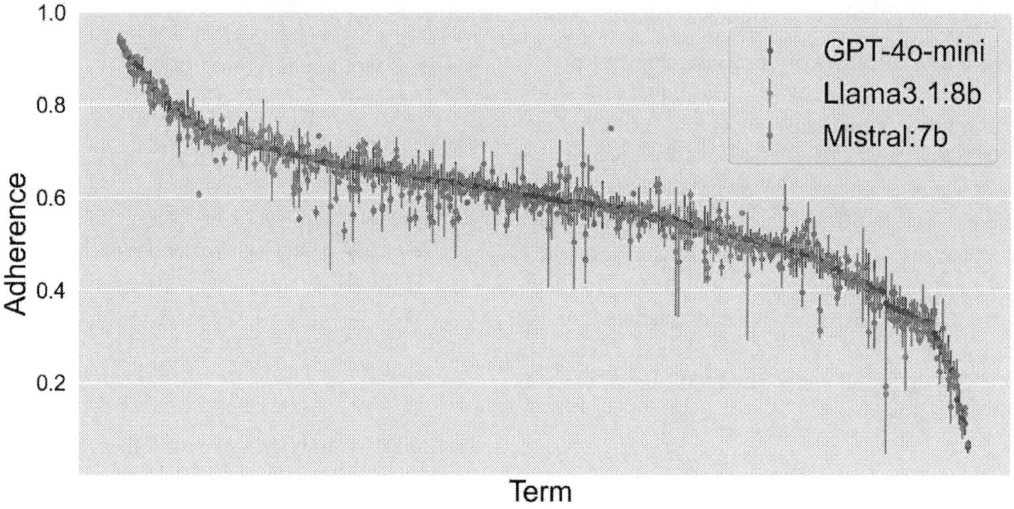


Figure 1: Distribution of SBERT adherence scores between LLM and official IPCC word definitions.

| Model | Adherence | Robustness | Num Words | Gunning Fog | Flesch-Kincaid |
|---|---|---|---|---|---|
| **GPT-4o-mini** | $0.59 \pm 0.15$ | $0.96 \pm 0.02$ | $34.3 \pm 51.5$ | $22.4 \pm 0.3$ | $19.4 \pm 0.2$ |
| **Llama 3.1 8B** | $0.57 \pm 0.15$ | $1.00 \pm 0.01$ | $39.7 \pm 61.4$ | $22.9 \pm 0.3$ | $19.9 \pm 0.2$ |
| **Mistral 7B** | $0.58 \pm 0.15$ | $1.00 \pm 0.00$ | $33.6 \pm 69.5$ | $20.8 \pm 0.3$ | $18.1 \pm 0.2$ |
| **Definitions** | - | - | $30.2 \pm 295.5$ | $19.7 \pm 0.8$ | $16.3 \pm 0.7$ |

Table 1: Adherence, robustness, and readability scores for various LLMs.

definition of "Projection" spanned the psychological ("Projection is a psychological defense mechanism..."), mathematical ("Projection is the process of transferring an image, shape, or data representation..."), and environmental ("Projection" refers to the process of estimating or forecasting future events") topics. This is to be expected, however, since the prompt did not constrain the model to a particular context. On the other hand, prompting without context gives a hint into potential ambiguities when adapting terms such as "Equity", "Exposure", and "Adaptation pathways" into the climate debate.

### 4.3 Readability

Table 1 shows the definitions' average lengths and readability scores. The scores indicate that both IPCC- and model-generated definitions are at the reading level of college graduates. Nevertheless, the IPCC definitions are significantly less complex according to both readability metrics and use fewer words than all model-generated definitions.

### 4.4 Ablation Case Studies

We perform three additional ablation studies using Llama3.1 8B, using the following prompts:

- **IPCC**: 'Define "[TERM]" in one sentence. Adhere to the official Intergovernmental Panel on Climate Change (IPCC) glossary without citing it.'
- **Readable**: 'Define "[TERM]" in one sentence. You must also make the definition understandable by a 10-year old.'
- **IPCC+Readable**: 'Define "[TERM]" in one sentence. Adhere to the official Intergovernmental Panel on Climate Change (IPCC) glossary without citing it. You must also make the definition understandable by a 10-year old.'

Table 4 shows the adherence and readability scores using the ablation prompt templates. Notably, the adherence score remains roughly unchanged using the IPCC-specific prompt. Instead, the readability prompt seems to have a greater effect, decreasing the Flesch-Kincaid score from $19.9 \pm 0.2$ to

| Model | Highest Adherence Terms | Lowest Adherence Terms |
|---|---|---|
| **GPT-4o-mini** | 1. East Asian monsoon (EAsiaM) | 1. Demand- and supply-side measures |
| | 2. Eastern boundary upwelling systems (EBUS) | 2. Poverty |
| | 3. Reducing Emissions from Deforestation and Forest Degradation (REDD+) | 3. Leakage |
| **Llama3.1:8b** | 1. East Asian monsoon (EAsiaM) | 1. Demand- and supply-side measures |
| | 2. Eastern boundary upwelling systems (EBUS) | 2. Leakage |
| | 3. Deliberative governance | 3. Poverty |
| **Mistral:7b** | 1. Eastern boundary upwelling systems (EBUS) | 1. Demand- and supply-side measures |
| | 2. East Asian monsoon (EAsiaM) | 2. Leakage |
| | 3. Reducing Emissions from Deforestation and Forest Degradation (REDD+) | 3. Poverty |

Table 2: Terms with the highest and lowest adherence scores between generated and official definitions.

| Model | Lowest Robustness Scores |
|---|---|
| **GPT-4o-mini** | 1. Projection |
| | 2. Equity |
| | 3. Adaptation pathways |
| **Llama3.1:8b** | 1. Exposure |
| | 2. Glacier |
| | 3. Forest |
| **Mistral:7b** | 1. Sea ice |
| | 2. Global mean surface air temperature (GSAT) |
| | 3. Ensemble |

Table 3: Terms with the lowest robustness score between the generated and official definitions.

$16.4 \pm 0.02$. Although the prompt specified language for a 10-year hold, the Flesh-Kincaid score still corresponds to a college reading level. The relatively high score may partly be explained by the increased sentence length in the LLM's attempt to elaborate and explain parts of the concepts. Table 5 shows case studies for the term "Radiative Forcing" for the official IPCC definition and ablations comparing the definitions generated from different prompts.

## 5 Discussion

The adherence scores suggest that all LLMs generally capture the core semantic meanings of official definitions. Intriguingly, all LLMs achieved similar average adherence scores and had many common outlier terms. This similarity may be due to the models being trained using similar methods and on roughly the same training data. Notably, the adherence score did not significantly improve when we explicitly prompted the model for IPCC definitions. These results imply that providing a climate context may not automatically align language models for a given terminology group. The models do not have perfect recall of definitions; instead, they operate based on probability distributions. Therefore, it is advisable to include the exact definitions in the prompts or LLM systems to ensure they are readily available for reference.

Regarding robustness, the five prompt templates tested did not result in significant variations in generated model definitions. However, there was a notable variability among several terms. As anticipated, the terms with lower robustness scores tend to have multiple meanings, such as "Projection", "Exposure", and "Equity". For instance, "Equity" displayed many definitions, reflecting its complex and multi-faceted meanings. This ambiguity aligns with discussions in recent sustainability reports, such as the UN's 2024 Emissions Gap Report, which dedicates an entire section to discuss different equity models (UN, 2024b). Thus, the robustness score can help target terms needing further standardization. However, we must also note that robustness is very dependent on the temperature settings of the models. In this paper, we use the default temperature for the models. However, model parameters play a significant role in the consistency and variability of model outputs. These variations could impact how the model presents terms to different users across time.

In terms of readability, both the IPCC and model definitions scored poorly across both readability metrics. This finding is consistent with previous studies, which suggest that sustainability texts are inaccessible to most readers. Notably, all model completions consistently received more complex readability scores than the already

| Ablation | Adherence | Num Words | Gunning Fog | Flesch-Kincaid |
|---|---|---|---|---|
| **LLama+IPCC** | $0.60 \pm 0.14$ | $38.1 \pm 45.1$ | $22.5 \pm 0.3$ | $19.4 \pm 0.2$ |
| **Llama+Readable** | $0.55 \pm 0.16$ | $43.4 \pm 58.6$ | $19.2 \pm 0.2$ | $16.4 \pm 0.2$ |
| **Llama+IPCC+Readable** | $0.58 \pm 0.14$ | $42.6 \pm 47.9$ | $20.2 \pm 0.2$ | $17.3 \pm 0.1$ |

Table 4: Adherence and readability scores for different ablation studies using Llama3.1 8B.

| Ablation | Radiative Forcing Definition |
|---|---|
| **Official Definition** | The change in the net, downward minus upward, radiative flux (expressed in W m–2) due to a change in an external driver of climate change, such as a change in the concentration of carbon dioxide (CO2), the concentration of volcanic aerosols or in the output of the Sun. |
| **Llama+IPCC** | Radiative forcing is the change in the balance between the incoming and outgoing radiation at the top of the atmosphere, usually expressed in watts per square meter ($W/m^2$), resulting from a specific perturbation, such as the increase in greenhouse gases. |
| **Llama+Readable** | Radiative forcing is the amount of extra energy that the Earth's atmosphere receives from the sun, usually because of something like pollution or a change in the atmosphere, which can make the planet warmer or cooler. |
| **LLama+IPCC-Readable** | Radiative forcing is the change in the amount of energy that the Earth's atmosphere receives from the sun, usually caused by human activities or natural changes, which can make the planet warmer or cooler. |

Table 5: Case Study: Ablation study using LLama 3.1 8B to define "Radiative Forcing" using three different prompting strategies. "IPCC" explicitly asks for a definition in line with the official definition, "Readable" for an easily understandable description, and "IPCC+Readable" combines the two.

intricate official definitions. This discrepancy may partly be attributed to the longer model responses. Moreover, increasing the readability proved difficult. Although the model used more straightforward terminology, prompting for readability made the model more verbose. Additionally, the readability metrics were not initially designed for single sentences, suggesting that using multiple sentences may yield a more representative assessment.

Future work could explore ways to improve accessibility by using LLMs to simplify language without compromising accuracy and incorporating relevant official glossaries as part of an in-context learning approach. One challenge will be balancing simplicity with accuracy. Adherence scores could offer a helpful framework for evaluating and refining these model outputs since they rely not on exact sentence matching but semantic meaning. Studies across more models and languages would further inform how LLMs represent sustainability.

## 6 Conclusion

This study provides a comprehensive framework for assessing the adherence, robustness, and readability of LLM-generated definitions of sustainability terms compared to official glossaries. While the LLMs capture the semantic meaning of most terms, there is significant variation, particularly for terms with multiple meanings or ambiguous definitions. In addition, IPCC and model definitions show low readability, highlighting the need for further work to simplify sustainability-related language without sacrificing accuracy. Moreover, the case studies show the difficulty in retrieving official definitions even using explicit prompting, indicating the need to include official definitions directly in the prompt. These findings highlight the potential of LLMs to support the environmental conversation but also underscore the importance of carefully aligning model outputs with established terminology to ensure clarity and consistency.

## Acknowledgments

I want to express my sincere gratitude to Professor Chris Piech for his continued support and encouragement. I also appreciate Maty Bohacek and Anjali Sreenivas's thoughtful comments and invaluable advice.

## References

Berk Atil, Alexa Chittams, Liseng Fu, Ferhan Ture, Lixinyu Xu, and Breck Baldwin. 2024. LLM Stability: A detailed analysis with some surprises. ArXiv:2408.04667 [cs] version: 1.

Ralf Barkemeyer, Suraje Dessai, Beatriz Monge-Sanz, Barbara Gabriella Renzi, and Giulio Napolitano.

2016. Linguistic analysis of IPCC summaries for policymakers and associated coverage. *Nature Climate Change*, 6(3):311–316. Publisher: Nature Publishing Group.

Max Callaghan, Carl-Friedrich Schleussner, Shruti Nath, Quentin Lejeune, Thomas R. Knutson, Markus Reichstein, Gerrit Hansen, Emily Theokritoff, Marina Andrijevic, Robert J. Brecha, Michael Hegarty, Chelsea Jones, Kaylin Lee, Agathe Lucas, Nicole van Maanen, Inga Menke, Peter Pfleiderer, Burcu Yesil, and Jan C. Minx. 2021. Machine-learning-based evidence and attribution mapping of 100,000 climate impact studies. *Nature Climate Change*, 11(11):966–972.

Robert Gunning. 1952. *The Technique of Clear Writing*. McGraw-Hill, New York.

IPCC. 2018. Annex i: Glossary. In V. Masson-Delmotte, P. Zhai, H.-O. Pörtner, D. Roberts, J. Skea, P.R. Shukla, A. Pirani, W. Moufouma-Okia, C. Péan, R. Pidcock, S. Connors, J.B.R. Matthews, Y. Chen, X. Zhou, M.I. Gomis, E. Lonnoy, T. Maycock, M. Tignor, and T. Waterfield, editors, *Global Warming of 1.5°C. An IPCC Special Report on the impacts of global warming of 1.5°C above pre-industrial levels and related global greenhouse gas emission pathways, in the context of strengthening the global response to the threat of climate change, sustainable development, and efforts to eradicate poverty*. IPCC. In Press.

IPCC. 2019a. Annex i: Glossary. In H.-O. Pörtner, D.C. Roberts, V. Masson-Delmotte, P. Zhai, M. Tignor, E. Poloczanska, K. Mintenbeck, A. Alegría, M. Nicolai, A. Okem, J. Petzold, B. Rama, and N.M. Weyer, editors, *IPCC Special Report on the Ocean and Cryosphere in a Changing Climate*. IPCC. In Press.

IPCC. 2019b. Annex i: Glossary. In P.R. Shukla, J. Skea, E. Calvo Buendia, V. Masson-Delmotte, H.-O. Pörtner, D.C. Roberts, P. Zhai, R. Slade, S. Connors, R. van Diemen, M. Ferrat, E. Haughey, S. Luz, S. Neogi, M. Pathak, J. Petzold, J. Portugal Pereira, P. Vyas, E. Huntley, K. Kissick, M. Belkacemi, and J. Malley, editors, *Climate Change and Land: an IPCC special report on climate change, desertification, land degradation, sustainable land management, food security, and greenhouse gas fluxes in terrestrial ecosystems*. IPCC. In press.

IPCC. 2022. *Climate Change and Land: IPCC Special Report on Climate Change, Desertification, Land Degradation, Sustainable Land Management, Food Security, and Greenhouse Gas Fluxes in Terrestrial Ecosystems*. Cambridge University Press.

Albert Jiang, Alexandre Sablayrolles, Arthur Mensch, Chris Bamford, Singh Devendra, Diego Chaplot, Florian De Las Casas, Gianna Bressand, Guillaume Lengyel, Lucile Lample, Renard Saulnier, Marie-Anne Lavaud, Pierre Lachaux, Teven Stock, Thibaut Le Scao, Thomas Lavril, Timothée Wang, William Lacroix, and Sayed. 2023. *Mistral 7B*. arXiv.

Marko Hekkert Julian Kirchherr, Denise Reike. 2017. Conceptualizing the circular economy: An analysis of 114 definitions. *Resources, Conservation and Recycling*, 127:221–232. Publisher: Elsevier.

J Kincaid, Robert Fishburne, L Richard, Brad Rogers, and Chissom. 1975. *Derivation Of New Readability Formulas (Automated Readability Index, Fog Count And Flesch Reading Ease Formula) For Navy Enlisted Personnel 1-1-1975*. Institute for Simulation and Training.

Meta. 2024. *The Llama 3 Herd of Models*. arXiv.

Jingwei Ni, Julia Bingler, Chiara Colesanti-Senni, Mathias Kraus, Glen Gostlow, Tobias Schimanski, Dominik Stammbach, Saeid Ashraf Vaghefi, Qian Wang, Nicolas Webersinke, Tobias Wekhof, Tingyu Yu, and Markus Leippold. 2023. CHATREPORT: Democratizing Sustainability Disclosure Analysis through LLM-based Tools. ArXiv:2307.15770 [cs].

Rebeka Lukman Peter Glavič. 2007. Review of sustainability terms and their definitions. *Journal of Cleaner Production*, 15(18):1875–1885. Publisher: Elsevier.

Bach Pham, JuiHsuan Wong, Samuel Kim, Yunting Yin, and Steven Skiena. 2024. Word Definitions from Large Language Models. ArXiv:2311.06362 [cs].

Py-Readbility-Metrics. 2019. [link].

Nils Smeuninx, Bernard De Clerck, and Walter Aerts. 2020. Measuring the Readability of Sustainability Reports: A Corpus-Based Analysis Through Standard Formulae and NLP. *International Journal of Business Communication*, 57(1):52–85. Publisher: SAGE Publications Inc.

UN. 2024a. [link].

UN. 2024b. Emissions gap report 2024.

Zonghai Yao, Nandyala Siddharth Kantu, Guanghao Wei, Hieu Tran, Zhangqi Duan, Sunjae Kwon, Zhichao Yang, README annotation team, and Hong Yu. 2024. README: Bridging Medical Jargon and Lay Understanding for Patient Education through Data-Centric NLP. ArXiv:2312.15561 [cs].

# Author Index

**Association for Computational Linguistics**
209 N. Eighth Street
Stroudsburg, Pennsylvania 18360

ISBN 979-8-3313-1888-8